THE ARTS AT A NEW FRONTIER

The National Endowment for the Arts

Nonprofit Management and Finance

Series Editor: VIRGINIA WHITE

GRANT PROPOSALS THAT SUCCEEDED
Edited by Virginia White

THE ARTS AT A NEW FRONTIER
The National Endowment for the Arts
Fannie Taylor and Anthony L. Barresi

VOLUNTARY NONPROFIT ENTERPRISE MANAGEMENT
David E. Mason

A Continuation Order Plan is available for this series. A continuation order will bring delivery of each new volume immediately upon publication. Volumes are billed only upon actual shipment. For further information please contact the publisher.

THE ARTS AT A NEW FRONTIER

The National Endowment for the Arts

FANNIE TAYLOR
AND
ANTHONY L. BARRESI
University of Wisconsin—Madison
Madison, Wisconsin

PLENUM PRESS • NEW YORK AND LONDON

Library of Congress Cataloging in Publication Data

Taylor, Fannie.
The arts at a new frontier.

(Nonprofit management and finance)
Includes bibliographical references and index.
1. National Endowment for the Arts. I. Barresi, Anthony L., 1934– . II. Title. III. Series.
NX22.T39 1984 353.0085′4 84-11676
ISBN 0-306-41569-0

A Division of Plenum Publishing Corporation
233 Spring Street, New York, N.Y. 10013

Printed in the United States of America

This Congress will consider many programs which will leave an enduring mark on American life. But it may be that the passage of this legislation, modest as it is, will help secure for this Congress a sure and honored place in the story of the advance of civilization.

—President Lyndon B. Johnson

Preface

Profound changes were taking place in American society during the period of the 1960s and 1970s when legislation for the National Foundation for the Arts and the Humanities was enacted and the agencies went into operation. It was a period of soul-searching by the American public when the cherished prejudices and civil inequities of the past decades were wiped out and old wounds began to heal; at the same time, however, the Vietnam War was creating new fissures and antagonisms.

Into this newly healing, newly questioning society, congressional action thrust the National Council on the Arts in 1964, and the National Endowment for the Arts in 1965. Their mission was to encourage and support the arts, and the men and women charged with this responsibility went about their work with the zeal and enthusiasm of religious converts.

The idea of even a minute amount of federal financial assistance to the country's chronically beleaguered and often impoverished artists and arts organizations seemed strange to a segment of the population that had existed in forgotten independence from government intervention. Many of the nation's artists and arts leaders were wary, partly because of the uncertainties and constraints of previous patterns of governmental support.

But when the Arts Endowment legislation was being brought into existence there was already clear indication that the cultural activities of the nation, as accepted for generations, were changing. Costs were rising, public attitudes and interests shifting, minority groups and diverse populations everywhere were demanding their own cultural expressions. The country's great arts institutions—the major museums, symphonies, operas—were beginning to feel increased funding pressures. New productions were not attempted; old productions were increasingly threadbare. Touring costs were becoming so high that many dance, theater, and musical productions were traveling only to major audience centers and cutting stage settings to minimal props. Many museums traditionally free to the public were beginning to ask for voluntary donations. At the same time, personal expression in the plastic arts exploded as everyone began to do his or her "own thing"—in macramé, pots, weaving, or bread sculpture.

But was federal assistance required to help change these conditions? The nation's cultural leaders examined the pros and cons skeptically. Would the arts be helped or hindered by the entry of federal funding into the precarious budgets of the arts organizations? Would federal bureaucracy lead into a kind of homogenized and universally acceptable mediocrity? Would subtle political considerations shade decisions? Would justifications for the use of public moneys begin to warp the aesthetic criteria by which artists had most often been guided? Would availability of public money (and the changing tax laws) shrink support from the Lord and Lady Bountifuls of the past? In short, was the introduction of federal funding good or bad for the nation's cultural enterprises?

Now, nearly two decades later, it seems appropriate to examine the initial policies and formative activities of the agency and try to understand how these developed in the first decade and to consider their effect on the arts in this country during the remainder of the century. Were there substantive changes in public attitudes that can be said to have resulted from the arts legislation? Did the Arts Endowment, through its grant-making capabilities, help or discourage private giving? Are the current outreach programs of major institutions, and the great proliferation of new arts groups in different segments of society, a result of the availability of federal funding or a consequence of affluence and a more open society?

Certainly there were major changes in cultural patterns during the period. State arts agencies were legislated in every state and special jurisdiction of America during the first decade of the Arts Endowment's operation, and they began to develop new regional influence. Symphony orchestras expanded their seasons and improved artistic capabilities. The labor unions that served the arts industry were increasingly visible. For a small but steadily growing audience, television began to give new audience support to some of the major opera, dance, and theater productions; because of the quality of the works produced, this set new critical standards nationwide. Service associations for the arts proliferated. Museum attendance in the early Seventies was running at more than 308 million visitors annually. Grantsmanship was becoming a way of life with most institutions.

But far deeper into the social fabric of the community than these manifestations of widespread support and interest in the arts ran the counterforce of insidious inflation. It was felt by arts institutions in the first decade of the existence of the Arts Endowment. As fast as federal funding expanded and new sources of private money could be developed, inflation swallowed them. Growing deficits became a prime concern for boards of directors.

Inflation struck at the financial roots of the arts. These "roots," often slender and unstable, and based largely on private giving and personal decisions to purchase tickets or works of art, were the traditional guarantee of independence for the product that had resulted from interaction between artist and audience and from skills of management. This trio maintained a self-sustaining symbiosis and integrity of communication between the consumer and the artist.

But times changed. The pressure of costs for presentation of the arts exploded beyond the capacity of the majority of auditoriums to generate ticket income and beyond the abilities of most museum managers to raise private money to house and routinely display works of art with adequate security. Increased demand raised costs. The individual artist, working in the performing arts, was pressured, too; his opportunities for creative outlets were curtailed. It was difficult, for example, for a symphony orchestra to rehearse a new work by a contemporary composer when there were no funds for extra rehearsals. It was difficult for a playwright to find production opportunities for a play or a musical theater show that would be able to sustain itself long enough at the box office to pay back costs.

The increased demand for the arts, as shown in growing audiences and new interest in personal participation, was tangible evidence, however, of changing public attitudes about the arts. They were becoming more integrated into the daily lives of the general public, especially through the universal impact of television.

Under the public pressure of this new and more democratic audience, vestiges of nineteenth-century elitist attitudes have gradually begun to disappear. More and more the critical verdicts depend on content and production excellence rather than time-honored sponsorships, and upon genuine interest rather than lip service.

The first National Council for the Arts, under Chairman Roger L. Stevens, understood the cultural changes that were fermenting in the country. The Council members, many of them artists themselves, recognized the need to nurture the individual artist in the face of growing mass production. They supported the nationwide maintenance of the highest qualities of presentation. With virtually no money—only $2.5 million in fiscal year 1966—the Arts Endowment, as a concept, began to have an impact throughout the country on what active national leadership and broad regional local support for the arts could do for America. The National Endowment for the Arts was the right legislation for the right time.

Both Roger Stevens and Nancy Hanks toured the country telling their story on every available platform to major arts institutions, their board members, educators, artists, civic groups, and old-line arts patrons, in big cities as well as whistle stops. There were cautious appraisals, loud and sometimes ill-advised praise, and sometimes equally ill-advised diatribes against "introducing the government into the arts."

Nonetheless, the creation of the National Foundation on the Arts and the

Humanities with its two great administrative branches, the National Endowment for the Arts and the National Endowment for the Humanities, was landmark legislation. There is reason to believe that the cultural thrust of the society has been affected markedly by the funding and policies. Some of these changes, as demonstrated by the National Endowment for the Arts, will be explored in this history of the agency in its first ten years.

In documenting this history the authors have been aware of the influence brought to the agency by members of the National Council on the Arts and the staff, a group of extraordinary people dedicated to the importance of the arts in our society. The result of this Council and staff leadership was a unique federal agency, remarkably free of the constraints of bureaucracy and political pressure, that actively opened opportunities for artists and arts organizations throughout the United States.

Acknowledgments

The authors have been helped by many individuals and institutions in the researching and writing of this book; and we are deeply grateful for the interest and encouragement we have received on all sides.

Our thanks go to the University of Wisconsin–Madison, where both of us have been supported by our departments and cheerfully urged on by our colleagues—major factors in the accomplishment of the task.

We are especially grateful to the William T. Evjue Foundation, the University of Wisconsin Consortium for the Arts, the University of Wisconsin Foundation, and the Wisconsin Foundation for the Arts, all of which helped to fund the research costs entailed in the project. In addition, the University of Wisconsin School of Music has been extremely cooperative.

Opportunities to document many aspects of the National Endowment for the Arts history were made available to us through individual interviews with some of the men and women involved with the agency during its formative years. These taped interviews have been invaluable resources and have provided insights into many decisions and situations. We are particularly grateful to the following for their willingness to be interviewed:* Roger L. Stevens, the first Chairman of the Arts Endowment; Nancy Hanks, the second Chairman; Livingston L. Biddle, the third Chairman; Walter F. Anderson, Program Director for Music; Richard Contee, Assistant Chairman/Management; Lawrence Halprin, member of the National Council on the Arts; Ruth R. Mayleas, Program Director for Theater; Lawrence L. Reger, Director of Program Development and Coordination; Clark Mitze, Program Director for Federal–State Partnership; Ana Steele, Director of Planning; Karel Yasko, Assistant Commissioner for Design, and staff at the Public Buildings Service, General Services Administration.

In addition, we had welcome correspondence and conversations with the

*Titles used are those of the interviewees at the period being studied.

following individuals: Schuyler Chapin, manager, Metropolitan Opera Company; Luna Diamond, secretary to the National Council on the Arts; Richard C. Diebenkorn, member of the National Council on the Arts; John S. Edwards, Executive Vice-president and General Manager of the Chicago Symphony Orchestra; Paul Engle, member of the National Council on the Arts; R. Philip Hanes, member of the National Council on the Arts; Doris Hering, executive director, National Association of Regional Ballet; Isaac Stern, member of the National Council on the Arts.

We were assisted by Ann Guthrie, Program Information staff member, who provided additional background material. Kristin P. Thelander and Trudy Woods assisted the research process. The dedication and typing skills of Genevieve Mittnacht brought the manuscript to readable completion. Virginia Barresi read copy assiduously. Carol Frykenberg was always helpful.

Finally, the authors owe a special debt to Virginia P. White, who urged us to attempt this history and brought us together with Plenum Press.

Much of the unpublished material that documents this history is filed in the archives of the Wisconsin Center for Film and Theater Research, sponsored by the University of Wisconsin–Madison and the State Historical Society of Wisconsin, and included within the Fannie Taylor Papers lodged there. Professor Taylor was a member of the staff of the National Endowment for the Arts on two occasions during the first decade of the agency's existence—as Program Director for Music under Roger Stevens and as Program Information Director under Nancy Hanks. The taped interviews referred to are also filed in these archives.

In conclusion, the authors would like to say that in the writing of this history of federal support for the arts much has had to be shortened and some things left out. Sometimes we are sure that programs and projects which would have been illuminating to discuss have been inadvertently omitted. The subject has endless ramifications; the results have numerous interpretations. We have tried to trace a steady course of development as the budget grew, in order to make a fair analysis. To the many creative minds and able hands that helped shape this course of this nation's growth in the arts—and who may not have been mentioned—we simply have to say we deeply regret any omissions that could have given the chronicle more depth and more excitement.

F.T.
A.L.B.

Contents

1

Development of Government Support for the Arts

. . . the right to study painting, poetry, music, and architecture.
—John Adams' letter to his wife, 1780

The years between 1966 and 1976 witnessed approaches to support for the arts never before attempted in our nation's history. For the first time, the federal government became substantially committed to the preservation and advancement of artists, arts organizations, and cultural opportunities for its citizens. Moreover, it accomplished these tasks with active cooperation from private, business, and foundation sectors. Through imaginative granting procedures which, in effect, extended federal dollars by matching them, the government was enabled to encourage artistic expression of quality, varied arts activities, improvements in arts education, and development of existing and future arts consumers.

Before this ten-year period, which was characterized by many other social changes as well, the arts in America had been supported primarily through the private sector—that segment of the population interested, willing, and able to provide financial stability to the arts. Whether the private support was for aesthetic enjoyment or extra-artistic purposes, these patrons provided enough help to allow the country's major arts organizations to remain relatively clear of financial problems. Private patronage for the individual artist was uncertain and often based as much on personality as on talent. On the other hand, public support through the federal government in nearly two centuries preceding the 1960s appears to have been available only in instances of practical necessity—when the services of artists were required for some public celebration or display, or when artists, like other citizens, faced unemployment or diminished private patronage.

Not until the sixth decade of the twentieth century did the American government provide arts support of any importance for reasons that might be described as cultural. Nearly 200 years of national growth had to pass before the average American citizen accepted the arts as another unexplored frontier, worthy of federal or state support for its development. The factors leading to this acceptance are many. In early years, most evidence seems to point to a combination of social and economic factors as motivation for legislation for this special sector of society, while artistic motivation was rarely considered or, at least, never appeared to have enough practical application to be appropriate for public expenditure. Beginning in the late 1950s, however, the arts began to receive broader public recognition as one of the ancient expressions of the aspirations of the human spirit.

Although throughout American history the arts have always been plagued with financial problems, usually solved in the nick of time with private largesse, by the 1960s new troubles threatened the nation's greatest artistic resources. Inflation began to deplete the financial reserves of many arts organizations. Costs of arts production steadily increased, and the ability of private patrons to bridge the widening gap between income and expenditures lessened with the dwindling value of the dollar and increasingly restrictive tax structures. Economists, evaluating the status of the arts in the 1960s, identified the economic problems contributing to these "income gaps" (the deficit that exists between income and expenditure) and predicted that such voids would widen and that additional sources of arts support would have to be developed if the arts were to remain active and vital influences in American life. The federal government, reacting to these economic "facts of life," slowly began to fashion arts funding programs under the aegis of the National Endowment for the Arts which in some cases provided direct assistance to artists, and in others creatively stimulated additional state and local sources of revenue from the private sector to arts organizations through matching grants.

Social considerations also influenced federal action in support of the arts. During the upheavals of the Sixties, many arts activists began to press for equal access to art experience by all segments of the nation's citizenry. They pointed out that the nation's diversified cultural heritage was a national resource worthy of government encouragement and support. Because the social climate of the period encouraged expression from previously anonymous sections of the population, ethnic and folk art in various forms began to assume more importance in the nation's cultural environment.

An aesthetic dimension must also be considered as contributing to government involvement in the arts in the 1960s. The Sixties were sometimes referred to as a period of "cultural explosion"—a time marked by a great increase of interest in the arts by many Americans. Whether it was actually an explosion or resulted from population growth, increased affluence, or broad-based education has often been debated. Whatever the reasons, there was an expanding audience for arts exhibitions and performances and a marked growth in amateur and professional arts activity throughout the country.

These factors certainly influenced the federal legislators; but sustained government assistance could not have been initiated or maintained without those people—whom we call arts activists—who were dedicated to the idea of legislated arts support. The lobbying of presidents, legislators, and governors by these concerned citizens became an important catalyst for the achievement of legislation in support of the arts with tax moneys. While there had been such individuals urging a general arts sustenance since our nation's beginnings, the realization of a *bona fide* granting agency awaited a favorable social, economic, and political environment. The National Endowment for the Arts, established during the administration of Lyndon B. Johnson, represented the journey's end on the long road leading toward substantial government involvement in the arts.

It would be wrong to assume that specific arts support by the central government did not exist before the 1960s. At least since 1790 there had been some government involvement, usually for rather restricted projects and in most cases for purposes other than ártistic. Generally, the instances of support were controlled by social, economic, and political priorities rather than by artistic considerations. To understand why this was the case, it is helpful to examine early-American society and to trace the developing arts involvement of the government to the ultimate establishment of the National Endowment for the arts.

History of Federal Arts Support to 1965

Religious, social, and geographic factors in colonial America fostered various multiple attitudes toward the arts. These attitudes, founded in religious convictions and reinforced by regional isolation and social and economic restraints, were responsible for divided opinions among the founding fathers concerning the value of the arts in American life.

In the Southern colonies, where the Church of England and, to some extent, the Catholic Church managed to establish religious leadership, a landed gentry emerged to control the social and economic environment. The rich cultural history of the churches plus the aristocratic tradition of the gentry and their available leisure time combined to foster favorable arts attitudes that resulted in the importation of art from Europe. Paul Henry Lang, in his book *Music in Western Civilization*, cites early examples of arts activities in the Southern colonies.[1]

> The southern cities, unfettered by restrictions, offered an inspiring spectacle. Charleston and Williamsburg, most aristocratic and most British of the colonial centers of wealth and culture in the South, were proud of their music, which echoed the latest fashion in England. The first recorded performance of an opera in America, in 1735, took place in Charleston. *Flora*, or *Hob in the Well*, one of the most successful one-act ballad operas . . . was the memorable piece . . . . Williamsburg,

> Virginia, owned a permanent playhouse as early as 1722, and some authorities vouch for an even earlier date. Maryland also welcomed concerts and theatrical performances; in 1752 the Kean and Murry Company offered there *The Beggar's Opera*, a performance particularly notable for its use of an orchestra instead of a mere spinet. Charles Theodore Pachelbel, a German musician . . . gave concerts in New York and Charleston in 1736, when such events were almost unheard of in New England.

Lang's comments picture a rich and varied arts life in the southern colonies. However, it should be noted that the supporters of the arts were the wealthy landowners and merchants. Lower classes—slaves, servants, tenant farmers, and craftsmen, as "inferiors" in the social structure of the time—were left to their own artistic devices. Although their economic resources may have restricted access to *new* European arts experiences, the permissive climate of these areas encouraged the perpetuation of traditional folk art by these less-leisured colonists. From these roots grew an art expression that was uniquely American.

New England colonists, in contrast to their southern counterparts, early rejected such artistic expression. Unlike the members of the more liberal churches of the South, the geographically isolated Puritans of Massachusetts Bay accepted only unadorned psalm-singing. Moreover, as other New England settlements grew, the absence of an aristocratic ruling class allowed a rigorously controlled theocracy to develop. Within this Protestant social structure the arts were viewed as idle diversion—a sin second only to adultery. Concerning music in early New England, Lang states:

> A society founded on theocracy legislates in terms of moral sins; consequently music, openly liked and practiced by the majority of Puritans in England, and, as we have seen, by the Pilgrim Fathers on setting sail for the New World, was proscribed by the second generation in America, firmly believing that its prohibition was an act pleasing to God. There was no secular amusement or music or any kind, vocal or instrumental, and the churches banished organs, which were introduced only in the eighteenth century.

Certainly, a society that adhered so strictly to its religious beliefs would probably react to most religious graphic art as idolatry—perhaps one of the reasons for the unadorned, severely simple, design of New England churches.

However, by the middle of the eighteenth century, music and limited graphic expression had found its way into New England life. Public concerts, under rigidly controlled circumstances, were sometimes permitted, but dramatic presentations continued to be vigorously opposed. Lang relates that a mid-eighteenth century performance by English actors in a Boston coffeehouse raised furious indignation. This performance of Thomas Otway's *The Orphan*, "a stark drama of passion and love in which many critics saw almost Shakespearian qualities," raised objections that may not have been based purely on religious prejudice. In fact, by this time rejection of dramatic activity was so ingrained in society that the city council, reacting to the public outcry, passed a law prohibiting all forms of theatrical entertainment. The New Englanders' fear that the arts would tend to disrupt the industrious life by encouraging wasted, idle use of leisure time existed up to the period of the Revolutionary War.

By the end of the eighteenth century, affluent members of the merchant class in urban areas began to make their influence known. Although their partronage of music, dramatic presentations, and the arts in general encouraged more liberal artistic attitudes, many New England residents still regarded performing and creative artists with scepticism.

The central colonies were somewhat paradoxical in their relationship to the arts. Artistic attitudes, while highly influenced by some religious prohibitions, were tempered by the proximity of the liberal South and by the influx of non-English immigrants. For example, in Pennsylvania the austere religious beliefs of the Quakers restricted artistic expression and acceptance; yet, by the middle of the eighteenth century, increased commercial importance, a mixed ethnic and religious population, and social interaction with the South caused the city of Philadelphia to achieve an active artistic life. In addition, the Bohemian settlement of Bethlehem, Pennsylvania, and German immigrants of Baltimore, Maryland, from the beginning encouraged and sponsored musical performances of high quality, while merchants in New York, descended from Dutch and German stock, eventually became strong patrons for the performing and graphic arts. In fact, this generous financial aristocracy was responsible to a large degree for creating an urban climate whereby New York City could develop into an important cultural center.

As the folk arts in the southern colonies developed, alongside the continuing tradition of a more tutored culture, the less affluent citizens in the central and northern colonies also fashioned art expressions that fulfilled their particular needs. Because these typically American expressions usually evolved free from the influences of traditionally accepted artistic forms, folk arts were often viewed as crude attempts at artistic creation. Not until the mid-twentieth century was there sufficient sophistication and critical perception to recognize in the folk arts their creative vigor, the importance of their adaptations of age-old ethnic traditions, and their expression of an innate need of mankind to foster beauty.[2]

All of these divergent points of view were represented in the first Congress. The attitudes of the representatives toward the arts reflected their religious beliefs, geographic locations, and social positions. On the one hand, they represented the middle-class northern farmer or craftsman whose egalitarian, Protestant work ethic caused him to regard artistic activity as impractical for anyone intent on earning a living; on the other hand, the wealthy landowner or merchant with a background of association with the arts valued them as an important way of life. These diametrically opposed attitudes became defined when legislators met in the Houses of Congress to consider some sort of satisfactory national arts policy and the philosophical positions are clearly displayed in the words and actions of John Adams and George Washington.

John Adams, a middle-class New England farmer, regarded the arts as life-enriching but nonessential to everyday existence. His practical, egalitarian attitudes motivate the low priority assigned to the arts in his national development plan. He wrote:

> I must study politics and war, that my sons may have liberty to study mathematics, philosophy, geography, natural history and naval architecture, navigation, commerce and agriculture in order to give their children the right to study painting, poetry, music, and architecture.[3]

This future President's plan was colored by his perception of the young nation's needs. The arts would achieve importance when the practical matters of everyday life were solved—when social, political, and economic stability were achieved.

George Washington, on the other hand, as one of the southern landed gentry, revealed his bias toward the arts when he observed that "the Arts and Sciences, essential to the prosperity of the State and to the ornamentation and happiness of human life, have a primary claim to the encouragement of every lover of his country and mankind."[4] The first President further demonstrated his conviction in 1790 when he recommended that Pierre L'Enfant, designer of the city of Washington, D.C., include an arts center in the plans for the nation's new capital city.

Because these opposing opinions are indicative of attitudes held by many in Congress, some sort of accommodation was necessary before a national arts policy could be adopted. It appears that an unwritten compromise, close to the Adams point of view but influenced by the Washington ideas, was reached. Thus, for nearly 200 years, the federal government would support only those arts endeavors that provided direct services for the government—only as a factor of *practical necessity*.

The Era of Practical Necessity

Perhaps the earliest instance of direct federal arts support occurred with the establishment of the United States Marine Band in 1790. Although it is likely that assorted military ensembles, such as fife-and-drum corps, may have existed prior to this time, the Marine Band was the first permanent musical ensemble of a large size to be supported by the federal government. However, its formation and support was not to fulfill artistic purposes but rather to provide military pomp for official ceremonies—a service considered of practical necessity. In later years, additional ensembles were to become common as the need for such services grew. The United States Military and Naval Academy bands date from the first part of the nineteenth century, while the United States Army and Navy bands were officially organized at the beginning of World War I.[5] Today, these ensembles are in actuality more flexible than their titles would lead us to believe. Nearly all of them can perform as orchestras by the addition of strings and the subtraction of some wind instruments. Moreover, in recent years a choral dimension has been added which increases their flexibility even further. In addition to presenting regular concerts, the varied ensembles provide music for government ceremonies, serve as public-relations vehicles, and assist at recruitment occasions.

Through the establishment of a national library and a national museum, the arts were also obliquely but importantly aided in the early years of the republic. In 1800, the national government founded the Library of Congress, which from the beginning maintained substantial music and art collections. The establishment of this institution was all the more notable because it occurred at a time when the nation's attention was focused on the development of material wealth and westward expansion.[6]

With the founding of the Smithsonian Institution in 1846, the government took another halting step into the area of arts support. James Smithson's will, which bequeathed his fortune for the establishment of an institution "for the increase and diffusion of knowledge among men," contained no specific references to the arts but the enabling legislation, in its surprising wisdom, included a gallery of art along with museums, a laboratory, a library, and lecture rooms.[7] It may be assumed that the inclusion of this facility reflected government recognition of the need for a repository for the national art treasures. As the years passed and the Smithsonian broadened its scope of activities through the sponsorship of publications, museums, art galleries, and public arts presentations, government's role also broadened in arts support as a practical necessity for a growing nation. It should also be noted that, until the establishment of the National Gallery of Art in 1937, the federal art treasures were housed primarily in the existing facilities of the Smithsonian Institution.

From its inception, the American government has employed artists, architects, and sculptors to construct and beautify federal properties. As August Heckscher, Special Consultant on the Arts to the Kennedy administration, stated, "Memorials, statues, murals, fountains, historic and decorative paintings, as well as works for public museums, are among the objects which government in some degree or another makes its own."[8] That federal properties should be impressive and beautiful seems to have been important to legislators throughout our nation's history. Perhaps the aristocratic tastes represented in some members of the early legislative bodies were more influential than one might suspect. In fact, isolated voices urging more extensive government involvement in arts matters spoke out at various times throughout these decades of sporadic public support engendered by practical necessity.

In 1874 and 1879, Representative Samuel Cox of New York introduced legislation to establish a federal council on arts matters.[9] Unfortunately, Cox's attempt to directly involve Congress in the nation's cultural development met with failure, caused, it would seem, by the reluctance of legislators to involve government in the financial support of projects and activities that they felt unimportant to the country's growth and development. In short, they considered this type of support impractical.

Practicality as a criterion is again evident in 1891. On March 3 of that year, the 51st Congress passed and President Harrison signed a bill incorporating a National Conservatory of Music.[10] A year later, the Conservatory opened its doors in New York City with Antonin Dvořák as its artistic director. This national arts school, which technically still exists since its charter set no expiration date, closed its doors several years later. Congress, unconvinced of its practicality, never made any provisions for its financial support, although there were repeated attempts to reactivate the Conservatory from 1919 to 1937.[11]

Early in the twentieth century, the national government took a potentially significant step toward arts involvement—a step that marked the first important legislation in recognition of the graphic arts and one that foreshadowed later legislation beneficial to all of the fine arts. On May 17, 1910, at the request of President Taft, Congress established a Commission on the Fine Arts to advise on public buildings, monuments, and parks in the Washington area and to advise generally on questions of the arts when required to do so by the President or by any committee of either house of the Congress.[12] Though the commission published a periodic report of its activities until it disbanded in the 1950s, it never completely fulfilled its mandate, because it restricted its attention to art and architecture in the District of Columbia unless specificially requested to broaden its scope.[13]

It is interesting to speculate about the possible influence of this commission and about why it failed to achieve the expectations of its founders. In effect, the commission—the first arts council to be established within the executive branch of government—could have been an important vehicle for arts encouragement. However, necessity for such federal support was apparently not perceived by the council or by Congress at that time. Because social, economic, and political stability allowed Americans to devote more attention to the arts than had been possible in the aggressive and restless nineteenth century, private support may have seemed sufficient. On the other hand, the commission, unaware of its potential as a force for federal arts assistance, may not have pursued the task because it had no real concept of this objective. Perhaps the combination of both factors contributed to the commission's ineffectiveness. Whatever the reasons, the fact remains that for the first three decades of the century arts subsidies from private patrons were considered sufficient to meet the financial requirements of the nation's artists and art organizations. Federal assistance to the arts was not judged imperative.[14]

The Era of Economic Necessity

With the stock market crash of 1929 and its accompanying economic paralysis, the flow of private arts patronage was reduced to a trickle. Inevitably, this economic dilemma swelled the number of unemployed artists of all types and talents. During the years 1929–1934, approximately 70 percent of the nation's musicians were unemployed and the remainder were earning a substandard living from the profession.[15] Numerous actors, painters, dancers, and writers were also experiencing similar tribulations.

In reaction to the economic crisis, the federal government responded with programs designed to provide jobs for out-of-work artists—programs specifically initiated in response to economic necessity.

> Between 1933 and 1943 the course of the arts in America was profoundly influenced by federal patronage. Out of the misery and despair thrust upon creative artists by the Depression grew a recognition of the need for substantial public support of the arts. Under a variety of "alphabet soup" labels—WPA, PWAP, TRAP—thousands of artists, writers, actors, and musicians found in the patronage of the federal government the freedom to create, and to preserve their skills.[16]

An examination of government efforts provides interesting insights into the nature of Depression arts activities. In November 1933, the Civil Works Administration (CWA) was inaugurated as a work replacement for the public dole. This program, administered on the local level but directed from Washington, employed needy artists to create, teach, and perform in a variety of work situations.

With the termination of the CWA in March 1934, its programs were transferred to the Federal Emergency Relief Administration. The Works Project Administration (WPA), which was legislated in 1935, supported the most comprehensive and well-publicized of the Depression programs: the Federal Art Project, the Federal Music Project, the Federal Writers Project, and the Federal Theatre Project.[17]

The Federal Art Project provided murals, sculptures, paintings, and other forms of graphic art for numerous buildings constructed with public funds. One has only to enter a Depression-vintage public building to see the effects of this program. The art works that have been preserved are frequently a tribute to the skills of artists temporarily supported by this government program.[18]

At its peak, the Federal Music Project employed 16,000 people. An estimated three million citizens attended 5,000 performances by WPA musicians each month and 132,000 children in 26 states were taught music by Music Project teachers.[19]

The Federal Theatre Project (FTP), perhaps the most controversial of the WPA arts projects, drew 90 percent of its participants from the relief rolls.[20] During its tenure, approximately 9,000 persons were involved throughout the country and 2,660 of these were returned to successful employment in commercial theatre. In New York City alone, about 4,000 theatrical artists were performing for largely unemployed citizens in a variety of settings. In other areas of the nation, FTP employees performed in playgounds, parks, and theatres to 25 million people—one-fifth of the population.

A perusal of FTP records reveals that dramatic productions were not confined to appearances in major cities. Such towns as Tacoma, Syracuse, San Bernardino, and Peoria, as well as New York, Boston, and San Francisco were recipients of FTP grants. Further investigation into play titles and authors shows that many of the productions, considered then as "experimental," are today regarded as standard American theatre literature. Unfortunately, the Federal Theatre Project had an early demise because it developed some powerful foes in Congress. In well-publicized congressional hearings, these legislators asserted that Communist influences were present in the dramatic themes and that many FTP personnel were avowed Communists. In her book on the Federal Theatre Project, Hallie Flanagan asserts that congressional opponents—with little personal knowledge of the project—effectively achieved its destruction. Only a few secure and brave congressmen, such as Senator Claude Pepper, rose to the project's defense. But their pleas were not understood and went unheeded.[21]

Although government motives for arts subsidies were economic, the results of these Depression projects proved artistically beneficial to artists and public alike.

> So while the crash marked the end of much, it was also the beginning of even more. The traditional guardians of public taste who held their mandate from the halcyon days of the 1890s and had triumphantly reasserted their claims of the nation's image in the 1920s, found their influence slipping away. Old patterns of patronage were largely gone by the end of the Depression decade. In spite of the heavy administrative overhead thought necessary to direct federal programs—with supervisors, inspectors and multiple juries—artists themselves began to be heard as social forces. They had now met the public in local art centers, argued over their highly visible public commissions, collaborated on the decoration of schools and libraries, and joined universities as "artists in residence." They were recognized members not of "high" society, but of society as a whole. Although in the immense government programs quantity may have blunted a sense of quality, contemporary art had entered the public consciousness and was not likely to retract once more into a cultural cocoon.[22]

As a result of this change in public awareness, several legislators initiated bills concerned with arts support. Early in 1937, Representative William I. Sirovitch of New York offered a joint resolution in the House of Representatives providing for the establishment of an executive department to be known as the Department of Science, Art, and Literature, whose head officer would have

Cabinet rank. In August of the same year, Representative John M. Coffee of Washington introduced a more definitive bill calling for the establishment of a Bureau of Fine Arts. This agency was to be composed of a commissioner appointed by the President, and six directors in theatre, dance, music, literature, graphic arts, and architecture. Provisions were also made for regional bureaus in various sections of the country, to be supervised by a regional director and four consultants.[23] But it was not until January 1938, when Senator Claude Pepper presented Coffee's bill in the Senate and when Representative Sirovitch brought his bill again before the Patents Committee, that serious congressional consideration was given to the issue.[24] Unfortunately, the convictions of these legislators were not shared by the majority of congressmen who, it may be presumed, still considered any support for the arts as a matter of reaction to necessity rather than support for the creativity of the arts.

This is another instance in the nation's history where prominent legislators unsuccessfully challenged their peers to acknowledge the importance of the arts in the quality of American life. The proposed agencies, unlike the already existing Commission on Fine Arts, would have possessed the power to allocate federal funds for the arts and the authority to develop and direct a national arts policy. Although congressional rejection was probably influenced by critical reaction to some of the Depression projects, as well as by an improving economic situation and the brewing international strife in Europe and Asia, it also seems possible that the legislators considered the idea impractical (even dangerous) for the nation. In any event, Congress chose to continue WPA legislation only until World War II, when war-related jobs supplanted federal-project jobs and entertainment units replaced the experimental work of the Thirties.

Government's role in arts funding during and just after World War II may be briefly characterized as "propagandistic" in intent. Artists of many types received assistance for activities related to morale improvement, attitude development, and even for the advancement of international understanding. In her book *Grants for the Arts*, Virginia White relates that in the early 1940s Nelson Rockefeller, President Roosevelt's Coordinator of the Office of Inter-American Affairs (OIAA), organized tours and cultural exchanges with Latin American countries. OIAA funds were allocated with the justification that such activities were useful in the creation of international good will. She adds that, as in the past, whatever modest arts support was provided during this period was usually disguised within non-arts programs.[25]

Throughout the 1950s, emphasis on practical necessity continued to color government arts policies. However, the trauma of the Holocaust had brought to American shores some of the most gifted, creative, and talented minds of the period. This infusion of artistic energy coupled with social, intellectural intellectual, and attitudinal changes in the citizenry resulted in a dynamic climate for the arts.

> The war brought to people of every economic class new knowledge about the world abroad, directly or indirectly introducing them to new ideas, new kinds of food and drink, and different types of entertainment. Many who had previously considered anything foreign undesirable, or at least unsuitable for everyday consumption, not only accepted such things but became genuinely and fervently attached to them. It was during World War II that the United States finally broke out of its isolation and even its dreams of isolation from the rest of the world. The effect on the arts in the country was explosive.[26]

The opening of America to the arts must also be examined from an economic and an educational standpoint. In the 1950s the standard of living had reached a level of affluence where many more of the nation's citizens could afford to turn their interest toward the arts. As John Adams had predicted, the nation had arrived at a place where the arts could assume importance in the lives of a large segment of the population. Moreover, it is possible that preceding generations of children, receiving some arts education in the schools, plus the Depression-generated arts presentations, had combined to produce an arts receptivity in many. Whatever the reasons, the postwar period witnessed the rumblings of what would later be referred to as a cultural explosion—that era of the Sixties and Seventies when arts interest, participation, and diversification would spread across the nation.

But, the federal government's response to these 1950 tremors was sporadic and indirect. With the exception of the tours sponsored by the State Department, White House dinners honoring outstanding artists, and indirect financial support in the form of income tax deductions for arts contributions, the government maintained its traditional policy of practical support for institutional uses only. This is not to say that certain new forms of federal arts support were not attempted, but they were, as Representative John Brademas stated, "introduced sheepishly and negated by laughter."[27]

Two significant federal actions occurred in the 1950s that were to affect future government efforts in arts support. Early in the decade President Truman tried to utilize the already existing Commission of Fine Arts in an advisory capacity, requesting that it investigate ways in which the arts could be aided on a national scale. The Commission, however, was dilatory and finally delivered its report to President Eisenhower in 1953. Although various recommendations were made, only one came to eventual fruition—the National Cultural Center, which was signed into public law on September 2, 1958. Five years later, as a result of a national tragedy, it was renamed for the late President John F. Kennedy. Senator J. William Fulbright and others in Congress initiated the legislation to rename the Center and authorize a matching grant of $15.5 million for its construction—the first concrete monetary evidence of federal arts support since the WPA days.[28]

The second significant action occurred in 1954. Nelson Rockefeller, an undersecretary in the Department of Health, Education and Welfare, persuaded President Eisenhower to sponsor legislation to create a National Council on the Arts.[29] Rockefeller developed a plan for a federal support agency based on the Arts Council of Great Britain. Congressional approval, however, was more difficult to obtain and the bill failed to receive the necessary votes. Nancy Hanks, who was working in the Rockefeller office at the time, recalled later that the bill was referred to in Congress as the "President's toe dance bill."

In 1960, when Nelson Rockefeller was elected Governor of the State of New York, he moved for the establishment of the New York State Council on the Arts. Nancy Hanks gives further insight into this event:

> When Mr. Rockefeller became Governor of New York, one of my jobs in the first administration was to coordinate the planning of legislation going through . . . . The day before the Legislature closed the first session, Governor Rockefeller said, "I forgot the arts bill, Nancy. Would you please get the old one that you typed in Washington and fix it up a little bit and let's introduce it."
>
> One of the legislative leaders said, "Nelson, under no circumstances are we going to introduce any more legislation and we're certainly not going to introduce an arts bill!" The arts bill was the first one going through the next session. And it was basically the same bill that had been developed in Washington in 1954, fixed up a bit.[30]

Hanks goes on to explain that the later federal legislation, though somewhat better in its wording, was also patterned after the 1954 bill.

Passage of the New York bill established that state agency as a pioneer in the field of government arts subsidies. Moreover, this agency gave experience to many people who would become influential in later federal arts efforts.[31]

Throughout the history of our nation, the federal government has usually responded when it perceived that its resources would be beneficial to the general welfare of its citizens. For years there was not sufficient pressure from the advocates of the arts to include them as a part of the general welfare and, previous to 1960, government funding was largely influenced by necessity and tempered by a traditional ambivalence toward direct support.

American congressional bodies included some legislators who embraced arts as ideal forms of expression, others who preferred the "homegrown" American folk arts to foreign imports, and still others who vigorously rejected all arts expression as unimportant and even detrimental to the national well-being. From these conflicting attitudes emerged a policy for federal properties and state ceremonies, and economic support for work programs and projects for unemployed artists. These two necessities influenced arts funding until the mid-twentieth century when another motivational factor, based to some degree on the two previous factors, assumed importance. For the first time, government support was proposed with the additional conviction that the arts were important to the well-being of man and, therefore, were deserving of liberal endowments from the public coffers.

To infer that events of the 1960s led completely away from practical and economic motivations toward humanistic federal assistance would be naïve and, indeed, misleading. However, a shift of cultural emphasis was making itself felt during this period, and the welfare of arts organizations and their publics became important ingredients in the formula of government support within "The Great Society." Stirring this mixture was an influential and determined group of arts advocates in league with legislators who shaped a national policy responsive to cultural necessity. The early 1960s marked the arrival of the federal government at the threshold of a new arts frontier.

Reference Notes

1. Quotations and information on the arts in colonial America were taken from P. H. Lang, *Mucis in Western Civilization* (New York: Norton, 1941), pp. 428, 691–694.
2. F. Taylor, "A Still Small Voice," *Musical America* (February 1963).
3. C. F. Adams, *Letters of John Adams Addressed to His Wife*, Vol. II, No. 178, Second letter, 1780 (Boston: Charles C. Little and James Brown, 1841), p. 68.
4. J. C. Fitzpatrick, *Writings of George Washington from the Original Manuscript, 1745–1799*, Vol. 21, December 22, 1780–April 26, 1781 (Washington: U.S. Government Printing Office, 1937).
5. R. F. Goldman, *The Concert Band*, Vol. I (New York: Rinehart and Company, 1946), p. 89.
6. J. R. Brademas, "The Arts and Public Happiness," *Music Educators Journal*, 27 (November 1969), p. 42.
7. V. White, *Grants for the Arts* (New York: Plenum Press, 1980), p. 89.
8. A. Heckscher, *The Arts and the National Government: Report to the President*, Senate Document N. 28 (Washington; U.S. Government Printing Office, 1963), p. 4.
9. U.S. Federal Government, *Congresional Record—House*, 43rd Cong., 1st sess., Vol. II, Part 3; and 46th Cong., 2nd sess., Vol. 10; Part 1 (Washington: U.S. Government Printing Office, 1874 and 1879), pp. 2078 and 21.
10. *The Statutes at Large of the United States of America*, Vol. 26 (Washington: U.S. Government Printing Office, 1891), p. 1093.
11. National Endowment for the Arts, "The National Council on the Arts and the National Endowment for the Arts During the Administration of President Lyndon B. Johnson: The History," Vol. 1 (Unpublished document available from the Lyndon B. Johnson Library, Austin, Texas, 1968), p. 3.
12. Federal government, *The Statutes at Large*, Vol. 36, 1911, p. 371.
13. National Endowment for the Arts, "The History," p. 3.
14. J. C. Taylor, "A Poignant, Relevant Backward Look at Artists of the Great Depression," *Smithsonian*, 10:7 (October 1979), p. 47.
15. W. F. McDonald, *Federal Relief Administration and the Arts* (Columbus: Ohio University Press, 1969), p. 587.
16. G. Monroe, *Fine Arts and the People*, a report of the Conference on the New Deal Cultural Project (Glassboro, N.J.: Glassboro State College, 1975), p. 1.
17. McDonald, pp. 367–370.

18. K. Yasko, taped interview, April 26, 1980, Madison, Wisc.
19. Brademas, "Public Happiness," pp. 42–43.
20. Quotations and information on the Federal Theatre Project were taken from H. Flanagan, *Arena: The History of the Federal Theatre* (New York: Benjamin Blom, 1965), pp. 333–436.
21. *Ibid.*
22. J. C. Taylor, "Artists of the Great Depression," p. 52.
23. Flanagan, "Federal Theatre," p. 325.
24. U.S. Federal Government, *Congressional Record—House*, 75th Cong., 1st sess., p. 8880.
25. White, "Grants," pp. 47–48.
26. Ibid.
27. Brademas, "Public Happiness," p. 43.
28. National Endowment for the Arts, "The History," p. 4.
29. N. Rockefeller, *Our Environment Can Be Saved* (New York: Doubleday, 1970), p. 112.
30. N. Hanks, "Overview from the Federal Chair," lecture, University of Wisconsin Summer Forum, *The Arts in the Changing Decade of the Seventies* (Madison, Wisc., July 21, 1980).
31. A. Barresi, "The History and Programs of the New York State Council on the Arts" (Unpublished doctoral dissertation, University of Michigan, 1973), pp. 104–107.

2

Reaching Legislative Consensus, 1960–1965

> In the eyes of posterity the success of the United States as a civilized society will be largely judged by the creative activities of its citizens in the arts, architecture, literature, music, and the sciences.
> —The President's Commission on National Goals (1960)

During the decades of the Fifties and Sixties, a tremendous expansion of interest in the arts in America occurred. This phenomenon, often termed in the popular press as a cultural "boom" or "explosion," was characterized as a seeking for cultural sustenance by an affluent population in a variety of settings and through a variety of experiences.

In 1958, *Newsweek* magazine published a series of articles entitled "New America." The last of these described Americans as "clamoring for culture" and stated that:

- More than 55 million Americans roam through art galleries and museums each year.
- Since 1939, about 2 billion paperback volumes have been bought from the counters of book and department stores and the racks of newsstands and drugstores.
- Some $400 million worth of records were sold last year [1957], about one-third of them classical, while the burgeoning hi-fi industry reckons that it sold nearly $500 million worth of amplifiers, turntables, speakers, and other bits of tweeting and woofing equipment to acoustical purists.[1]

The article cited other examples to illustrate the spread of culture across the country. In Rexburg, Idaho (pop. 4,253) and Glendive, Montana (pop. 5,254), thriving symphony orchestras existed. Across the nation more than 6,000 amateur painters were studying their craft while, in as small a place as Rangely, Colorado, 467 of the total 808 citizens raised $2,250 to present a concert series in the town. Even Birmingham, Alabama, a predominantly industrial, blue-collar city, was sponsoring its seventh festival of the arts and was expecting more than 100,000 people from all over the South to attend.

The thoroughly researched 1965 Rockefeller Panel Report on the performing arts provided additional statistics. It stated that 1,401 symphony orchestras existed at that time, more than double those existing in 1939; that the 754 groups presenting opera were almost double those existing in 1955; that the 40,000 theatrical enterprises had increased 15 percent over the previous ten years; that the number of dance companies in America had grown to a total approaching 200; and that the $400 million paid for admission to the performing arts had approximately doubled since 1950.

Cultural interest seemed to be at an all-time high during the early 1960s and it appeared that Americans were the world's largest consumers of culture. But why should such a condition have existed? What factors were responsible? Although a variety of explanations have been put forth in an effort to account for this cultural growth, none seem of themselves to be completely satisfactory.

One might, at first, attribute the "explosion," if that is what it was, to the rapid population growth; but it appears that increased arts participation was not proportionate with population increase.[2] Leisure-time availability has often been offered as an explanation because the work week was reduced from 50 hours in 1929 to 39 hours in 1958. However, demographic studies by economists Baumol and Bowen revealed that arts events were characteristically attended by professional persons—not the blue-collar population who made up the largest proportion of the national workforce. Still others have asserted that increased affluence of Americans allowed them the luxury of arts participation—that is, citizens had more money for cultural endeavors. This would seem a plausible explanation until one realizes that professional arts organizations of this period were experiencing extreme financial hardships.

Perhaps the answer to the increased arts interest was a combination of the above demographic and financial conditions and other more subtle sociological influences. Several generations of expanded arts education in the schools could have awakened a latent awareness of the arts which reached an active participation phase when corresponding factors of affluence and social mobility were added. Some sociologists even claim that the drive for the attainment of culture was the result of a desire for "firm, tradition-backed values on the part of people increasingly unsettled by the state of the world." Further, they viewed this interest as a "reaching for snobbish, prestige-giving activities which were once monopolized by the leisure classes," an interesting but somewhat cynical assessment of what might have really been for some, at least, a search for life-enriching experiences.[3]

One factor mentioned by almost everyone who has investigated the "culture boom" is that of immigration to America from Europe as a result of World War II. Artists, writers, and musicians came to America as part of a massive group of educated people with highly developed attitudes and appreciations for the arts. Because the arts had played such an important part in their lives in Europe, these new citizens sought to establish a cultural climate in the United States that would fulfil their desires for continuing arts experiences. As these people dispersed throughout the country, they impressed those around them with their artistic zeal and, by their example, encouraged other Americans to join them in arts experiences.

Whatever the accumulation of reasons, the fact remains that more Americans than ever before were seeking contact with the arts in a cultural climate that some characterized as revolutionary. Although eminent commentators, such as critic Stanley Kauffmann and composer Igor Stravinsky, despaired for artistic quality in a period where the arts received such popular support, it must be remembered that "most revolutions proceeded in confusion and entailed participation of the untutored."[4] They hoped that as public sophistication increased, so would levels of artistic quality.

Patterns of Arts Support prior to 1965

Although there was increased interest in the arts, most of the expansion may be characterized as amateur. While acknowledging the importance of amateur activity, the Rockefeller Panel Report quotes unsettling statistics about the status of the professional performing arts in the early 1960s: The American people may have experienced an extraordinary awakening to the performing arts, but comparatively few are ever exposed to any live professional presentations. By way of rough illustration:

- Broadway, historically the creative center of American theatre, has reduced its output from an average of 142 productions per year during the thirties to 63 in 1963–64 and its playhouses have diminished in number from 54 to 36 in the same span of years.
- The number of commercial theatres in the country dropped from 590 in 1927 to barely 200.
- Of the 1,401 symphony orchestras, only 54 are composed predominantly of professional musicians.
- In the entire country there are only five or six dance companies that meet high professional standards and possess any real degree of institutional stability; only one approaches giving year-around performances.
- Of the 754 opera-producing groups, only 35 to 40 are fully professional,

> and not more than 10 of these provide performances more than 15 days a year.[5]

The Panel concluded that, while amateur activity stimulated interest in professional arts activity, furnished young artists with initial experiences, and provided live performances where none might have existed otherwise, the ultimate responsibility for the highest levels of creativity and quality rested with professional artists and arts organizations. Despite the apparent grass-roots interest in the arts throughout the country, the basic financial health of professional artists and arts groups showed little or no significant improvement.[6]

The key to understanding this paradox rests in several factors. First, the production of professional artists, working and performing principally in the major urban areas, was for the most part inaccessible to a large segment of the nation. Funds for the distribution of art works or for touring activities by performing artists were restricted by tight finances. Second, the ability of the private sector to bridge traditional deficits between what artists earned and what they expended was reduced drastically by the ravages of inflation. The costs of production were rising to such a degree and amount that traditional sources of income were rapidly becoming inadequate.

Private Contributions

At one time in the nation's history, the income gaps of arts organizations could be bridged by wealthy private donors—patrons with large fortunes and cultural enthusiasms. Often these individuals or families established trust funds that sustained the artist or arts organization through periods of financial distress. As inflation eroded the dollar's value, the effectiveness of such trusts was reduced accordingly. In some instances, arts groups that were once able to sustain themselves from the interest paid on trust accounts were forced by inflation to draw on the principal. Such practices were extremely perilous to the financial strategies and stability of artists and arts organizations.

After World War II, patterns of private giving began to shift from the few large donors to numerous small patrons. By the middle 1960s, roughly 90 percent of all private donations came from individuals as tax-deductible gifts. Though these gifts were often small, they were the most important single source of contributions. In 1969, the American Symphony Orchestra League reported that "88 percent of the total number of donations made to symphony orchestras' annual maintenance funds were in amounts of less than $100 and averaging $37." These donations accounted for approximately 40 percent of the total annual contributed dollars received by symphony orchestras.[7] Private contributions to all of the arts in 1968 amounted to between $240 and $350 million.[8]

Although donations to the arts over the years became more numerous, the amounts donated became smaller. The steadily worsening effects inflation on these arts dollars reduced their buying power. Private patrons alone could neither completely subsidize deficits nor increase support sufficiently to maintain even traditional levels of activity. Rudolph Bing, general manager of the Metropolitan Opera Association, informed the Rockefeller Panel that arts organizations would have to broaden their bases of support in the coming years. This action could only be accomplished if arts groups would become more imaginative and effective in developing programs to serve the artistic needs of the community, and if the public were made aware of the significance of the work done by artists and arts organizations.[9]

Foundation Support of the Arts

Over the years, philanthropic giving by foundations of various types has assumed increasing importance. This kind of funding took a new direction during the 1960s when educational projects replaced the traditional health and welfare projects as recipients of the major portion of philanthropic grants. It may be surmised that this development was due to several factors: first, the federal government, after World War II, assumed greater responsibility for health and welfare matters through the initiation of federal agencies and programs designed to address these areas of public concern and, second, the scientific advances of the Soviet Union had caused a national feeling of educational inferiority which resulted in a reexamination of many educational programs. Teaching Johnny to read, do mathematics, and develop scientific understanding became a national priority that affected educational establishments throughout the country. Foundations, reacting to the educational impetus, espoused this priority by providing money for educational programs. Arts and humanities advocates, believing that instruction in their areas was also important, sought support from foundation sources as well.

Baumol and Bowen reported that, in 1964, a total of $850 million or 6 percent of the total private philanthropy was provided by foundations. Of the 24,000 organizations of the foundation variety existing at that time, 16,000 were presumed to qualify as active foundations and these were increasing at a rate of about 1,500 a year.[10] The Foundation Center, an independent organization monitoring activities of foundations, further estimated that two-thirds of the assets of the 50 largest foundations were traceable to bequests received since 1939 and that one-third of this amount was obtained in the 1950s. These 50 foundations accounted for more than half of all foundation assets.[11]

During the early 1960s, 4 to 7 percent of foundation philanthropy was devoted to the humanities which included many types of arts endeavors. In fact, in 1963 and 1964, the performing arts were the main beneficiary within the humanities category. Thirty-five foundations awarded grants of $10,000 or more to the performing arts while, of the 6,000 foundations of substantial size, only 65 made any grants of that amount to the humanities. Arts grants played a crucial role in the operation of many arts organizations—without these gifts many groups, including dance troupes, regional theatres, opera companies, and symphony orchestras, might not have survived.[12]

Despite these significant instances of support, foundations in general provided only a small proportion of arts contributions, a situation that seemed unlikely to change substantially, especially in the case of smaller foundations. The Rockefeller Panel reported that many artists had not adequately made their case for foundation support, and also asserted that arts groups, in comparison with other claimants on foundation resources, suffered "all too often from poor management and inadequate planning."[13] Moreover, economists Baumol and Bowen stated that foundation support for arts endeavors was often withheld from groups with unbusinesslike organization and administration. They further revealed that the awarding of "seed money" for innovative projects required artists to attract more permanent forms of financial support in order to continue the project after foundation funds were withdrawn—an ability not adequately developed by most artists and arts groups.[14] Finally, the Rockefeller Panel advised artists to become more articulate in their requests for foundation contributions.

> Whether they are approaching a national or local foundation, arts organizations must state their case coherently and fully. This is not a matter of public relations technique but of making a reasonable attempt to project future programs and needs and demonstrating a conscientious effort to develop other sources of funds. In many communities the argument for support must begin at the most basic level. Arts leaders must be prepared to discuss the nature of the arts, why they are important, and why foundation support of this still-minority interest is justified. They must work hard because the case for the arts is less readily evident than that of education or medicine. The case must be well thought through and be understood by everyone who expects to make headway with the foundations or any other potential source of support.[15]

By way of conclusion, the Panel cautioned artists to recognize that foundation resources were not limitless and that they could not be viewed as "cure-all solutions." Foundations, on the other hand, were encouraged to accept artists as they did scientists and educators and were admonished to "increase their interest in the arts and in doing so to recognize the necessarily speculative element in the development of the arts."[16]

The Ford Foundation, possibly the most generous contributor to the arts during this period, developed a granting procedure under W. McNeil Lowry that addressed itself in part to the problems of artists in attracting more permanent sources of support. By adopting a matching grant concept, used so successfully by the Arts Council of Great Britain, the Ford Foundation encouraged artists to seek funds from other private sources to match those provided by the foundation. In effect, this procedure broadened the financial base of artists and, in many cases, stimulated matching contributions to continue the funding of a project even after temporary foundation moneys were withdrawn.[17] When the National Endowment for the Arts was established, the congressional legislation incorporated this effective funding strategy.

Corporate Support for the Arts

Corporate support for the arts during the sixth decade of the twentieth century was viewed as a relatively untapped financial resource. Although corporations had contributed to many philanthropic causes, arts projects had claimed a small portion of their donations.

The Internal Revenue Code of 1935 had introduced tax provisions permitting the deduction of charitable contributions for corporate income tax purposes up to a maximum of 5 percent of taxable income, but the provision was not widely utilized. By the year 1966, business had contributed just over 1 percent of taxable income to these causes. This sum amounted to roughly 5 percent of the total philanthropic giving provided in that year.

In more concrete terms, corporate philanthropy rose from $30 million in 1937 to about $512 million in 1962. These contributions, claim Baumol and Bowen, rose faster than corporate profit. (In 1936, corporate giving amounted to less than one-half of one percent of profits, and in 1966 it was well over one percent.) It must be remembered, however, that a relatively small portion of this money was awarded to the arts.[18] C. Douglas Dillon, former chairman of the board of Dillon, Read & Company, former Secretary of the Treasury, and the first chairman of the Business Committee for the Arts (BCA), claimed that in 1966 contributions to the arts by corporations amounted to only $22 million—a "mere three percent of business contributions for *all* philanthropic purposes, which totaled $750 million."[19]

To encourage business support of the arts, a group of business leaders assembled in 1967 at the suggestion of David Rockefeller, chairman of the Chase Manhattan Bank, and set up the Business Committee for the Arts. Although BCA membership included the presidents and board chairmen of some of the country's and the world's largest corporations, its philosophy was community-oriented in that every business, regardless of its size, was encouraged to support the arts of its community in some fashion.[20]

As a rationale for increased corporate contributions, arts advocates argued that a firm, wishing to function well in a society, should embrace charitable giving as a primary corporate concern. Dillon implied that if companies would regard such donations as a community responsibility they would receive substantial nonmonetary dividends.

> Companies that do become involved are reaping unexpectedly rich returns in good

> will from their customers, from their employees, and from the communities in which they are established. There is no public service that business can undertake that will yield more dividends of good will than support of the arts.[21]

Despite the urging of arts advocates, only about half of the nation's largest corporations gave something to the arts in 1965. However, it should be noted that discrepancies on estimated annual arts support figures result from differences in the interpretation of what constitutes such a contribution. Commenting on this situation, Virginia White stated:

> If deductible business expenses that benefit the arts are included, the figure is not the same as it is if only direct donations to artists or arts programs are taken into account. Just as corporations make "in kind" donations of equipment and products that do not show up on their giving estimates, they also support the arts in ways other than through traditional philanthropy. The increasing use of contemporary art in the decor of corporate offices or building lobbies, for example, provides a large, new outlet for the work of modern artists and an opportunity for their work to be seen by a large audience, while it serves to make the offices and the buildings more interesting and attractive.[22]

Regardless of how one interprets the somewhat confusing and often conflicting statistics, it is commonly agreed that corporate arts contributions were at best minimal during the 1950s and 1960s. Corporate leaders, in general, seemed to find it difficult to justify to stockholders the expenditure of company profits on arts projects that yielded few, if any, tangible returns.

However, corporations showed interest in arts projects that would enhance their corporate image in the community and in the nation. Arts advocates, such as the Business Committee for the Arts, recognized this fact and assumed a more aggressive posture in their quest for the corporate dollar. To compete with more traditional philanthropic causes, advocates presented rationales for business support that stressed visibility as an asset to corporate development. Using this approach, they pointed to the growing public interest in the arts and encouraged business leaders to recognize that arts contributions could enhance the corporate image in the community and in the nation, positively affect corporate sales and services, assist in the recruitment of quality personnel, and stimulate to some degree the growth of additional commerce and industry.[23] This approach seemed to have an effect as corporate contributions during the 1960s gradually began to increase.

Another factor was influential on corporate giving. While corporations recognized that arts production was not business oriented, they were reluctant to provide funds for projects that were not administered in a "businesslike" manner. As community and business leaders, they began to seek out "career-minded young people to manage the affairs of cultural institutions."[24] Such actions were influential in the initiation of the new profession of arts administration—administrators with an understanding of business and the arts who assisted artists within cultural organizations and within state and local arts councils.

The Arts in a New Sociological Position

Increased public interest of the 1950s and 1960s placed the arts in a new sociological position. Previously, many artists and arts organizations had been somewhat removed from the mainstream of American life. The arts were considered by many to be exclusive diversions of a select group of people with sufficient leisure time, cultural background, and income to indulge their interests. As these advantages became available to more citizens, the traditional insularity of artists and cultural institutions began to vanish. Innovative programs of the late 1960s placed professional arts activities in new circumstances and surroundings, making them available to previously excluded segments of the population. In a sense, the "imposing walls of culture" began to crumble as the arts achieved a more significant place in the lives of Americans. As the decade progressed, this factor allowed arts advocates to make an even stronger case for support from private and government sources. In his book *Culture and Company*, Alvin Reiss characterizes this sociological shift in these terms:

> For many years, the arts case was virtually unknown. In spite of some trail-blazing efforts at the community level and some broad promotional efforts by national service organizations in the arts, culture was of small concern to the average citizen. Then, in 1965, the dam burst.[25]

Three landmark events occurred that year. First was the publication of the Rockefeller Panel Report, *The Performing Arts: Problems and Prospects*, which clearly articulated the arts cause to the general public. The fact that this report was made by a prestigious organization caused it to become front-page news. Second, congressional passage of the Elementary and Secondary School Act authorized schools to "develop innovative projects which could utilize the services of arts groups and cultural resources in their communities."[26] Finally, the passage of the National Foundation on the Arts and Humanities Act of 1965 allowed the federal government to become a small but official patron of the arts. In that capacity, it could only give out modest sums of money because of its extremely small appropriation. More important, however, it could consistently and forcefully make a case for the arts to the private sector. In brief, this federal agency, over the years, became a bridge between artists and private patrons.

Important Events Leading to the Passage of Arts Funding Legislation

After World War II, a larger proportion of the American public than ever before had become receptive to the arts. However, while amateur endeavors requiring little financial aid were flourishing, professional artists were faced with dwindling support from traditional sources. Rising production costs and the devastating effects of inflation rendered formerly adequate arts subsidies insufficient to cope with ever-widening income gaps. These circumstances activated a chain of events that eventually led to direct government involvement in arts funding.

For clarity, it seems appropriate that the growth of government be examined from two vantage points: first, those general actions by government personnel that influenced the development of government interest; and, second, those specific pieces of legislation that influenced the course of federal arts commitment.

General Actions by Government Personnel

After World War II, both the Truman and Eisenhower administrations exhibited interest in the national arts scene. In 1952, President Truman had requested that the existing Commission on Fine Arts examine ways in which the arts could be aided by the federal government. The commission report, finally delivered to President Eisenhower in 1953, recommended among other things the establishment of a National Cultural Center which the President signed into Public Law 85-874 on September 2, 1958.[27] President Eisenhower, at the urging of HEW Undersecretary Nelson Rockefeller, also encouraged the establishment of an advisory arts council which was supported by a few influential congressmen.[28]

President Kennedy's personal commitment to the arts was highly influential in creating a climate that was conducive to cultural recognition. His support—manifested in various ways such as the participation of poet Robert Frost in the inauguration ceremony, White House dinners honoring outstanding artists, and his personal attendance at arts presentations—provided a new kind of media visibility for the arts and fostered government consideration of them.

In 1961, the intervention of the Labor Department in the Metropolitan Opera strike was a significant step along the road to government arts involvement. Arthur Goldberg, the Secretary of Labor for the Kennedy administration, brought the forces of the Department of Labor into action as arbitrators. In the arbitration award, Goldberg stated that "the nation must come to accept the arts as a new community responsiblity and part of this responsibility must fall to the federal government."[29] The results of this action, in addition to lending importance to cultural considerations by the national government, also established the concept that artistic activities and institutions were national resources worthy of government attention. Moreover, the intervention supported the idea that artists were working citizens, performing a vital service, and worthy of a suitable living wage. Finally, it demonstrated that the arts could be important to the economic well-being of a geographic area since peripheral business around the Metropolitan Opera were, to a large degree, dependent on the financial success of that institution.

Early in 1962, President Kennedy appointed August Heckscher, former director of the Twentieth Century Fund, as Special Consultant on the Arts to the President. Kennedy asked Heckscher to prepare a special report on the relationship between the arts and the federal government. On June 11, 1963, Heckscher submitted his report.

In this highly publicized document, the President's special consultant encouraged the implementation of ideas that some legislators had been supporting over the past decade, but which had received little political or legislative recognition. The Heckscher report came out at a crucial time; it became a blueprint for government arts involvement since most of the suggestions made in it eventually received legislative approval.

Three major suggestions emerged that were implemented over the next several years.[30] First, Heckscher recommended the permanent establishment of the post of Special Advisor on the Arts within the Executive Branch. In the description of the advisor's duties, he stated:

> Besides the policy planning and review functions which formed the major part of the original assignment, he should be available for advice on all matters pertaining to the arts which arise in the course of the administration's work. He should be the President's liaison with the National Cultural Center, and should sit on panels and meetings where matters of Federal architecture, design, graphics, etc., are being disucssed.

Second, the report recommended the establishment of an Advisory Council on the Arts within the Executive Office of the President. This agency would play an essential role in the establishment of an orderly and representative structure for dealing with the arts.

> Its basic function is to continue and fill out the work of study and gathering information begun with the limited resources of the speical consultant; to review Federal policies and make recommendations for improving design; to recommend long-range programs; and to assure the active participation of the artistic community in the Government effort.
>
> The special advisor can call upon the Council and its specialized committees for assistance. The Advisory Council will thus become part of the machinery through which advice is provided to the various agencies of government as they endeavor to set up arts committees of their own, to organize competitions, or otherwise raise the level of design.
>
> The President will appoint the Chairman of the Council, who presumably will be the special advisor.

Finally, Heckscher suggested the establishment of a national arts foundation which "would be a means of administering grants-in-aid, generally on a matching basis, to states and institutions setting up arts councils." The proposed foundation might also make available grants for projects proposed by artists or cultural institutions, thereby enabling it to consider the "support of experiments designed to increase attendance, to foster creativity and introduce contemporary works to

r services on an experimental basis." Since the founda-
ting cultural diversity, innovation, and excellence, it
ies to carry the deficits of artists or arts institutions.
s from legislators who would oppose the entrance of
ent into the cultural funding arena, Heckscher concluded
with these comments:

> What is sketched here represents the beginning of what could become a permanent policy giving form to the relationship between government and the arts. It is a limited policy; for government's role in this area must always be marginal. It is a policy not copied after European models, but keyed to the particular conditions of diversity and decentralization prevailing in the United States.
>
> There will always remain those who feel that art and government should exist in different spheres, having nothing to do with each other. But in fact the Government of the United States comes up constantly against choices and decisions where esthetic considerations are involved. In today's world, moreover, artistic talent and creativity are resources vitally important to the Nation, and the well-being of the people is related to progress in the arts as surely as to progress in fields such as recreation and education where government's responsibility is fully recognized.
>
> Although government's role in the arts must always remain peripheral, with individual creativity and private support being central, that is no reason why the things which government can properly do in this field should not be done confidently and expertly.

On June 12, 1963, President Kennedy established the President's Advisory Council on the Arts by Executive Order No. 1112. There seems to be ample evidence that the President used the machinery of the executive order out of frustration with the House of Representatives' reluctance to give legislative status to this advisory body. Kennedy's statement concerning the council's establishment subtly reflects these feelings. He said:

> Establishment of an Advisory Council on the Arts has long seemed a natural step in fulfilling the Government's responsibility to the arts. I acknowledge the support of members of both Houses for this measure. I am hopeful that the Congress will give the Council a statutory base, but meanwhile the setting up of the Council by Executive action seems timely and advisable. Accordingly, I am establishing the President's Advisory Council on the Arts within the Executive office, to be composed of heads of Federal departments and agencies concerned with the arts and 30 private citizens who have played a prominent part in the arts. Private members will be drawn from civic and cultural leaders and others who are engaged professionally in some phase of the arts. . . . An Executive Order is being issued today defining the scope and structure of the Council and I shall shortly announce the names of those private citizens I am asking to serve.[31]

Although the Council never convened because of the death of the President in November, the idea continued to receive support in Congress until it finally received statutory acceptance. When it was enacted into law, most of the council composition and duties outlined in Kennedy's statement were included within two bodies—the National Council on the Arts and the Federal Council on the Arts.

After Lyndon B. Johnson assumed the presidency, he appointed a Special Assistant to the President on the Arts—the first full-time arts consultant in America's history. The man selected, Roger L. Stevens, a prominent theatrical producer, was appointed on May 13, 1964, and charged with the development of Congressional support for the establishment of a permanent arts agency. Stevens immediately began to lobby congressmen for the passage of legislation.

In August 1964, Stevens appeared before the National Democratic Platform Committee to urge increased federal recognition and support for the arts. The resulting statement—the first of its kind to be included as a political plank—pledged the party to "encourage further support of the arts, giving people a better chance to use increased leisure and recognizing that the achievements of art are an index of the greatness of a civilization."[32]

The stage had thus been set for the passage of significant arts legislation although the eventual enactment of such laws was a slow, tortuous process for those supporting them, filled with impassioned dialogue, skillful legislative manipulation, and pure persistence on the part of arts advocates in both houses of Congress.

Rationale for Passage of Arts Legislation

Throughout the twentieth century, "conservative" politicians espoused the free enterprise system as the primary economic guiding principle. Government's role, they believed, was to expedite matters so that this system would work efficiently. "Liberals" also supported this idea, but have traditionally shown concern as well for those areas of our culture that did not receive the full benefits of the free enterprise system. Social welfare, education, and health, they believed, were legitimate matters of concern for government intervention. Moreover, they maintained that the rule that should determine the government's relation to the arts is basically the same as that which shaped its role in general. As Abraham Lincoln eloquently stated:

> The legitimate object of government is to do for a community of people whatever they need to have done, but cannot do at all, or cannot so well do, for themselves, in their separate and individual capacities. In all the people can individually do as well for themselves, government ought not to interfere.[33]

Supporters of arts legislation and their opponents were divided into liberal and conservative camps. Politically, arts advocates were generally liberal Democrats and Republicans while opponents were often bipartisan conservatives. Moreover, legislators from urban centers with active cultural environments were initiators and supporters of arts bills while those from less developed situations tended to represent the conservative opposition.

As a rationale for government involvement in cultural matters, drafters of the legislation pointed out that the arts were traditionally identified with great cultures and that the survival of the arts in America was of major importance. They also claimed that the quality of life of the nation's citizens would be improved and enhanced by a widened access and exposure to the arts. Because the arts were a national resource, because a large segment of the population had demonstrated an interest in arts activities, and because professional arts production was hampered by financial problems, the arts should be fostered, nurtured, and even funded by the federal government.

In a *New York Times* article entitled "New Cultural Climate" (1961), Senator Jacob Javits of New York stated that he believed the people of the country were ready, through their elected representatives in Congress, to enact a federal program to help the development of our "nation's cultural resources" in the performing and visual arts. The article continued:

> I have been trying to get Federal help for the arts since 1949 and this is the first year that I am confident our country has reached the point when the needed public support can be marshaled to bring about the adoption of the legislation.[34]

Another Javits article, appearing in the February 17 (1961) issue of *Backstage,* stated that the election of the culturally-inclined President Kennedy, and examples provided by the British and Canadian arts councils and by state arts councils, would increase the likelihood for passage of arts legislation during that session of Congress. He also identified an important factor that had previously hampered legislative affirmation:

> . . . one of the main blocks to previous legislation introduced in the House, Representative Barden of North Carolina, no longer heads the Committee on Labor and Education. Representative Barden pigeonholed nearly all such bills in the past but the new head of the committee is Congressman Adam Clayton Powell, of New York, who is expected to move all such bills along quickly. More liberal committee heads in both Houses of Congress are now receptive to legislation aiding the arts and a mail campaign could convince the recalcitrants.[35]

To fully comprehend the gist of the Javits statement, one must first understand the process by which a bill moves through Congress. Often, hearings on a proposed piece of legislation are held by interested Senate and House members in their respective committee rooms. Witnesses with expert knowledge are invited to testify concerning the proposed legislation and their testimony is taken into account in the final drafting of the legislation. Because approval of both the House of Representatives and the Senate is required for passage into law, sponsors in both houses must introduce the legislation into the appropriate chamber.

Both houses then submit the legislation for consideration by a Congressional committee with appropriate jurisdiction. It is probable that the bill will then be assigned by the jurisdictional committee to a special subcommittee for discussion before it returns to the complete committee for consideration.

The legislative process of Congress allows a great deal of power to the committee chairmen and committee members. For example, it is possible for a dissenting chairman to stall a bill by deferring its placement on the Congressional calendar. A majority of committee members may refuse to report the bill out of committee if they do not want it considered by the complete House or Senate. A bill stalled in committee until the close of a session is, in effect, "killed" and, if the sponsor wishes, must be reintroduced in the next session of Congress. However, if a majority of members from the appropriate house wishes to release the stalled bill during the session, these Congressmen may "petition the bill out of committee" by obtaining the required number of signatures.

If a bill receives favorable consideration in committee, it is "reported out" to the complete chamber of Congress for debate, after which amendments are offered and voted on. At this point the bill may either come up for a vote by the total membership or be "recommitted" to committee for further consideration.

When the House and Senate pass similar versions of a bill, a simple concurrence by both chambers is all that is necessary. Where House and Senate versions vary considerably, they are submitted to a joint committee of both houses for compromise solutions. Revised versions are then returned to each house for approval. Of course, there are subtle variations in this procedure depending on particular circumstances, but in general this is the route followed by a bill before it reaches the desk of the President for his signature.

The constitutional system of checks and balances requires that the President, representing the Executive Branch of government, sign any bill before it can become law. Usually, his refusal to sign a bill or his outright veto will prohibit a piece of legislation from becoming law. Only a two-thirds vote of the House and Senate membership can override his veto.

During the early 1960s numerous bills in support of the arts were introduced in the House and Senate. Most of these fell into one or more of three categories:

1. Those bills advocating the establishment of an Advisory Arts Council.
2. Those bills advocating the establishment of a national arts agency with funding capabilities.
3. Those bills that proposed a plan to assist state-sponsored arts programs by granting each state a specified sum in matching federal funds.[36]

For brevity, only those pieces of legislation that eventually achieved passage will be examined.

Attempts to Establish a National Advisory Arts Council

The concept of an Advisory Council on the Arts and a Foundation for the Arts was the subject of lively debate by legislators during both the Eisenhower and Kennedy administrations. The Senate in 1956 had already passed a bill to establish such a Council but the House had failed to concur. After testing the political waters in 1961, House advocates realized that attaining both a Council and a Foundation would be impossible because of the opposition in House membership. The advocates decided instead to work for the passage of a bill to establish an advisory council as an initial step toward the eventual achievement of an advisory group and a funding agency. Representative Frank Thompson of New Jersey, a long-time advocate of arts legislation, introduced H.R. 4172 in the 87th Congress.[37]

The House bill proposed a council that would act as a coordinating body between private and governmental activities in the arts. Specifically, it would "recommend ways to maintain and increase the cultural resources of the United States; propose methods to encourage private initiative in the arts; cooperate with local, state, and Federal departments and agencies to foster artistic and cultural endeavors; and strive to stimulate greater appreciation for the arts by the nation's citizens."

As part of the Department of Health, Education, and Welfare (HEW), the Council was to be composed of private citizens appointed by the President. The members were to represent, in approximate proportions, the major arts fields of music, drama, dance, literature, architecture and allied arts, photography, graphic and crafts arts, films, radio, and television.

House debate on H.R. 4172 was punctuated with pro and anti Council statements. Advocates spoke of the importance of the arts in the quality of life and the nation's place in history. An advisory council, they felt, would begin to accomplish these goals. The bill's opponents argued against its passage mainly on fiscal grounds: "With the nation $290 billion in debt," stated Representative Howard Gross of Iowa, "an additional $200,000 each year for a council might be better deferred until we have a balanced budget in this country and start retiring the Federal debt." Representative Howard Smith of Virginia (Judge Smith), an outspoken foe of arts legislation and powerful chairman of the House Rules Committee, took a different tack. He sarcastically questioned which endeavors would be considered artistic:

> What are the arts? And here is where I display my ignorance. I do not know . . . I suppose fiddle players would be in the arts and the painting of pictures would be in the arts. It was suggested that poker playing would be an artful occupation. Is this going to subsidize poker players that get in trouble?

Both of these conservative congressmen as well as others who spoke were seeking to maintain the traditional stance of government toward assisting the arts only in instances of practical necessity. The more liberal legislators, however, were striving to develop a new legislative position—that the arts were the proper concern of government and that federal support was a matter of cultural necessity. Although, on September 21, 1961, this bill was defeated on the House floor, the pro-arts arguments had been forcefully presented and they were to gain additional adherents in later sessions of Congress.

The National Arts and Cultural Development Act: Senate Approval

If the impetus for government arts support was somewhat tentative in the House of Representatives, it was considerably stronger in the Senate. During the early deliberations of the 88th Congress, the Senate considered a bill that was a combination of three pieces of legislation presented in the 87th Congress by Senators Hubert Humphrey of Minnesota, Joseph Clark of Pennsylvania, and Jacob Javits of New York.[38] The combined bill presented under the cosponsorship of Senators Humphrey, Javits, Clark, Pell, and Ribicoff consisted of two title segments. Title I was concerned with the establishment of an Advisory Council on the Arts within the Executive Office of the President and Title II provided for the institution of a National Arts Foundation to "award grants-in-aid to private groups and States in support of programs and projects" which would make significant contributions to the arts.[39,40]

On December 20, 1963, the National Arts and Cultural Development Act (S. 2379) came up for a vote on the floor of the Senate. While reviewing the bill's content, Senator Claiborne Pell stated that during hearings before his subcommittee 50 distinguished representatives of American cultural life "whole-heartedly and enthusiastically" supported its enactment. The hearings also revealed that private financial sources alone could no longer sustain American cultural activities; that a financial crisis existed in the arts; and that, by ignoring the plight of the creative arts, the government was relinquishing "one of the great advantages over the communists."[41] Obviously, arts advocates at the hearings may have been indulging in a bit of flag-waving when they characterized the arts as a natural resource and a cause for national pride. They were introducing and the Senator was endorsing the issue of cultural superiority as a rationale for federal arts support.

During the course of the debate, other Senators echoed Pell's justifications for passage and cited instances where state governments were initiating programs to encourage arts development. It was implied that the federal government should follow the example by instituting a program that provided a national plan for cultural progress. This, they felt, could be accomplished most effectively through the establishment of a National Arts Council and a National Arts Foundation.

Only one of the bill's opponents spoke during this short debate. Senator

Strom Thurmond of South Carolina, at that time a Democrat, raised several issues for consideration. The first issue referred to the constitutionality of federal arts subsidies. Senator Thurmond attacked this issue because arts advocates based much of their rationale for governemnt involvement on the "general welfare" clause of the Constitution. He maintained that:

> The general welfare provision of the Constitution does not authorize the Congress of the United States to engage in programs of this type. It gives no legislative power per se to the Congress, but merely acts as a further restraint upon actions which are taken under authority granted elsewhere in the Constitution.[42]

Thurmond next addressed the matter of artistic control by government. He reminded the Senate that the Supreme Court had ruled "that the Federal Government has the power to control that which it subsidizes and experience proves that when the Federal Government has the power, that power is eventually exercised." In short, if the government furnished the money, it could and would control arts production regardless of any safeguards provided within the legislation. He further warned that inevitable federal control would eventually lead to sterility of thought and production and stifling of the truly creative mind.[43]

During ensuing speeches in support of the legislation, arts advocates were quick to remind Senator Thurmond that the question of constitutionality as it pertains to the general welfare clause was open to interpretation and that the sums appropriated would hardly be enough to control any magnitude of arts production. Moreover, the bill's provisions for combined support from federal and private sources would counteract any efforts by either sector to influence the quality of artistic activities. Their arguments won the day and the Senate passed the National Arts and Cultural Development Act.

The relative absence of organized opposition in the Senate demonstrated the traditional willingness of that body to accept arts legislation. Resistance on the House of Representatives, however, was still inhibiting complete legislative consensus.

House Passage of the National Arts and Cultural Development Act of 1964

When Roger L. Stevens was appointed to the post of Special Assistant to the President on the Arts in May 1964, he immediately began the difficult task of urging House members to pass pending pieces of cultural legislation. Bill H.R. 9586 to establish a National Council on the Arts, which President Kennedy had hoped for, was still locked in the powerful House Committee on Rules. The Rules Committee chairman, Howard W. Smith, was an opponent of arts legislation and refused to allow the bill to be reported out for consideration on the House floor. Roger Stevens, as his first task in his new Special Assistant role, "made the journey daily from the White House to the Hill during the month of July and talked with a number of Congressmen."[44] Still, the bill was bottled up.

In a recent interview, Roger Stevens described the personal approach that he used to get the National Arts and Cultural Development Act released from Judge Smith's powerful committee. Stevens was finally able to get the act released from Judge Smith's iron grip by enlisting the help of one of Judge Smith's good friends, Robert Fleming, head of the Riggs Bank. Stevens told Fleming he was working on a bill which he was having trouble getting out of the Judge's committee. Fleming, a man of many interests who, as a Washingtonian, wanted the city to become arts-oriented as a national capital should be, dictated a letter immediately to Judge Smith and sent it over to him. Within a few days the bill was reported out.[45]

Livingston L. Biddle, former assistant to Senator Pell and later chairman of the Arts Endowment, remembers that the reluctance of the House of Representatives to accept Title II of the Senate passed bill was apparent early in the House deliberations. When the bill "went over to the House side," Biddle commented, "the House eliminated the foundation part and only left the advisory council in place."[46]

On August 20, 1964, the House debated H.R. 9586, a scaled-down version of the National Arts and Cultural Development Act already passed by the Senate.[47] Representatives favoring the arts viewed the acceptance of this reduced bill as a way of getting their foot in the door. They reasoned that by first achieving an advisory council they would later be able to muster support for a federal arts foundation. Opponents, on the other hand, saw this "sanitized" version of the Senate-approved bill as ineffectual and nonthreatening.

During the course of the debate, pro and con arguments similar to those raised in earlier congressional sessions were made. At one point, however, a new aspect of federal cultural support was introduced. Representative John E. Fogarty of Rhode Island stated that he would "reintroduce in the next session of Congress" a bill calling for the creation of a National Arts Foundation and a National Institute of the Arts and Humanities. This was the first time in the congressional debates on federal arts legislation that anyone had formally suggested linking support for the humanities with funding for the arts. Fogarty's comment was almost lost in the lively discussion, but his idea was to gain increasing importance when later sessions of Congress considered ways of providing federal arts subsidies.

After the debate was concluded, a vote of the House membership was taken and the National Arts and Cultural Development Act of 1964 was passed by a vote of 213 to 135. After repeated attempts in previous congressional sessions, this long-awaited legislation—the first step toward active government involvement in the arts—was finally achieved in the House of Representatives.

On the next day, August 21, 1964, the Senate took up consideration of H.R. 9586. Senator Pell stated that he regretted that the Title II portion of the original Senate bill (providing for a foundation to make grants-in-aid) did not receive endorsement by the House. "Nevertheless, I feel that the bill we have before us constitutes an important step forward in the bettering of our cultural vitality."[48] Along with other senators who voiced similar disappointment, he urged a consensus vote from the Senate.[1] After the consensus vote was achieved, Senator Humphrey rose to address the Senate. He said:

> But I say with a note of happiness tonight that we waited many long years for the elected representatives of the people of the United States to authorize by statute the establishment of a National Council on the Arts to promote the development of the arts in the United States. This is a great day, it seems to me, for the cultural life of the nation.

On September 3, 1964, just after the Democratic Convention, President Johnson signed Public Law 88-579, establishing the first National Council on the Arts.[49] The President now had the congressional mandate to assemble an advisory arts council.

During the early months of 1965, the President and his special arts advisor, Roger Stevens, were considering the first appointments to the National Council. In February, Senator Javits, one of the most ardent advocates of arts legislation, became impatient with what he perceived to be a delay in the Council implementation. When he persistently chided Stevens about the matter, Stevens appealed to the White House for immediate action. (In fact, the 24 Council members were already selected and about to be named by the President.) To convince opponents of the legislation that the Council was a reality and to calm the fears of Senator Javits, Stevens was given permission to announce the names on February 23, 1965.[50] They were:

Members with terms expiring in 1970 (6-year terms):

Albert Bush-Brown, President, Rhode Island School of Design
Paul H. Engle, poet, writer, teacher
Ralph Philips Hanes, Jr., President, Arts Council of America
Oliver Smith, theatrical designer, producer, painter
Isaac Stern, musician
George Stevens, Sr., film director and producer
Minoru Yamasaki, architect

Members with terms expiring in 1968 (3-year terms):

Leonard Bernstein, composer, conductor
Anthony Bliss, President, Metropolitan Opera Association
David Brinkley, NBC News
Warner Lawson, Dean of the College of Fine Arts, Howard University

*Senator Javits sought to salvage some portion of the funding concept for which he had striven so long. He offered a proposal for administration consideration that would invest the council with the authority to accept bequests, gifts, and donations which could be used for the benefit and objectives of the council until some other means of funding could be provided. The Javits proposal was officially read into the *Congressional Record* and shortly thereafter a vote on consensus was taken.

William Pereira, architect, film producer
David Smith, sculptor
James Johnson Sweeney, writer, museum director
Richard Rodgers, composer

Members with terms expiring in 1966 (1-year terms):
Elizabeth Ashley, actress
Agnes DeMille, choreographer
Ralph Waldo Ellison, writer, lecturer, teacher
Father Gilbert Hartke, Head of Speech and Drama Department, Catholic University of America
Eleanor Lambert, Honorary Member, Council of Fashion Designers of America
Gregory Peck, actor
Otto Wittman, museum director
Stanley Young, author, publisher, Executive Director, American National Theatre and Academy
(Ex-officio) Dr. S. Dillon Ripley, Secretary, The Smithsonian Institution.[51]

Development of the National Foundation for the Arts and Humanities Legislation

With the National Council on the Arts in place, the administration could now turn its attention to the attainment of a government agency with "sufficient funds to assist actively in American cultural development." President Johnson, in his State-of-the-Union message, provided a strong impetus for the creation of such an agency by stating: "To help promote and honor creative achievements, I will propose a National Foundation on the Arts."[52]

While Senate willingness to support such legislation had been demonstrated in several previous sessions of Congress, House approval was less certain. Roger Stevens, therefore, turned his attention to lobbying House members. Because there was considerable support in the House of Representatives for establishing a National Foundation on the Humanities as well, the administration began in mid-February to try to determine whether it should transmit legislation to Congress asking for an arts foundation, a foundation for both the arts and humanities, or two separate foundations. It was felt that combining congressional support for both the arts and humanities would enable both to secure adequate funding.[53]

Concerning the joining of the arts and humanities, Livingston Biddle related that in 1964 a "blue-ribbon" committee of scholars was organized and entitled the Commission on the Humanities. Chaired by Barnaby C. Keeney, president of Brown University, and backed by the American Council of Learned Societies, the Council of Graduate Schools in the United States, and the United Chapters of Phi Beta Kappa, the commission met to consider the need for instituting a national program for the humanities.[54] The Commission Report published in the fall of 1964, which recommended the establishment of a National Foundation for the Humanities, triggered an immediate response in Congress from Rep. William Moorhead of Pennsylvania and Sen. Ernest Gruening of Alaska. Both Congressmen introduced legislation in their respective Houses for the creation of a humanities foundation.

But it was Senator Pell of Rhode Island who spearheaded the development of combined arts and humanities legislation. Livingston Biddle stated:

> Claiborne Pell, because of his understanding of the value of scholarship and because Barnaby Keeney was president of Brown University in his home state, felt very strongly about the developing legislation for the humanities. His own educational background included both arts and humanities, and his first legislative initiatives were for the arts.

Biddle further said that he, as Pell's assistant, worked with the Senator to develop alternative formats of the legislation to incorporate the humanities which were then submitted to the Bureau of the Budget.

> The Bureau of the Budget people said that there was no chance of the Administration accepting two new foundations. At this point, also, the humanities people were very insistent on their approach and the arts people were just as insistent on their side.[55]

The resulting legislation, presented in both the House of Representatives and in the Senate, joined together the arts and humanities under one foundation with two *separate but equal* Councils and Endowments. Although accounts about the development of the legislation vary to some degree, it is certain that Congressional leaders—Senator Pell in the Senate and Representative Thompson in the House—and the Johnson Administration worked together to create the structure of the National Foundation on the Arts and Humanities Act.

In mid-February of 1965 Senator Pell and Congressman Thompson conducted separate and joint special subcommittee hearings on arts and humanities legislation. Forty-nine persons prominently involved in these areas testified and provided favorable and enthusiastic support for the proposed legislation. On March 10, 1965, Subcommittee Chairmen Pell and Representative Thompson requested that the President transmit to Congress the administration's bill for the establishment of a National Foundation on the Arts and Humanities so that Congressional committee work could proceed.

House and Senate special subcommittees worked on the bills during the spring and into the summer of 1965. The Senate Committee on Labor and Public Welfare reported out an amended version of the Act (S. 1483) which the

Senate passed by a voice vote on June 10, 1965. House deliberations, however, were slower. It was not until June 24, 1965, that the House Committee on Education and Labor reported out H.R. 6050 to establish a foundation and ordered a "clean bill" introduced. This order resulted on July 8th in H.R. 9460 being reported out of Committee for consideration by the total House membership. This action set the scene for a spirited and sometimes humorous debate on the floor of the House.[56]

Provisions of the National Foundation on the Arts and Humanities Act

It seems appropriate at this point to discuss the legislation already approved by the Senate and about to be debated on the floor of the House.[57] The National Foundation on the Arts and Humanities Act sought to establish a new independent agency within the Executive Branch of government with two funding wings called endowments: a National Endowment for the Arts and a National Endowment for the Humanities.

Each Endowment's activities were to be supervised by a presidentially-appointed group of 26 citizens prominent in their respective disciplines—a National Council on the Arts and a National Council on the Humanities. Within each Endowment the Council chairman was to serve as chief executive officer receiving his appointment from the President with the advice and consent of the Senate.

In addition to the two National Councils, a single Federal Council on the Arts and Humanities was to be set up to serve as an advisory body to both Endowments. The function of this joint Council was to advise and consult with the two Endowment chairmen; to assist in the coordination of the work of the two Endowments; to coordinate the programs of the Foundation with related programs of other federal agencies, to plan and coordinate appropriate participation in major and historical events; and to divide appropriately between the two Endowments such gifts as might be directed to the Foundation, rather than to one of its Endowments.

Nine officials from established government agencies and departments with projects and programs in the arts and humanities were to comprise the federal Council membership. They were:

The Chairman of the National Endowment for the Arts
The Chairman of the National Endowment for the Humanities
The U.S. Commissioner of Education
The Secretary of the Smithsonian Institution
The Director of the National Science Foundation
The Librarian of Congress
The Director of the National Gallery of Arts

The Chairman of the Commission on Fine Arts
A member designated by the Secretary of State

The bill offered protection against domination and control of the arts and humanities by Endowment chairmen or other government officials. Section 4(c) of the Act stated:

> In the administration of this Act no department, agency, officer, or employee of the United States shall exercise any direction, supervision, or control on the policy determination, personnel, curriculum, or the administration or operation of any school or other non-Federal agency, institution, organization, or association.

Drafters of the legislation also assumed that the make-up of the National Councils would be a deterrent to government interference. Council members would make recommendations to the Endowment chairmen on applications for assistance and, because they were private citizens representative of their respective areas in the arts and humanities, Council participants were expected to be sensitive and resistant to any form of government control.

The bill's granting provisions specified that applications for grants were to be made to the chairman of the appropriate Endowment. In general, the Act intended that the Humanities Endowment would be concerned primarily with scholarly endeavors in the arts and humanities while the Arts Endowment would focus on artistic creativity and arts development. *

Activities to be funded by each Endowment were generally described in the Act. The Arts Endowment would consider funding professional productions of significant artistic merit that gave emphasis to creativity and the maintenance and encouragement of professional excellence; productions that would otherwise be unavailable to Americans in many areas of the country; projects that encouraged and assisted artists to achieve professional excellence; works that assisted in the development of public appreciation and enjoyment of the arts; and relevant projects and research in arts planning. Much of the funding for the Arts Endowment would be in the form of matching grants to assist arts organizations and state arts agencies.

The Humanities Endowment, on the other hand, was planned to concern itself with more scholarly activities. Its projects would reflect activities in the

*Funding for the Foundation was to be authorized by Congress with each Endowment receiving $5 million for three fiscal years—1966, 1967, and 1968. These funds were not the total amounts possible. A major objective of the legislation was to stimulate private philanthropy for cultural activities on national and state levels. For these purposes an additional annual maximum appropriation of $5 million went to the Humanities Endowment. The Arts Endowment was authorized $2.25 million to match funds donated by private sources, and $2.75 million to enable each state having an arts agency to receive an annual grant of up to $50,000 on a matching basis. States without an arts agency were eligible to receive a one-time grant of up to $25,000. This grant would enable a state to conduct a survey as a preliminary step to establishing an arts agency.

development of a national policy for the promotion of progress and scholarship in the humanities through research grants to individuals or groups; in the development of fellowships or grants to individuals or institutions for training or workshops in the humanities; in fostering, through financial support, public understanding, and appreciation for the humanities; and in providing financial support for publications of scholarly works in the humanities. Because the purposes and activities of this Endowment were so different from the Arts Endowment, it was not required to abide by the matching grant concept.*[58]

The Foundation Act described here represented the basis for action throughout the next decade for the two Endowments.

Passage of the National Foundation on the Arts and Humanities Act in the House of Representatives

On September 15, 1965, the House of Representatives deliberated the passage of the National Foundation on the Arts and Humanities Act of 1965 (H.R. 9460). Sponsored by 114 House members, with Representative Thompson of New Jersey as the chief sponsor, the bill was vigorously supported by bipartisan liberal congressmen and adamantly opposed by those with conservative leanings.

A comparison of the *Congressional Record* reports of the Foundation debate and the one for the National Cultural Development Act of 1964 reveals the names of numerous Congressmen who lent support to both pieces of legislation. In addition, this bill attracted the support of representatives who had formerly offered, at best, token agreement. This increasingly positive attitude toward cultural legislation was noted by Representative John Lindsay in the March 13, 1965, issue of *Saturday Review of Literature.* He commented that more than 100 bills in favor of arts funding were introduced in the 89th Congress and that "even Congressmen who would have left the floor in dismay four years ago were now declaring themselves in favor of it."[59] The implication of his statement seems clear: the influence of the humanities component added to the arts was reflected in the number and content of the cultural bills introduced in the 89th Congress and in the number of co-sponsors for the Foundation Act.

The debate was lively.[60] Congressmen supporting the legislation stated the

*The Act enumerated, though in broad terms, the scope of endeavor included within the humanities and arts. Humanities areas included the study of "language, both modern and classic; linguistics; literature; history; jurisprudence; philosophy; archeology; the history, criticism, theory, and practice of the arts; those aspects of the social sciences which have humanistic content and employ humanistic methods." The term "arts" included "music (instrumental and vocal), dance, drama, folk arts, creative writing, architecture and allied fields, painting, sculpture, photography, graphic and craft arts, industrial design, costume and fashion design, motion pictures, television, radio, tape and sound recording, and the arts related to the presentation, performance, execution, and exhibition of such major art forms."

rationales: cultural necessity, reaction to the nation's scientific emphasis, educational opportunities in the arts, and the stimulation by government of funding from private sources. Each of these issues was raised frequently by various speakers as they sought to convince uncommitted legislators to vote for the Foundation concept. Moreover, the arguments both pro and con influenced later development of the Arts Endowment's philosophy, funding procedure, and programs.

During the period of the early 1960s, government had considered arts support as a matter of cultural necessity. In the mid-1960s members of Congress for the first time supported arts legislation for the aesthetic welfare of the nation's citizens. Early in this debate, Congressman Claude Pepper, formerly a Senator and advocate of arts support during the 1930s, rose to speak in favor of the bill.

> I introduced legislation in the 75th Congress, 3rd session, January 21, 1938, S. 3296, a bill to set up a Bureau of Fine Arts and again in the 76th Congress, 1st session, I reintroduced this bill on August 5, 1939, as S. 967. . . . Now in the 1960s we are still debating the merits of Federal support. The difference now is that it is not so much a question of humanitarian relief for the destitute artist as it is a question of relief to meet the fundamental needs of our people.

Congressman Lloyd Meeds of Washington described these fundamental needs as special concepts when he said:

> And what are these concepts? They are truly "big ideas" that man has contemplated and wrestled with since the beginning of enlightened civilization. They are concepts dealing with truth, God, beauty—concepts that provide the very foundation and justification of man's very existence. . . . The great civilizations of the world have all established their place in history not merely as great military powers, as great centers of commerce or as nations possessed of scientific and technical knowledge. They have also given the world superb achievements in art, music, history, the theatre, literature, philosophy, and stagecraft. We are a great nation. But we have not reached our potential. . . . The humanities and all they encompass, the arts in all their manifestations, must thrive. This bill . . . gives impetus and encouragement from which, hopefully, all mankind will benefit.

Other representatives echoed similar sentiments and went on to warn of the dangers of exclusive national and government focus on purely scientific matters. Congressman Robert Giaimo of Connecticut stated that, in the interest of national defense, the educational system of America was distorted so that sciences dominated the classrooms while the humanities, "the essence of all civilization," were shunted aside. Congressman Sidney Yates of Illinois added that "the Federal Government has long testified to the development of science and technology in this nation but that it has largely ignored corresponding inspirations to the arts and humanities." Numerous other congressmen urged passage of this bill so that the National Foundation on the Arts and Humanities could achieve at least partial parity with the National Science Foundation.

Of particular concern to many in the House were the Act's provisions for the many forms of public education. Representative William F. Ryan of New York commented that the bill would strengthen education in the arts and humanities at the elementary and secondary school levels through grants for purchases of equipment, programs in schools, and institutes for teacher training. Giaimo believed that, because the arts are essential to the intellectual and spiritual growth of the adult population, "the government must recognize its responsibility to provide arts experiences for that segment of citizens—it should furnish equal access to arts experiences for those persons with interest in such activities." Representative Henry Helstoski of New Jersey further amplified this position when he stated:

> In the past there has been a tendency to bring culture and art to persons in the higher income group, and it is up to us to take the initial step toward bringing artistic productions to the grasp of more of our American people.

Obviously, the national educational priorities so evident during this period led arts-inclined legislators to recognize the impact that educational rationales would have on passage of the Act.

As a final reason for passage, advocates pointed to the apparent paradox existing between the increased interest in the arts occurring in the country and the steadily worsening financial situation faced by professional artists. Commenting on this situation, Congressman Jacob H. Gilbert from New York observed that "the performing arts cannot depend entirely on local benefactors, societies and civic groups." The lack of private funds to support the arts and humanities, he felt, presented a "grave financial crisis." Other arts advocates mentioned that many artists, existing on salaries far below the national average income, might forsake the arts to search for more lucrative endeavors unless new sources of funding for the arts could be found.

That the National Endowment for the Arts could relieve the financial crisis in the arts by stimulating additional sources of income from private, corporate, and foundation donors was another point made by some of the bill's backers. Congressman Yates reinforced this point.

> Of course, H.R. 9460 will not serve as a panacea for the ills troubling the arts today. But this legislation will serve as a catalyst to encourage more gifted people toward a profession in the arts and it will encourage the public to take a greater interest in the arts and to contribute more to their support.

This statement, it appears, was made to reassure protectors of "free enterprise" that government was not seeking to assume the full responsibility for arts support. Speakers for the bill noted that the yearly appropriation was merely sufficient to stimulate artistic activity. The Endowment would have to help artists attract additional sources of private support if the arts were to thrive.

Opponents of the legislation were, for the most part, very specific in their objections. Led by Representatives Robert Griffin of Michigan and Harold Gross of Iowa, they reacted to issues concerned with the necessity for government funding of the arts, the consequences of government "intervention" into arts matters, the expense of cultural funding, and the lack of specificity about cultural activities that could receive subsidies—recurring themes that would affect future Endowment policies and procedures.

Congressman John J. Rhodes of Arizona, after stating that the "bill was reported by the Committee on Education and Labor after only 15 minutes of consideration," proceeded to read into the *Congressional Record* the minority report of dissenting committee members. It maintained that the newly-established National Council on the Arts "was created by the Congress [in 1964] to study and analyze the state of the arts in this Nation and to make recommendations concerning methods to encourage and improve the arts." The proposed legislation, the report continued, was not based on any such study or recommendations; was, in fact, already in subcommittee hearings before the Council was even appointed; and was a threat to "the very foundations of our Nation's cultural activities." It further asserted that state domination of the arts in the Soviet Union should be "a sufficient warning against experiments of this nature in this country." The report concluded with the warning that the prospect of "political interference in the arts should be repugnant to all Americans," and that the arts would cease to thrive if subjected to "the deadening hand of Federal bureaucracy."

Congressman Paul Findley of Illinois questioned whether concerns for the arts and humanities were justified. He observed that, at that moment, the number of students achieving degrees in the humanities was greater than those receiving science degrees. He further observed that American literary arts were most productive in periods when there was no government input. His statement implied that government assistance was unnecessary and even detrimental to the development of *all* the arts because the availability of federal moneys would lead to nonproductivity.

Other opponents were more specific about the consequences of what they perceived to be government "intervention" rather than assistance. Representative William S. Broomfield of Michigan put forth the argument that federal support would lead to government control which would, in turn, result in "mediocre art and a Federal straitjacket over creativity." Representative Thomas B. Curtis of Missouri referred humorously to what he called the "Curtis Law" which stated that government money drives out private money—the availability of government support reduces the obligation for support from the private sector.

Whether the American people even wanted artistic experiences of "high quality" was questioned by Representative Findley when he compared the sparse attendance at a moderately-priced Bach concert in Constitution Hall with the record audiences for a similarly-priced showing of the movie, *Mary Poppins*. He further questioned whether the result of the legislation would be to create audiences for the arts or to train additional artists "way beyond the public demand."

Finally, Congressman Robert Duncan of Oregon attacked the bill's phrasing that referred to the fostering of excellence in the arts by stating that what is "artistic excellence to one is often absurd nonsense to another." Excellence, he maintained, is a problem of definition and personal preference. Support of particular art forms should be left to those who value them:

> I submit that the United States [government] has no business setting arts standards or attempting to influence them; that inevitably the establishment of a national foundation to encourage excellence in the arts would become a foundation determinating [sic] what constitutes excellence in the arts and financing its judgments and prejudices with the public's money.

The power vested in the chairman of the Endowment for the Arts proved to be another area of contention. The fear that the chairman would become an "arts czar" was voiced by Representatives Broomfield and Griffin. Even Congressman Ogden Reid of New York, a backer of the legislation, was concerned about whether the Congress should establish an arts council "where the authority is lodged with the Chairman and not with the Council itself." The chairman, he felt, should act with the *approval* rather than with the *advice* of the Council since advice was not binding on the actions of the chairman. Congressman William B. Widnall of New Jersey noted that cultural organizations also feared the sole power of the chairman to award or reject grant requests. He reported that the American Symphony Orchestra League's director, Helen M. Thompson, at an emergency meeting in Pittsburgh, had been highly critical of the power conferred on the chairman and "had advised the league's nationwide membership to oppose giving the arts and humanities Chairmen such extraordinary and unusual powers." Widnall further contended that a "blue ribbon committee" of the American Symphony Orchestra League had brought these concerns to the attention of Roger Stevens before the bill was drafted, but the League's suggestions were ignored.*

Congressman Albert H. Quie of Minnesota voiced concern about possible conflicts of interest in the case of Roger Stevens. Because Stevens was a successful theatrical producer and a board member of the Metropolitan Opera Association, the National Symphony Orchestra, and the John F. Kennedy Center for the Performing Arts, Quie questioned his impartiality and offered an amendment which stated that the Arts Endowment chairman should be appointed by the President with the advice and consent of the Senate. When Representative Thompson pointed out that the National Arts and Cultural Development

*It should be noted that ASOL did not officially oppose the legislation, but that its reservations were used by opponents of the Foundation concept as evidence of weakness in the proposed bill.

Act provided for this procedure, Quie responded that, when Stevens was reviewed by the Senate, it had been for the position of chairman of the National Council on the Arts, not the National Endowment for the Arts. The power to decide on the distribution of funds, Quie felt, altered the situation and demanded a more vigorous Senate examination. Quie's amendment, which was firmly defeated on the House floor, was directly aimed at Roger Stevens since future chairmen under the stipulations of the NFAH Act of 1965 would be required to receive Senate confirmation.

Opponents drew attention to other areas of concern—the bill's "elaborate" structure and the potentially escalating expenses resulting from ever-increasing arts activities and bureaucratic growth. Representative Griffin observed that the Act's organizational structure was complicated and that one who sought to understand its provisions could "easily get lost in a maze of councils and foundations." Representative Bert Bandstra of Iowa echoed these sentiments when he suggested that the bureaucracy created by such an elaborate structure would divert a significant portion of the appropriation toward agency operation and away from those for whom it was intended—humanities scholars and artists.

Similar fears were voiced by Representative Charles R. Jonas of North Carolina. He predicted that Endowment programs would grow enormously over the years to a sum which was "three, four, or five times greater than that appropriated in the proposed legislation." As an example of budget escalation, he pointed out that the National Science Foundation had grown from about $4 million a year to $530 million a year in a decade and a half. Other opponents cautioned that the national budget, already operating at a deficit, should not be subjected to programs with potential for such enormous growth. Only after a balanced budget was achieved should such programs be considered. It is possible that these conservative legislators, made gun-shy by the multiplicity of "Great Society" programs, saw the Foundation Act as another financial hardship inflicted on an already beleaguered national budget.

The final area of objection centered on the lack of specificity about which activities would be classified as the arts and which the humanities. Throughout the debate, Representative Gross, in his self-appointed role as watchdog of the federal budget, repeatedly requested a definition of a "humanities practitioner." Although this traditional foe of cultural legislation was attempting to poke fun at the Act's intent, he was also questioning the broad scope of activities included in the arts and humanities categories. Perhaps his most caustic, yet amusing, comments were contained in the amendments he put forward:

> On page 3, line 19, after the word "dance," insert the following: "including but not limited to the irregular jactitations and/or rhythmic contractions and coordinated relaxations of the serrati, obliques, and abdominis recti group of muscles—accompanied by rotatory undulations, tilts, and turns timed with and attuned to the titillating and blended tone of synchronous woodwinds."

Thus, the Congressman facetiously introduced belly-dancing as an art form! When that amendment was defeated he, still undaunted, offered another: On page 3, line 25, strike the period and add the following: "including but not limited to baseball, football, golf, tennis, squash, pinochle, and poker." Gross maintained that since great skill, study, and practice (all qualities of excellence in arts production) were required to perform all of the above well, they should be considered arts and as such should receive arts funding. When reminded by Representative Findley that these activities could probably be included under performing or folk arts, Gross expressed bewilderment. Findley and he then went on to attack the principle of subsidizing what they perceived as undefinable activities in the arts and humanities. Before the amendment was voted on, Findley commented:

> Last year, in consideration of the proposal for a National Arts Council, we on the minority side predicted that this would soon lead to a Federal subsidy program for everything from belly dancing to ballet, from Handel to the hootenanny, and from Brahms to the Beatles. We overlooked the fact that probably it would cover from Tschaikovsky to cheesecake. The language presently before us is broad enough to cover it all plus the activities the gentleman mentions.

While both of these congressmen recognized that the amendment would be defeated, their attack was based on their belief that this kind of funding was another example of a federal "boondoggle"—tax money spent for activities that should be personally supported by those individuals who enjoy them and are willing to pay for them.

Arts and humanities advocates recognized two of the previous arguments as potentially damaging to their cause: 1. passage of the National Foundation on the Arts and Humanities Act could lead to cultural control by the government; and 2. the elaborate administrative structure of the Foundation Act might inhibit national arts production. Although numerous proponents addressed various aspects of these issues, Representative William S. Moorhead of Pennsylvania offered the most effective responses.

Moorhead maintained that the proposed legislation gave adequate protection from undue government interference in Foundation matters. Although the chairmen of both Endowments and the members of the Federal Council would be considered government employees, "the 26 board members of each of the two endowments [National Councils] would be very independent of government and hopefully men of stature sufficient to withstand any improper pressure." An added measure of protection for the Foundation's independence, he continued, would be provided by Section 10(a)(2) which authorized the Foundation to receive private donations and Section 11(b) which sought to inspire such gifts by authorizing additional appropriations to match private donations. "Thus in the National Arts and Humanities Foundation we are creating not an institution of

Government but an institution designed to be able to talk back to Government." Obviously, Moorhead saw the input from the private sector as an effective deterrent to government control of Foundation practice.

The Congressman also saw the make-up of the Arts Council and the Humanities Council as deterrents to Foundation interference with those institutions and individuals receiving assistance. In any struggle between the Foundation and educators or artists, Council members—persons of eminence in the fields of the arts and humanities—"would almost assuredly be on the side of academic and artistic freedom." The pluralistic function of the Foundation, Moorhead maintained, would add to the freedom. The combination of federal and private funding would reduce greatly the possibility for government control while freeing scholars and artists to pursue excellence in their respective fields: "The old saying is: 'He who pays the piper calls the tune.' But, I submit to you that, if there are enough people willing to pay the piper, he can select his own tune."

Representative Moorhead then addressed the question of complexity of the Foundation's administrative structure. He mentioned that he, too, was bothered by the bill's apparent complexity and favored a single foundation of science, arts, and humanities. Such a simple concept had been rejected by the Act's drafters, he explained, because artists and humanists feared that they would be "swallowed up" if "newborn on the government scene they were, in effect, made part of the 15-year-old National Science Foundation." The establishment of one foundation with jurisdiction over both the arts and humanities, another simple concept, presented additional problems because artists felt they would be outnumbered by humanists and therefore given lesser consideration. The establishment of two separate and distinct foundations—one for the arts and another for the humanities—was rejected because, first, two foundations would be just as difficult to administer, if not more so, than the two endowments; second, two separate smaller foundations would be less able to match the prestige of a single National Science Foundation; and third, the two-foundation concept did not allow for the often-interrelated activities of the arts and the humanities. With these factors in mind, Moorhead claimed that the drafters of the legislation chose what they perceived to be the most simple and effective structure possible: one foundation with two separate but equal endowments.

Finally, Congressman Moorhead explained that the Federal Council on the Arts and Humanities, made up of officials associated with other government agencies having programs in the arts and humanities, would act as a coordinating body for the two endowments while reducing the possibility of duplication of programs among government agencies. The Congressman concluded his response to opponents by stating that the bill's structure had the approval of persons in the arts and letters, bipartisan support in Congress, and the backing of the Johnson administration.

After a complete reading of the bill by the clerk, Rep. Griffin made one last motion to "kill" the legislation by moving to recommit it to the Committee on Education and Labor. A voice vote was taken by the Speaker of the House and the motion was defeated. A vote for passage or rejection followed, resulting in the House passage of the National Foundation on the Arts and Humanities Act of 1965. On the following evening, September 16, 1965, the Senate concurred by a voice vote with the House-passed version of the bill.[61]

Congressional assent was finally achieved. Now, only the President's signature was required to make this long-cherished dream of cultural advocates a reality.

Executive Approval of the National Foundation on the Arts and Humanities Act

On September 29, 1965, the National Foundation on the Arts and Humanities Act came into being when President Johnson signed Public Law 89-209. At the Rose Garden signing ceremony, attended by 250 congressional, humanist, and cultural leaders, the President stated:

> In the long history of man, countless empires and nations have come and gone. Those which created no lasting works of art are reduced today to short footnotes in history's catalogue.
>
> Art is a nation's most precious heritage, for it is in our works of art that we reveal to ourselves, and to others, the inner vision which guides us as a nation. And where there is no vision, the people perish.
>
> We in America have not always been kind to the artists and scholars who are the creators and the keepers of our vision. Somehow, the scientists always seem to get the penthouse, while the arts and the humanities get the basement.

The President proceeded to outline some specific, positive proposals for the Foundation to consider. He proposed the creation of a National Theatre, support for a National Opera Company and a National Ballet Company, the creation of an American Film Institute, commissioning of new works of music by American composers, support of the nation's symphony orchestras, and residency programs for artists in schools and universities. He concluded:

> But these actions, and others soon to follow, cannot alone achieve our goals. To produce true and lasting results, our states and our municipalities, our schools and our great private foundations, must join forces with us . . . .
>
> What this bill really does is to bring active support to this great national asset, to make fresher the winds of art in this great land of ours.
>
> The arts and humanities belong to the people, for it is, after all, the people who created them.[62]

Along with the chronicle of the congressional legislation, it is worth recalling that there was a very human, personal, and emotional involvement in the achievement of these pieces of legislation. How the idea of the Council and the

Endowment originated and how they were implemented has as many versions as the people involved.

When Senator Javits reviewed his early congressional attempts in support of arts legislation for the *Congressional Record*, he made a plea not only for passage of the proposed bill but also for recognition of his own persistent efforts. Certainly, his personal role in the final achievement of federal support is well-documented in speeches, articles, and congressional action.

When asked if he felt that the development of the Arts Endowment in the sixties was part of the changes of that decade or a long-term idea coming to fruition, Roger Stevens did not attempt to analyze the impetus, but simply said, "I was asked to be Assistant to the President for the Arts, and I felt that there ought to be an arts council, and I put it through. It was as simple as that." Stevens added that Senator Pell in later years believed that he started the project; John Brademas felt that he should have credit. "But," Stevens added, "Frank Thompson was the fellow that was really in there. And Humphrey. Humphrey never got credit. The two senators who pushed the thing through were Humphrey and Javits. Senator Pell was a key supporter who had the very helpful idea of securing the support of the education lobby."[63]

Livingston Biddle recalled that he came to Washington in 1963 to work for Senator Claiborne Pell as a special assistant and generalist. Pell asked him if there were any new areas appropriate for legislation that he would like to examine. After a month or so of reflection, Biddle asked the Senator if he would like to do something for the cultural well-being of the country. "There had been some efforts," recalled Biddle. "There was the effort made by Senator Javits going back to the Forties; Senator Claude Pepper, then-Representative from Florida, had been connected with some efforts; Senator Hubert Humphrey was also involved. But nobody had really put together a concerted effort." With Pell's concurrence, Biddle began researching what other countries were doing for the arts, discovering as he worked that almost every other civilized country was giving them extensive support. As a result of his research, Biddle drew up several proposals for legislation which he submitted to the Senator.

Biddle remembered that Senator Pell gave the project strong support, and that, little-by-little, other members of the Senate also began to give it attention.

> The nucleus of the senators from the very beginning included Senators Scott and Clark from Pennsylvania, Humphrey, Fulbright, obviously Pell, and maybe one or two more, and certainly Javits, because he was the most important member in those days to give a bipartisan feelings. On the House side it was Frank Thompson and Congressman Reid from New York. McDade was involved in the early part of it, and so of course was John Brademas. But it was Adam Clayton Powell, chairman of the full committee in the House, who gave the most. He brought the bill up for special consideration in the 89th Congress when the days were dwindling down to almost none.[64]

Nancy Hanks also recalled an involvement with early legislation. She remembered typing a bill in 1954 for Nelson Rockefeller and Oveta Culp Hobby at the Office of Health, Education, and Welfare. "It was beautifully typed, there wasn't an error, and it was referred to as the 'toe-dance bill.' That was the end of that bill, I can tell you." Hanks added that the 1954 bill served also as a model for the later federal arts legislation.[65]

Violinist Isaac Stern recalled that he grew up in San Francisco with Pierre Salinger, who became Press Secretary to President Kennedy. When thinking about establishing a national advisory council on the arts, the President talked to Stern who, in turn, spoke to Jacqueline Kennedy because of her interest in the arts. Stern felt that the President had planned to put a political advisor in as chairman, and Stern and Salinger sought the advice of Supreme Court Justice Abe Fortas, who was also an accomplished amateur violinist and prominent arts advocate. All these events occurred shortly before the President's tragic trip to Dallas.

Stern's perceptions of Roger Stevens also provide interesting insights into the first chairman's influence.

> He was a theatrical producer, a businessman, and a very successful fundraiser for the Democratic party. He was acceptable on all fronts. Because money came so easily to Roger Stevens in his professional life, he thought it useful only as a tool to do really worthwhile things. He stood between the Council and all criticism and pressures. He was an impenetrable buffer.[66]

Although the recollections vary and the importance of various protagonists waxes and wanes according to the perceptions of the teller, one important factor emerges: Without the dedication and special abilities of many individuals and their persistence, imagination, and good humored ability to handle both criticism and ridicule, arts legislation would never have passed. Roger Stevens was probably right: The achievement of arts legislation was not so much a social trend of the sixties as it was the culmination of personal efforts on the part of many committed men and women who cherished the arts.

The journey to the threshold of active government arts support had been long and arduous. Passage of the National Foundation on the Arts and the Humanities Act of 1965 marked the beginning of a new chapter in the history of American arts development.

Reference Notes

1. "The Clamor for Culture," *Newsweek*, February 10, 1958, pp. 98*ff*.
2. W. Baumol and W. Bowen, *Performing Arts—the Economic Dilemma* (New York: The Twentieth Century Fund, 1966), p. 333.

3. *Newsweek*, "Clamor," pp. 98*ff.*
4. *Ibid.*
5. Rockefeller Panel Report, *The Performing Arts, Problems and Prospects* (New York: McGraw-Hill, 1965), p. 15.
6. *Ibid.*
7. "Summary of League Testimony for Senate Finance Committee on Tax Reform Act of 1969, H.R. 13270," *Newsletter of the American Symphony Orchestra League* (June–November 1969), p. 3.
8. G. Chagy, Ed., Business in the Arts '70 (New York: Paul S. Eriksson, 1970), p. 51.
9. Rockefeller Panel Report, p. 74.
10. Baumol and Bowen, "Economic Dilemma," pp. 333–339.
11. Foundation Library Center, *Annual Report* (1964), p. 14.
12. Baumol and Bowen, p. 340.
13. Rockefeller Panel Report, p. 95.
14. Baumol and Bowen, pp. 344–345.
15. Rockefeller Panel Report, pp. 97–98.
16. *Ibid.*, p. 107.
17. Baumol and Bowen, p. 344.
18. *Ibid.*, p. 329.
19. C. D. Dillon, "Business and the Arts," *Cultural Affairs*, 5 (1969), p. 10.
20. V. White, *Grants for the Arts* (New York: Plenum, 1980), p. 210.
21. Dillon, "Business and the Arts," p. 10.
22. V. White, *Grants—How to Find Out About Them and What to Do Next* (New York: Plenum, 1979), p. 22.
23. Chagy, pp. 37–39.
24. A. H. Reiss, *Culture and Company* (New York: Twayne, 1972), p. 39.
25. *Ibid.*, pp. 40–41.
26. *Ibid.*, p. 41.
27. A. Heckscher, *The Arts and the National Government—Report to the President*, Senate Document No. 28 (Washington; U.S. Government Printing Office, 1963), p. 2.
28. N. A. Rockefeller, *Our Environment Can Be Saved* (New York: Doubleday, 1970), p. 112.
29. J. R. Brademas, "Government, the Arts and Public Happiness," *Music Educators Journal* (April 1966), p. 43.
30. Quotations and information on potential governmental activities in support of the arts were taken from Heckscher, "The Arts," pp. 27–28.
31. U.S. Federal Government, *Congressional Record—Senate*, 88th Cong., 1st sess., Vol. 109, Part B, June 13, 1963 (Washington: U.S. Government Printing Office, 1963), p. 10814.
32. *National Democratic Party Platform*, Section "One Nation, One People" (Atlantic City, N.J.: Statement for convention delegates, 1964, available in Fannie Taylor Papers, Wisconsin State Historical Society Archives, Madison, Wisc.).
33. Rockefeller Panel Report, p. 112.
34. U.S. Federal Government, *Congressional Record—Senate*, 87th Cong., 1st sess., Vol. 107, Part 6, May 11, 1961 (Washington: U.S. Government Printing Office, 1961), p. 7824.
35. *Ibid.*, Vol. 107, Part 3, March 8, 1961, pp. 3444–3445.
36. *Ibid.*, May 11, 1961, p. 7824.
37. Quotations and information on House of Representatives debate of H.R. 4172 were taken from U.S. *Congressional Record—House*, 87th Cong., 1st sess., Vol. 107, Part 15, September 20, 1961 (Washington: U.S. Government Printing Office, 1961), pp. 20497–20503.
38. U.S. Federal Government, *Congressional Record—Senate*, 87th Cong., 2nd sess., Vol. 108, Part 17, October 12, 1963 (Washington: U.S. Government Printing Office, 1963), p. 6440.

39. *Ibid.*
40. *Ibid.* The National Arts and Cultural Development Act contained granting procedures developed earlier by the Arts Council of Great Britain, the Canadian Arts Council, the New York State Council on the Arts, and various private foundations. The bill stated that grants to private groups could not exceed one-half of the total cost of any project or production, although a percentage of the foundation's funds would be set aside for special direct-assistance grants where the application of the matching grant principle was not practical. Grants to state agencies would be made on a 50% matching basis. The act authorized appropriations not to exceed $5 million in the first fiscal year of operation and $10 million for each year thereafter. When the Senate session ended, a final decision on this legislation had not been reached. The bill was held over to the next session as unfinished business.
41. *Ibid.*, 88th Cong., 1st sess., Vol. 109, Part 19, December 20, 1963, p. 25263.
42. *Ibid.*, p. 25264.
43. *Ibid.*
44. National Endowment for the Arts, "The National Council on the Arts and the National Endowment for the Arts during the Administration of President Lyndon B. Johnson: The History," Vol. 1 (unpublished document available from the Lyndon B. Johnson Library, Austin, Texas, 1968), p. 6.
45. R. L. Stevens, taped interview, Washington, D.C., January 30, 1980.
46. L. L. Biddle, taped interview, Washington, D.C., December 22, 1980.
47. Quotations and information on House of Representatives debate of H.R. 9586 were taken from U.S. Federal Government, *Congressional Record—House*, 88th Cong., 2nd sess., Vol. 110, Part 16, August 20, 1964 (Washington: U.S. Government Printing Office, 1964), pp. 20652–20663.
48. Quotations and information on Senate consideration of H.R. 9586 (S. 2379) were taken from U.S. Federal Government, *Congressional Record—Senate*, 88th Cong., 2nd sess., Vol. 110, Part 16, August 21, 1964 (Washington: U.S. Government Printing Office, 1964), pp. 20923–20925.
49. National Endowment for the Arts, "The History," p. 7.
50. *Ibid.*, pp. 10–11.
51. *Ibid.*, pp. 11–12.
52. *Ibid.*, pp. 9–10.
53. *Ibid.*, p. 10.
54. Biddle, taped interview.
55. *Ibid.*
56. National Endowment for the Arts, "The History," pp. 15–16.
57. Quotations and information on the provisions of the National Foundation for the Arts and Humanities Act were taken from U.S. Senate Committee on Labor and Public Welfare, "National Foundation on the Arts and Humanities—Questions and Answers," prepared at the request of Senator Claiborne Pell, Chairman of the Special Subcommittee on the Arts and Humanities (Washington: U.S. Government Printing Office, 1965), pp. 1–4.
58. U.S. Federal Government, *Congressional Record—House*, 89th Cong., 1st sess., Vol. III, Part 18, September 15, 1965 (Washington: U.S. Government Printing Office, 1965), p. 23981.
59. J. V. Lindsay, "A Congressman Looks at the Arts," *Saturday Review*, March 13, 1965, p. 23.
60. Quotations and information on House of Representatives debate of H.R. 9460 were taken from *Congressional Record—House*, September 15, 1965, pp. 23941–23981.
61. National Endowment for the Arts, "The History," p. 22.
62. *Ibid.*, pp. 22–23.
63. Stevens, taped interview.

64. Biddle, taped interview.
65. N. Hanks, "Overview from the Federal Chair," lecture, University of Wisconsin Summer Forum, *The Arts in the Changing Decade of the Seventies* (Madison, Wisc., July 21, 1980).
66. I. Stern, personal communication, November 9, 1979.

3

The Roger Stevens Years

> We cannot merely buy and sell culture in the marketplace; it must be fought for, earned, and won.
> —Roger Stevens, speech at University of Oklahoma, 1965

"If Stevens didn't exist, we would have to invent him," once remarked Abe Fortas, former justice of the Supreme Court.[1] The Fortas comment sums the quality of this complex and brilliant man appointed by President Johnson to be the first chairman of the National Council for the Arts and the National Endowment for the Arts.

The situation of the agency in its fledgling months might be compared to the sudden emergence of a new teenage film star—the audience was clamoring for more, the trade was demanding hundreds of pieces of action, while the young vulnerable star needed a sense of direction and was short on all resources except newness, glamor, and talent.

Into this precarious scenario came Roger L. Stevens, former theatrical producer and high-flying real estate investor, to take charge of the agency, direct its first efforts with the advice of a distinguished national council, and steer its course through a Congress still not wholly convinced of its value.

When he walked into a room, Stevens took command by the force of his physical being. He was a natural leader to whom people deferred, often unconsciously, sometimes reluctantly. It was fortunate that he radiated leadership by his presence because he was often inarticulate—precise in his meaning but obscure in delivery.

A favorite quip of the Arts Endowment staff in the early years (when the office was located on the 11th floor of a building at 18th and G Streets) was "watch out, Roger's been giving an elevator grant again." The reference was to his propensity for suggesting to a would-be applicant he had met in the elevator, and for whom he had no other small talk, that the applicant should talk to one of the program directors at the chairman's request.

In spite of the amused frustration implied, Stevens was fair and even-handed in his discussions of grant applications and paid close attention to the ideas and concerns of the National Council for the Arts, a body of men and women with strong opinions and attitudes bred by fame and the judgmental capacity resulting from successful experience. Stevens, himself, was always willing to gamble on creative ideas, but he carefully assessed the track record before taking the gamble.

When Stevens began his tasks, the climate in America had some of the aspects of the lull before the storm. The economy was awash in affluence. By mid-1966, the gross national product (GNP) had reached an awesome rate of $727 billion. United State military pressures were increasing in Vietnam and the mood of the nation (some of it, at any rate) was fairly optimistic about that conflict. There was change in the air but its full impact was totally unpredicted. When President Johnson signed the bill creating the National Endowment for the Arts on September 29, 1965, he had commented in his direct, often blunt fashion, "somehow, the scientists always seem to get the penthouse while the arts and humanities get the basement." It was a time for high endeavor, high culture, and extension of the New Frontier. The Arts Endowment was a natural development.

The man appointed by President Johnson to lead the new agency was uniquely qualified to develop the policies outlined by August Heckscher in his 1963 report to the President. Stevens understood how to handle the problems raised by the diverse financial needs of the various art forms, from penniless dance to affluent film, and he possessed the prime qualification of a genuine love and understanding of the arts.

Roger Stevens' Background

Roger Lacey Stevens was born in Detroit, Michigan, on March 12, 1910, the son of Stanley Stevens and his wife, Florence Jackson. His father was a well-to-do real estate broker who sent his son to the Ivy League prep school, Choate, in Connecticut, where he graduated in 1928. When the Depression struck his family fortunes and he was forced to cancel his enrollment at Harvard, Stevens decided to live at home and attend the University of Michigan at Ann Arbor.

Restless, he left the university after his freshman year and looked around for any job he could find. He tended a gas station for $12 a week; he polished gears on a Ford assembly line; he worked in a real estate office where he earned nothing but began to learn the tools of the trade that became his career. During this period he began his lifelong habit of reading, often as many as five books a week. Discovering the riches of the public libraries, like many other Depression youngsters he devoured Shaw, Joyce, Shakespeare, Fielding, Proust, Thomas Mann, Pirandello, and that writer beloved of youth in the Thirties, Thomas Wolfe. Although he said of himself at the time that "the truth of the matter is that I was quite a good-for-nothing," the habit of omnivorous and retentive reading was permanently imprinted. In later years he commented that of all the things that can make people happy, "I'd put literature first. Many people," he added, "need other people around them, but I don't if I've got books."[2]

When the Depression released its hammerlock on the economy, Stevens embraced real estate and his creative insights and instinct for gambling on quality found their metier. In 1933 he had joined the Hamman Real Estate Exchange, a well-known Detroit firm, on a commission basis because he was unable to find a job that paid a salary. Within a year he became the firm's leading salesman. He saw opportunity in the bankrupt buildings of the Detroit area, gained control, and sold them for profit as the economy slowly improved. By the time he was 26 years old he was making $25,000 a year and had accumulated assets of $50,000—a not-inconsiderable sum for those times.

In 1937 he married Christine Gesell, an undergraduate at the University of Michigan and niece of Yale child-psychologist, Arnold Gesell, whose pronouncements on childrearing were household maxims for every family of the period. The two young people took off on a six-month honeymoon around the world.

When he returned to Detroit and the real estate brokerage business, Stevens found himself in the expanding world of the 1940s. At this point in his life, he began to ask himself whether there was not more to existence than buying and selling real estate. His love of books suggested the world of the arts.

Stevens discovered the Detroit Theater Guild. It was a new world, receptive to his instinct for gambling on his taste and his generational identity with the new emerging society. Although he would not then have recognized that his association with the Detroit group was part of a cultural trend of the period, it was a fact that a regional theater had first claimed his attention. It gave him the opportunity to develop his skills in the administrative needs of the arts—skills that were to give him a breadth of perception that would be of inestimable value to the country three decades later. He found an answer to another personal need. He began to meet interesting people and he discovered in the world of the theatre a warmth and intensity that complemented his own somewhat reserved personality.

In the late 1940s Stevens met the brilliant producer, Alfred de Liagre, Jr., and announced that he was preparing to begin his own career in the theatre by buying the old Belasco Theater, a characteristic ambition for a young real estate accumulator. De Liagre cautioned him that owning a theatre did not automatically put lights above the marquee and persuaded him, instead, to invest in the new de Liagre production, *The Madwoman of Chaillot* by Jean Giraudoux. The play won the Drama Critics Award in 1949 as the year's best production. Stevens had found the key to his life's work.

Broadway welcomed the likeable young Midwesterner with money in his pocket and stars in his eyes. He met Robert Whitehead and the two started a producing firm. Soon he was appointed to the board of the American National Theatre and Academy (ANTA) and the Phoenix Theatre. The Playwrights Company made him a partner in association with Robert Sherwood, Maxwell Anderson, and Elmer Rice and, until 1960 when the group dissolved, he cooperatively produced such hit plays as *The Fourposter, Cat on a Hot Tin Roof*, and *The Bad Seed.*[3]

In 1951, with his real estate partners Alfred R. Glancy Jr. of Detroit and Ben Tobin of Hollywood Beach, Florida, Stevens engineered one of his most arresting productions. Through an imaginative and intricate design of deals and loans, he formed a syndicate to buy the Empire State Building for $51.5 million, a record figure at that time for the price of one building—even the world's tallest. Three years later the syndicate sold Manhattan's most conspicuous spire for a profit of close to $10 million.[4]

In 1954 *The New Yorker* described him as "Broadway's busiest producer last year" and interviewed him in his office at 1554 Broadway. In this building, it reported, were quartered the Playwrights Company, of which Stevens was a member; the Producer's Theatre, of which he was president; the City Investing Company, a theater-owning corporation of which he was a director; ANTA, of which he was treasurer; and the Victoria Theatre, owned by the City Investing Company.[5]

Not everyone was impressed, however. Playwright Marc Connelly, who wrote *Green Pastures*, called him a "stage-struck shrewdie who brings nothing to the theater but a knowledge of real estate. The only thing you can say for him is that he keeps employment at a high level." In itself that was not an inconsiderable achievement in the precarious economy of the professional theater.[6]

In 1955 *Variety* called him "the most prolific producer in modern Broadway history,"[7] and in 1956 a press release from the Playwrights Company stated,

> With experience of only six years in the professional New York theatre, Roger L. Stevens is today the most active, successful and respected theatrical producer on the Broadway scene. No less than 15 plays currently operating either in New York or on tour were financed either wholly or in part by this colorful and industrious patron of the arts. This represents roughly one-quarter of what will be the entire Broadway output this year.[8]

The London newspapers called him "the skyscraper king." Interviewers remarked on his disconcerting habit of looking straight into the distance, apparently not seeing the individual talking to him. These same interviewers, however, noted that he retained what he heard. Stevens was vague about the reasons for his success; he seemed to work steadily without hobbies or small talk to pass the time; but he took pride in his integrity as a businessman. "Nobody ever loses on my deals," he maintained.[9]

His friends described Stevens as a natural coordinator, a persuasive salesman, willing to take chances. E. J. Kahn Jr. wrote "in times of stress he often adopts the disconcertingly phlegmatic attitude of the experienced gambler, which, of course, is essentially what he is—the high class variety of gambler known as speculator."

His energy and enthusiasm for the theater never flagged. He was involved with at least 40 shows with the Playwrights Company and some 30 other Broadway productions during this period. In addition to the works of Eugene O'Neill, Tennessee Williams, T. S. Eliot, Dylan Thomas, Shaw, and Shakespeare, he produced Leonard Bernstein's pace-setting *West Side Story*. In the middle of all these gala opening nights and quiet closings, he was still by day the risk-taking real estate man, buying and selling hotels and developing commercial centers in Seattle and Boston.[10]

Stevens Joins the National Political Scene

It was time, however, for a new challenge. Stevens found it with the advent of Adlai Stevenson on the national political scene. An ardent backer of the candidate from Illinois, he joined the Volunteers for Adlai Stevenson in 1952 and began raising funds. Four years later the *New York Times* reported his appointment as chairman of the finance committee of the Democratic National Committee. It was the beginning of a long involvement with the national Democratic fortunes, even though at the time he had no desire to take a job in Washington.[11]

Nearly a decade after he had been fired with interest in the political process, Stevens became Special Assistant to the President on the Arts. On August 20, 1964, he spoke before the platform committee of the Democratic national convention in Atlantic City because a bill creating a National Council on the Arts had been passed by the Senate and was now ready for action by the House of Representatives.[12] Stevens stated, "The part the arts will play in the Great Society has been greatly advanced." President Johnson, a strong advocate for arts support, was actively working for the bill's passage. "The purpose of the Arts Council," Stevens said,

> was to offer recognition and assistance in encouraging and promoting the nation's artistic and cultural progress. It is clearly stated in the Act that, while the growth and flourishing of the arts depend on freedom, imagination and individual initiative and that, while the encouragement and support of the arts are primarily a matter for private and local initiative, these are appropriate matters of concern to the Federal Government.

He also spoke about the development of support for the John F. Kennedy Center for the Performing Arts, of which he was chairman. Since September 2, 1961, when Kennedy had originally appointed him to the Board of Trustees, Stevens had been working to resolve the problems of locating, constructing, and funding this mammoth complex of auditoriums for the National Cultural Center. To assist him in this endeavor, Congress had made a significant $15.5 million matching grant to the Center when it was renamed for the slain President. Stevens folded this responsibility into his title as Special Assistant to the President on the Arts as readily as he had handled a dozen different and complex real estate deals in the past.

Continuing the platform statement, Stevens said that for a nation with a $600 billion national income and a $100 billion federal budget, the funds available to the arts were woefully limited—foundations and corporations were only making a small percentage of their funds available. Moreover, he pointed out that, "since the shock of Sputnik, there has been too much emphasis on science and technology." He added what might be described as his credo for the job he faced. "While money cannot create art, it can be one of the tools in helping its creation. Talent should not fail to reach its full development because of lack of funds or availability of education."

In this speech he set two goals: "1. giving proper recognition to the artist and his place in society; and 2. developing an audience that will appreciate his accomplishment." Both goals became increasingly important as Stevens began to work with the members of the National Council for the Arts and the demands of the arts world.

Stevens' pragmatism in pursuit of support for the artist is well-illustrated in his suggestions on how to achieve the first goal. "without any additional legislation, there are a number of ways in which the government can aid the artists without any direct subsidies." He mentioned hiring the best artists and architects to plan the design and construction of new buildings; improving the quality of postage stamps, coins, and posters by using the top artists of the country; recognizing outstanding work in the field of the arts by establishing White House Awards; changing tax laws which he felt were unfair to the artist; preserving buildings and landmarks of artistic and historic value; making government surplus property available to art schools and councils as was being done for medical and other institutions; urging corporations to include the arts along with other charitable contributions to the fullest extent of their tax deduction; asking foundations to contribute to the arts in the same proportion as in other fields; helping the newly formed Cultural Affairs Branch of the Department of Education to be as effective as possible in its program for the arts; and encouraging and aiding the arts councils being formed in cities and states.

Stevens, the real estate broker, also pointed to ways in which the museums, auditoriums, and theatres—cultural resources to which every community large or small should be entitled—could be assisted by self-liquidating government loans. "There is no reason why government cannot furnish loans for this purpose as they have done for the good of the country in many other fields when private financing has been difficult." He added that the government could increase the use of traveling art exhibits, as the Smithsonian Institution had done, by transporting them into remote areas where many people had never had the opportunity to view great works of art. (Seven or eight years later this suggestion came to a lively reality in the Artrain, sponsored by the National Endowment for the Arts during Nancy Hanks' tenure as chairman.)

The second goal specified by Stevens in the platform speech involved developing an audience for the arts which he considered a longer-range project. "It must start fundamentally with the education process," he said, "and it also requires personal commitment. It is important to remember that for the true appreciation of the arts, an individual will actually receive as much in enjoyment and pleasure as he is willing to put forth in effort." This is Stevens the inveterate reader speaking. But he goes on as the businessman:

> Additionally, there is the practical fact that, if there were a much larger audience, many unemployed musicians and artists would find work, and there would be a greater market for the works of painters and sculptors. If the audience for the arts were increased to the extent to which the country is capable, many interesting new job opportunities would be available.

The platform speech was part and parcel of the activist philosophy of the period that motivated the political action of the Congresses of the Great Society.

The National Council for the Arts

The democratic process had moved along its slow but inevitable way and the National Arts and Cultural Development Act, creating the National Council for the Arts (Public Law 88-579), was signed by President Lyndon B. Johnson on September 3, 1964.

Stevens then added a third dimension to his duties as special assistant to the President and as chairman of the board of Kennedy Center. He was appointed chairman of the National Council for the Arts by the President on February 23, 1965. When the Senate confirmed his nomination on March 9, 1965, he moved into the job with three strong alliances. He had the support of the President of the United States; he was given a vigorous and prestigious Council to work with; and he had his previous experience as real estate investor, political fund raiser, and theater producer.[13]

The 24 Presidentially-appointed members of the Council who were to serve with Stevens were a notable group of men and women representing many areas of the arts and arts administration. Their first Council meeting was held at the White House April 9, 1965, when President Johnson presided over the formal swearing-in of the members in the Cabinet Room. The occasion, attended by all the new Council members with the exception of Richard Rodgers and Minoru Yamasaki, was a euphoric time for all the people who had struggled for years to make recognition of the arts a legitimate concern of the government. The members went from the swearing-in ceremony into session in the Fish Room of the White House. Their afternoon meeting was at Decatur House on Lafayette Square. On April 10, the all-day session was held at the new Museum of History and Technology of the Smithsonian Institution.[14]

The members of the first Council included a glamorous array of names in the arts, each of them well-known and respected in their particular areas and some internationally famous. In addition, the pocket-sized staff working at that time in the old Executive Office Building was also present at the first sessions. The staff included Frank H. Crowther, Charles C. Mark (consultant), Diana Prior-Palmer, Luna Diamond (secretary to the Council), and Romlee Philipson (secretary to the staff).[15] Of this group, only Mrs. Diamond continued in the agency for an extended period, giving valued and uniquely enthusiastic service for many years.

There was also an important group of invited guests attending the first meeting: Senator Claiborne Pell, chairman of the Special Subcommittee on the Arts and Humanities of the Senate Committee on Labor and Public Welfare; Congressman Frank Thompson, Jr., chairman of the Special Subcommittee on Labor of the House Committee on Education and Labor; George D. Cary, Deputy Register of Copyrights; Richard N. Goodwin, Special Assistant to the President; and Dr. T. W. Taylor, assistant to the secretary of the Smithsonian Institution.

Once sworn in, the Council was immediately dealt a blow, the kind of disappointment that Congress in its infinite wisdom and inattention to detail can manage so effectively. Congressman Thompson explained the problem. When Public Law 88-279 establishing the National Council on the Arts was reproduced, the words *per annum* had been inadvertently dropped from the appropriations section as passed by Congress. Although the intention of the act was clearly for a permanent Council functioning on a continuing basis, the error hampered its effectiveness. Thus, while Congress had intended to provide "such sums as may be necessary, not to exceed $150,000," dispensed on an annual basis for administration purposes, because the *per annum* reference was omitted the Council was going to be left with only $150,000 for its authorized lifetime!

Obviously, something had to be done at once. The Council passed its first hopeful resolution requesting funds:

> *Resolved:* The National Council on the Arts unanimously requests that the Congress establish the Council as a permanent agency by amending Public Law

88-579 to allow for an annual appropriation of $150,000 for administrative purposes.[16]

However, when the final appropriation was made, Congress only provided $50,000 for the Council's expenses in the fiscal year 1966. What occurred from that miniscule budget for the first nine months of Council operation (from September 1964 through June 1965) is a startling example of what dedication to a dream can effect. The Council would have had no staff if Stevens had not personally paid several salaries.[17] People bought their own supplies, stamps, and newspapers and worked with missionary intensity as the budget page from the 1964–65 *First Annual Report reproduced as Table 1* indicates.

But there was other business for the first Council to attend to at its historic first meeting.[18] Both Senator Pell and Congressman Thompson detailed the intent and background of the legislation, then before Congress, which called for the establishment of a National Foundation for the Arts and Humanities. These proposals were receiving strong support. Media commentator David Brinkley said that the current session of Congress was an historic moment for the arts in America and that this small beginning could have great significance for the

Table 1
National Council on the Arts: Status of Funds—FY 1965
(as of June 30, 1965)

Object Class	Explanation	Amount
	Funds Available	$50,000
110	Salaries and wages	33,771
120	Overtime	135
130	Holiday pay	46
140	Personnel benefits	855
211	Travel	7,934
241	Printing	1,002
251	Payments to commercial contractors	2,531
257	Payments to general supply fund	8
259	Payments to working capital fund	135
261	Office supplies	515
262	Operating supplies	339
264	Newspapers and periodicals	30
268	Technical publications	88
271	Telephone, local	141
272	Long distance toll charges	99
274	Postage and fees	29
311	Office equipment	1,431
	Total funds obligated	$49,089
	Unobligated balance	$ 911

country. The Council then passed another resolution supporting the President's position on the establishment of a foundation for the arts and humanities.

The Council evidenced its first interest in the relationship of education and the arts by inquiring whether the funds appropriated under the Teacher Training section of the pending legislation—which was to strengthen the teaching of the arts and humanities in elementary and secondary schools—would be administered by the Council or the Office of Education. Congressman Thompson said that the grants or contracts for this training with institutions of higher learning would be administered directly by the Office of Education. The project was quite separate from the Arts Endowment, even though it had been tacked onto the bill as Section 13. Chairman Stevens kept track of the possibility for integrating the work of the two agencies and obtaining additional sources of funds. He returned to the arts in education idea frequently in subsequent years.

Even while "hamstrung" by a lack of funds, Stevens lost no time in setting up substantive issues for the Council to discuss and on which to make recommendations. Because he understood that the source of power is action, he immediately moved to take positions that could develop the active strength of the Council.

First Council Meeting

During these first Council sessions, the members distributed themselves into subgroups, acting in effect as panelists on subjects for which they had special interest and expertise. Stevens suggested that if future funding became available the Council might also want to utilize outside panels of experts to offer "advice and recommendations" as well as providing "a means of engaging increased numbers of private citizens in this fledgling partnership between the Federal Government and the arts world." At the time, however, all the Council could do was help the chairman in his role of advising the President and persuading and influencing other federal agencies to use their funds to help the arts.[19]

The Council set itself two purposes to cover a wide reference: enlarging audience participation in the arts, and providing opportunities for wider professional activities and training.

Stevens had invited George D. Cary, Deputy Register of Copyrights, to attend the first meeting to explain the provisions of the Copyright Revision Act of 1965. Cary stated that the laws of the United States differ from those of most European countries about the "rights-of-creation" concept. The U.S. law assumed that a creative work was ultimately and rightfully the property of the people. For a stated period of time the copyright holder was given exclusive use of his work as a stimulation to further creative activity. It developed in the discussion that copyright is basically a protection for written works—any work which could be defined as a creative work of written or substantive form. Performances, however, could not be copyrighted under the law as written. At the

April 10 meeting, the Council approved a resolution directed to the chairman of the House and Senate Judiciary Committees, where the copyright legislation would fall, and urged passage of the new copyright law:

> The National Council on the Arts expresses its views that modernizing and strengthening the copyright protection afforded to authors is of the utmost importance to the creative activity on which the strength and endurance of our cultural progress largely depends.[20]

The Council resolved that a subcommittee of its members was needed to recommend a table of organization and procedures for the Council to be presented at the second meeting. Stevens appointed Anthony A. Bliss, a New York lawyer and the president of the Metropolitan Opera, to head the committee. The Council suggested that the chairman appoint another subcommittee to define purposes and objectives of any study that might be made of the cultural resources of the United States. This subcommittee was appointed and duly made its report at the second Council meeting. The fact that other government agencies routinely collected data on the arts, even though the material might be somewhat unfocused, and that the Council had no current funds to support such an extensive survey caused the members to accept the report and table it, while broadly encouraging "closer cooperation among the various governmental and private agencies compiling statistics of benefit to the arts."

Thus, at this first and historic meeting, the Council vigorously set out broad goals to pursue—goals that did not involve attempting to spend nonexistent Council funds but rather sought pockets of support in other public and private agencies and ways of enhancing the status of the arts in the United States. As a result of their deliberations, the Council generated 14 recommendations, many of which would be echoed for the next decade.

> Fine Arts Decoration of Federal Buildings
> That the Federal Government require as mandatory the expenditure of 1% of the total cost of federal buildings for fine arts decoration at the time of construction, and that the selection of art and/or artists by GSA be made with the advice of experts from outside the Government.
> That the Federal Government earnestly encourage the expenditure of 1% of the budget for fine arts on buildings built with any federal funds, through FHA or urban renewal programs.
>
> Education Television
> That additional legislation be passed to assist educational television stations to carry out significant programming in the Arts.
>
> Public Service Time on Television
> The Council urged that the Federal Communications Commission define public service time as including, specifically, time used for the dissemination of the Arts and information about the Arts.
>
> National Parks
> That in establishing or expanding Department of Interior museums and other facili-

ties, including those in the national parks, more attention be given to the nation's cultural heritage, and that more cultural attractions of a performance nature be programmed in our national parks.

Taxes

The Council went on record as being opposed to the following taxes:

The excise tax on musical instruments; The excise tax on theatre tickets; The exclusion of artists from self-employed retirement programs; The various income-tax provisions regarding royalties from creative works, and recommended that the period over which income from the sale of works, including royalties, can be averaged, should be extended.

Creation of Arts Facilities

The Council urged that, wherever possible, art facilities be included in already existing federal construction and renewal projects.

Surplus Property

That the regulations governing the opportunities to purchase federal surplus property be broadened to include cultural agencies and institutions.

The Florence Agreement

That the United States join other leading nations of the world in adopting the Florence Agreement, regulating the import and export of cultural and educational items.

Artists' Housing

That continuing effort and study be directed toward the problem of housing the professional artist.

Quality of Design

The principle of encouraging the highest possible quality of design, wherever the Federal Government is involved, from architecture to postage stamps, was adopted by the Council.

International Art Exhibitions

The Council went on record as believing that American representation at the great international art exhibitions, such as *Biennales* of Venice and Saõ Paulo, are matters of national concern, and should be supported by the Government. The Council further believes that the Smithsonian Institution, being a governmental agency concerned with the Arts, is the logical agency to organize these exhibitions, in cooperation with other museums.

In this respect, the Council enquired if Sections 4 and 5 of the pending legislation (S. 1483) could be interpreted as restricting the work of the proposed Foundation to activities within the United States, and hence barring participation in international festivals, exhibitions, and programs. The Council agreed that a clear mandate to carry out international programs was desirable for the Foundation, and requested the Chairman to take the necessary steps to clarify the issue.

Arts Administration

The Council believes that one of the greatest needs of arts organizations is able administrators. It was recommended, therefore, that the Council cooperate with the Arts and Humanities Branch in the U.S. Office of Education in efforts to develop formal arts administration courses.

Arts in Education

That the Arts and Humanities Branch of the U.S. Office of Education study what is being done by the state boards of education with a view to improving and developing

> arts education in secondary and elementary schools, and that recommendations based on this study be presented to the National Council on the Arts for its action.
>
> International Film Festival
> That the National Council on the Arts favors the establishment of an annual International Film Festival to be held in Washington, D.C. The objectives of this Festival would be the elevation of standards, an incentive to excellence, and Government recognition of films as a major art form.[21]

The foregoing list exemplifies the concern of the First Council for what the Nobel prize-winner Glenn T. Seaborg described as the "greatest challenge of our times." Seaborg, writing in *American Education* in September 1966, claimed that "in a democratic society, the real quality of life is represented not only by economic and social change, but by the welfare—the well-being—of the individual in that society." He stressed the need to maintain the opportunity for individual growth in an overwhelmingly technological world and the need for "ways to support the humanities and the arts so that they can have the economic freedom to reflect some of the truths that a nation needs to have revealed to itself."[22]

The Council concluded its first meeting with a formal statement about the long-awaited and much-needed national recognition that the arts are a public necessity. "The Council cannot create artists," it stated, "but it is passionately dedicated to creating a climate in which arts and the artist shall flourish."[23]

There was an odd interlude between the first and second Council meetings. On June 14, 1965, the President and Mrs. Johnson were hosts at the White House for a Festival of the Arts which had been put together by the Princeton historian and writer Eric Goldman with the aid of others in government service. This was the first time in the nearly 200-year history of the United States government that an actual festival, encompassing all the performing and visual arts, had been presented at the White House. As Harold Taylor, the former president of Sarah Lawrence College, described it, it was a "coming-of-age of America in the field of the creative arts," a recognition of the fact that America was no longer neglecting the arts and that, in fact, the "cultural explosion" of the Sixties had been acknowledged by federal and state governments with economic and political support.[24]

But the political support was the undoing of the festival. The shadow of the Vietnam war and Johnson's foreign policy fell across the day and ruined a brave effort to light new paths for the arts. One of the invited guests was the poet Robert Lowell, who accepted President and Mrs. Johnson's invitation and then reconsidered his decision in a letter to his hosts which he released to the newspapers.

> I thought of such an occasion as a purely artistic flourish, even though every serious artist knows that he cannot enjoy public celebration without making subtle public commitments.
>
> After a week's wondering, I have decided that I am conscience-bound to refuse

your courteous invitation. I do so now in a public letter because my acceptance has been announced in the newspapers and because of the strangeness of the Administration's recent actions.

Although I am very enthusiastic about most of your domestic legislation and intentions, I nevertheless can only follow our present foreign policy with the greatest dismay and distrust. What we will do and what we ought to do as a sovereign nation facing other sovereign nations seems to hang in the balance between the better and the worse possibilities.

We are in danger of imperceptibly becoming an explosive and suddenly chauvinistic nation, and we may even be drifting on our way to the last nuclear ruin.

I know it is hard for the responsible man to act; it is also painful for the private and irresolute man to dare criticism. At this anguished, delicate and perhaps determining moment, I feel I am serving you and our country best by not taking part in the White House Festival of the Arts. Respectfully yours, Robert Lowell.

Perhaps Lowell underestimated the impact of his public refusal but it curdled the bright promise of the evening. Among the guests who were present were several who took the occasion to make political statements.

Author John Hersey commented in a preamble before reading from his own works. "Let these words be a reminder. The step from one degree of violence to the next is imperceptibly taken and cannot easily be taken back. . . . Wars have a way of getting out of hand." He then proceeded to read from *Hiroshima*.

Mark Van Doren made the introductions of the luminaries and commented on his own ambivalence about coming to the festival in view of Robert Lowell's abstention. "It raised the question among all poets," Harold Taylor writes in his analysis of the impact of the evening, "including those who had not been invited, whether or not the relation of the arts to politics was so direct that attendance at a Festival committed one to the politics of its sponsor."

Author Dwight MacDonald was perhaps the most graceless guest of all. He came to the festival evening with a petition for the other guests to sign which repudiated the President's foreign policy. Mrs. Johnson in *A White House Diary* recalled that there was some uncertainty about the number of signatures he obtained, whether four or seven from the 300 guests. "I'll take a 293 to 7 majority anytime!" wrote the First Lady.

She discussed the fact that the *New York Times*, the *New York Herald Tribune*, and even the *Washington Post* seemed to have gone out of their way to report the incidents, with apparent delight "in faulting their country and their President." She continued, "But do you think that was news? No, it was the fly on the top of the feast and, indeed, feast it had been. We had thrilled to Helen Hayes, Marian Anderson, Roberta Peters, the whole cast of *The Glass Menagerie*, Catherine Drinker Bowen, and poet Phyllis McGinley—all playing on the White House stage in one day."[25]

But the festival incident was a sour note in an otherwise exciting summer for the arts and artists in the United States as, step-by-slow-step, the bill to create the National Foundation for the Arts and Humanities moved through Congress.

Second Council Meeting

When the second meeting of the Council was convened June 24-27, 1965,[26] the Senate had just passed S.1483, an amended bill to establish the National Foundation for the Arts and the Humanities. As the Council was meeting on June 24, the House Committee on Education and Labor reported out H.R.6050, which also was concerned with establishing the Foundation, and ordered a clean bill to be introduced. Progress was being made; the Council was optimistic.

There was also a note of sadness as the Council approved a resolution expressing its sorrow about the death of one of its members, the distinguished American sculptor David Smith, who had been killed in an automobile accident. He was replaced on the Council by Herman David Kenin, international president of the American Federation of Musicians.

Kathryn Bloom, director of the Arts and Humanities Branch of the U.S. Office of Education, was on hand throughout the sessions as an observer, as was Livingston L. Biddle, Jr., special assistant to Sen. Claiborne Pell. Biddle later became Stevens' deputy and much later was appointed as the third chairman of the National Endowment for the Arts in 1977.

The Council received and adopted the Anthony Bliss report on its organizational structure; it resolved that its members should "remain as free as possible from affiliation with organizations, associations, institutions which could conceivably have an influential relationship with the Council or the Endowment for the Arts" (a forward projection since neither the National Foundation nor the Endowments had yet been approved by Congress). The executive staff was also prohibited from becoming affiliated with such organizations. The Council stressed, however, strong cooperative arrangements with professional organizations, the Office of Education, and local, state, and federal agencies concerned with the arts.

Kathryn Bloom, whose innovative work as director of the Arts and Humanities Branch of the Office of Education was becoming nationally known, spoke to the Council about the primary concern of her office—the use of art for educational purposes. She felt that there were many areas where the new Council could assume some of the undertakings that had fallen in the past, almost by default, to the Office of Education. One of the needs, she commented, was to improve the level of administration in the arts throughout the nation. At the final Sunday morning session, Francis Keppel, Commissioner of Education, also joined the group and stressed the importance of the arts in the overall programs of his agency.

Other resolutions were approved by the Council: on education and the arts, including matters of curriculum changes; on new testing procedures to locate talent; on the utilization of resident artists and artist-teachers; on improving leadership and administration in arts institutions; and on the possibility of honoring the nation's outstanding artists by a presidential citation or medal.

The Council's Committee on the Performing Arts recommended a particularly ambitious (and probably not well thought out) goal, that there should be created and developed "at such time as federal funds, together with private and other public funds are available, national companies in all branches of the performing arts—including a National Repertory Theatre, a National Opera Company, a National Ballet Company, a National Youth Symphony, a Heritage Theatre of Folk Forms." These new companies were to be composed of the most qualified managers, directors, and performers available in America.

> Until such time as these various national companies are formed and financed, it is recommended that certain pilot projects in the various categories of the performing arts, and in the various regions of the country, be undertaken at once—such pilot projects to act as experimental and contributory efforts to the final formation of the national companies.

The resolution also stressed the intention to encourage existing independent professional companies to provide their services and talents as sources for permanent national companies.

In the future this resolution was to lead to strong support for a wide variety of experiments: for regional theaters, an ill-fated national chamber orchestra, the ambitious but often troubled American Film Institute, emergency help to the American Ballet Theatre, critical aid to the Boston Opera Company directed by Sarah Caldwell, and many other projects—some vigorous and some better as dreams than as actualities. All these ideas were full of the excitement that characterized the wide-ranging arts movements of the mid-Sixties and reflected the creative enthusiasms of the members of the first Council.

The Council also voted to undertake studies of several so-called pilot projects in the repertory theater field—all contingent, of course, on the future availability of money for such tasks. It further urged that a national film archive recording great dances be developed before the "choreography is lost to posterity," and it encouraged film training and education for Americans interested in expanding "the frontiers of achievement in motion pictures." Formal recognition was given to the nation's museums as being worthy of support as "an integral part of our nation's growing educational and cultural complex."

At this meeting the Council also summarized its areas of concern: the need for help to arts institutions of quality; the lack of opportunities for artists; the need for education in and about the arts (especially the building of a large and more discriminating audience); and the lack of communication within the arts. These concerns would have profound influence on Council activities and the future development of the impending National Endowment for the Arts.

Studies Prepared for Council Use

In its effort to assess these national problems, the Council asked for studies by the staff.[27] Summaries of these studies were included in the first annual Council report.

In the fall of 1964 the Office of Education had examined the impact of the fledgling state arts councils on higher education and invited the National Council on the Arts to cooperate in developing, distributing, and ultimately compiling a questionnaire which was sent to some 25 state arts councils, or would-be councils. Consultant Charles C. Mark then visited the states to solicit information from state leaders and from university representatives. The final report made to Roger Stevens in January 1965 was used in making recommendations to the President and Congress about federal relationships to the states.

The U.S. Office of Education received a proposal that it and the Council jointly sponsor three metropolitan locations for a pilot program utilizing resident professional theaters. These groups, organized with professional directors and actors of the highest quality available, would offer theatrical presentations to schools in their respective surrounding areas. The educational premise for such a proposal was that "students who see well-produced, live theatrical performances of the classics will have a much greater interest in their classroom work." This plan had the additional benefit of offering repertory training for actors and directors, and employment opportunities—always a clinching argument when federal largesse was discussed in the expanding sixties.

Another proposal that bears the imprint of real estate broker Stevens' interests and experience was the development of low-cost artist housing. The Housing and Home Finance Agency had indicated willingness to cooperate with the Council to develop such plans; legislation covering disposal of surplus government property was examined with the hope that museums and other arts institutions could become eligible to receive properties along with schools, colleges, public health organizations, and other similar groups.

The Council staff investigated opportunities for audiences in cities of over 25,000 to attend professional productions in the arts. The Council resolved to coordinate the "fragmentary" research work being done by national organizations concerning the country's cultural resources. It also voted to encourage other federal agencies in the use of their resources to amass pertinent social and economic data. It is interesting to note that 1965 also marks the publication date of the seminal Rockefeller Panel Report, *The Performing Arts: Problems and Prospects*, which stated that "among the key problems of the performing arts in America today are the lack of sufficient data and a central source of information." The appearance of this study and its wide acceptance is evidence that the need for substantive information was perceived by many arts activists.[28]

The Council staff reported that in cooperation with the Office of Economic

Opportunity pilot projects in three Job Corps camps had been undertaken to make cultural activities a part of the general exposure program for Corps enrollees. There was a suggestion that similar pilot projects might be set up at other levels of the Poverty Program including Headstart and Community Action.

"A clear assessment of the Federal Art Projects of the thirties" and its influence on the present American world leadership in painting was suggested in cooperation with the National Collection of Fine Art and the Archives of American Art.

Most interesting of all in this imaginative and forward-looking list of projects and goals, prepared by the staff at the Council's instigation, was the proposal for the American Film Institute to be established at a postgraduate level and staffed by professionals from all areas of the film industry. "The training offered . . . would encompass every aspect of filmmaking from the original idea to the end product."

Throughout the first Council report there is a sense of excitement and discovery, scarcely repressed by its bureaucratic language. The dreamed-about projects became a moveable feast for all the arts, so long seated at the bottom of the federal table. Suddenly, there was a chance to work with the Office of Education and share in its enormous funding and clout in a nation convinced in the Sixties and post-Sputnik era that education (particularly in the sciences) was the cure for all ills. Suddenly there was a possibility of expanding into all the states, trailing the aura of federal encouragement (and, it was hoped, money). There were opportunities ahead for artists to pursue their art, to live decently, and to earn a living from doing what they did best. Livingston Biddle recalled those early years when he was sitting in on Council deliberations, first as Claiborne Pell's special assistant and later as deputy chairman to Roger Stevens.

> I can almost see them as they sat around the table. Isaac [Stern] and Agnes [DeMille] always sat next to each other and you knew when things were going to get very exciting. Agnes would put her glasses up like this and Isaac would rest his on the top of his head, and they would start.
>
> I think from the very beginning they all were concerned about the creative life of the arts and that they were not concerned about the small sum of money as much as they were about how to evolve something that had a creative value—though it might be difficult really to look at the first grants and say this was the direction the Endowment took right from the start.

But Biddle did indicate that many of the initiatives of the Endowment, when funding expanded during the chairmanship of Nancy Hanks and later during his own tenure as chairman, had had roots in the first Council deliberations. "Everybody will say that Artists in the Schools began in the Seventies; but it didn't. It began in 1966 when we put a few poets in a few classrooms in New York State and New York City."[29]

But in June 1965 it was not yet time for grant-making. Congress still had to act; the nation still had to be better informed about the needs of the arts. Roger Stevens lost no time in setting out to stump the country. At the end of the first Council report is a five-page listing of speeches, conferences, advisory group meetings, television and radio appearances, mostly made by Stevens himself, in which he sought to examine and suggest the needs of this new constituency that had been presented to him by the President. Clearly, there was no lack of imagination or energy, no dulling of what August Heckscher called the "sharp edge of excellence" in the input into their new responsibilities of the Council members or the chairman. The arts in America could not but benefit from this vigorous espousal in a country bursting with prosperity and fervor to build a better world.

Stevens Responds to Criticism

Inevitably, there were critics of the whole idea of government in the arts, and very specific criticism of Roger L. Stevens as chairman of this questionable venture. Concern was raised in Congress that a businessman, even one as skilled and creative as Stevens, could not possibly handle the delicate issues raised by the arts. His years of involvement with the Broadway theater, his original interest in regional theatre, were discounted as the glamorous entertainment of an inveterate gambler. His quiet, steady love of literature was never mentioned in these public questions. To try to dispel the criticism, Stevens released a prepared statement on October 8, just nine days after President Johnson signed Public Law 89-209 on September 29, 1965, which created the National Foundation for the Arts and the Humanities.

> There have been inquiries as to whether there is a conflict of interest in my position as chairman of the National Council on the Arts and I would like to clear up any possible misconceptions and allegations made during the past few days.
>
> First, there is an important job to be done in the field of the arts and humanities as indicated by the mandate given us by Congress. I am proceeding to the best of my ability and judgment to carry out this responsibility.
>
> I am perfectly willing to declare unequivocally that no organization with which I have an affiliation will be entitled to funds from any government program with which I am associated.
>
> At the time of my appointment as chairman of the National Council on the Arts I resigned from all business and nonprofit organizations that might have any possible conflict with my present position. The only organizations in the arts with which I am affiliated now are the Metropolitan Opera Association and the American Shakespeare Academy which are nonprofit organizations and any organization I might join would be in the same category.
>
> I feel in carrying out my duties as chairman of the National Council on the Arts it is important to be thoroughly familiar with as many developments in the field of the

arts as possible by being a member of nonprofit organizations, as long as there is no financial conflict.

There has been some discussion of royalties that may accrue to me from plays. As soon as the first class production of a play is finished, the title of the play reverts to the author. It has been suggested that such royalties be put in trust. This is impossible to do because, as has been stated, the ownership reverts to the author and all control remains in his hands.

I would like to further state that at the time I accepted the position I had many personal commitments including those to employees who have worked with me for many years. I have had to pay very substantial amounts as a result of the continuing deficits incurred by these commitments. I would be glad to open my books to confirm these substantial financial losses.

I have worked four years as chairman of the John F. Kennedy Center without any compensation, traveling a minimum of 250,000 miles for this organization and on behalf of the National Council on the Arts, to bring to the country a greater knowledge of their activities. At least ninety percent of the cost of this travel has been paid personally. For this I expect nothing in return, for I believe it is the duty of every American citizen to serve his country when asked.

As President Johnson has said concerning the arts legislation: "The Congress will consider many programs which will leave an enduring mark on American life. But it may well be that passage of this legislation, modest as it is, will help secure for this Congress a sure and honored place in the story of the advance of our civilization."

I am delighted to serve, to the best of my ability, under his leadership to see that these new programs fulfill the promise for which so many people have worked so long and so hard.[30]

The National Endowment for the Arts Becomes Law

Critics notwithstanding, Stevens had a mission. On September 29, 1965, the National Foundation for the Arts and Humanities had become law: an independent agency, housed in the Executive Branch, and for budgeting purposes included with the Department of the Interior. The National Council was transferred from the Office of the President to the Arts Endowment by the same act, to advise the chairman on policies, programs, and procedures and make recommendations on applications for financial aid. Stevens set out to build a staff for the new agency to handle these applications—a staff which would be required to move artistic mountains with a budget the size of a toy shovel.

Congress authorized, through Public Law 80-209, appropriation of $10 million to be divided between the Arts and Humanities Endowments, for the fiscal year ending June 30, 1966, and for the two succeeding years as well. In addition, $2.25 million was authorized annually to the Arts Endowment and $5 million annually to the Humanities Endowment (the so-called "Treasury Funds") to match unrestricted donations made to the agencies. The Arts Endowment also received $2.75 million annually for state arts agency programs, subject to matching provisions, to become effective in fiscal year 1967.

Congressional authorizations have great political and public relations impact, but the actual appropriations worked on by the Bureau of the Budget (later known as the Office of Management and Budget), located in the Executive Branch, may be considerably less than the congressionally-approved ceiling. Table 2 indicates the authorization figures and the actual funding for the arts during fiscal years 1966 and 1967.[31]

First Program Staff

The Endowment program staff assembled by Roger Stevens was made up of an interesting group of men and women drawn from all parts of the country and from many disciplines who represented varying points of view about the central mission.[32] In the rhetoric of the socially-conscious Sixties, raising the quality of life in America held a top priority. Thus, as the mission to bring federal help to the beleaguered artists and arts organizations took on special importance, the varying backgrounds and experience of the staff were unique assets to the agency.

Stevens continued to wear three hats—as chairman of the Arts Endowment, special assistant to President Johnson on the Arts, and chairman of the board of trustees of the John F. Kennedy Center. His deputy, Livingston Biddle, Jr., who joined the Arts Endowment in November 1965, was a former newspaper reporter and novelist who had been special assistant to Senator Claiborne

Table 2
National Endowment for the Arts Authorizations and Appropriations (in millions)

	PL 89-209 Authorization	FY 1966[a] Appropriation	FY 1967[b] Appropriation
Grant programs and pilot projects in fiscal 1966–1968	$5 million	$2.5 million	$4 million
State assistance beginning July 1, 1966 (FY 1967)	$2.75 million	Not authorized for this year	$2 million
Federal funds to match unrestricted donations	Not to exceed $2.25 million	Appropriation not to exceed $2 million determined by amount of unrestricted gifts received	$2 million less any amounts appropriated in fiscal 1966

[a]Supplemental Appropriation Act of 1966 (October 31, 1965).
[b]Department of the Interior and Related Agencies Appropriation Act of 1967 (May 31, 1966).

Pell of Rhode Island from 1962 to 1965, with a primary responsibility for arts and humanities legislation. Frank H. Crowther, Stevens' special assistant and speech writer, had a background as a writer–editor with the Democratic National Committee and had done news and public-affairs work in radio and television.

The general counsel for the Foundation was Charles B. Ruttenberg, whose sound legal understanding of the problems of the struggling young agency was developed in part from his previous work as deputy general counsel to the National Science Foundation. Ruttenberg was part of the "shared staff" of the National Foundation serving both Endowments, as was the first NFAH administrative director, Robert W. Cox.

Charles Christopher Mark, who took over the Office of State and Community Operations (later known as the Federal–State Partnership) as its first director, had worked with Stevens and the Council as a consultant while the agency was being formed. He was a University of Wisconsin–Madison graduate and had served as director of both the Greater St. Louis Arts and Education Council and the Winston-Salem Arts Council.

In the Visual Arts area, Henry Geldzahler was hired as a consultant, although he functioned from the outset as the program director. Having pursued a degree at Yale and graduate work at Harvard, he later became associate curator of American Art and Sculpture at the Metropolitan Museum of Art and was well-known on the New York art scene.

Caroline Kizer was in charge of the "Creative Writing" area, later renamed the Literature Program. She was the author of several books of poetry, the founder and editor of *Poetry Northwest*, director of the Association of Literary Magazines of America, and had been a poet-lecturer on American literature in East and West Pakistan under the auspices of the Department of State.

Ruth Mayleas, the first program director to "come aboard," took over theatre and dance as a combined function during the first year. She was a Cornell University graduate, had been associated with the Hanya Holm School of Dance, had edited the *ANTA News Bulletin* and the Regional Theater section of *The Best Plays of 1964–65*. She had also been assistant director of the U.S. Center, International Theatre Institute (USITT), director of the National Theatre Service Department for ANTA, a board member of USITT, and vice president of the *Drama Desk*.

Paul Spreiregen headed the Architecture and Design Program. He was a graduate of the Massachusetts Institute of Technology, a former Fulbright scholar to Italy, author of several works on urban design, and a member of the Committee of Architects and Planners for the Federal Commission for the Reconstruction of Alaska.

David C. Stewart was assigned the Education and Public Media Programs. He had degrees from Columbia and Case Western Reserve Universities, had taught dramatic literature and production at Robert College in Istanbul, at

Vassar College, and at Case Western Reserve. He had been a director of the National Educational Television office in Washington, D.C., and executive director of the Joint Council on Educational Broadcasting.

Fannie Taylor, Music Program, was a graduate of the University of Wisconsin–Madison and professor and director of the Wisconsin Union Theater at Madison where she had had many years of experience in programming and managing a cultural facility. She was a founding member and executive secretary of the Association of College and University Concert Managers (ACUCM) and editor of the ACUCM *Bulletin*. Lucy Bremner was her assistant.

In addition to the program desks, there were several special offices. The Office of Program Evaluation, where applications were reviewed fcr eligibility and referred to the appropriate program area, was headed by June Batten Arey. She came to the Arts Endowment from Winston-Salem, North Carolina, with a strong list of credits in public information, fund-raising, and volunteer service on the boards of the Symphony Association, Civic Ballet, Gallery of Fine Arts, and Children's Theatre. Later, Mrs. Arey became director of the Dance Program when it was separated from the Theatre area.

The Office of Public Affairs, where information and materials describing the Council and Endowment activities were prepared, was directed by Eleanor Pollock, former women's editor of *The Evening and Sunday Bulletin* in Philadelphia and *The Philadelphia Record*. She had been editor-in-chief of *Cue* magazine, managing editor of *Charm*, and assistant to the director of the women's division of *Look*.

The Office of Research was directed by Sureva Seligson, a graduate of New York University, who had been assistant to columnist Charles L. Bartlett and director of the research division of the Democratic National Committee. Also working as a young assistant in this office was Ana Steele, who was to remain with the Arts Endowment for many years as one of its steadiest and most resourceful researchers and planners.

The Office of Grants, where applications were reviewed to ensure that they were in compliance with grant policies and requirements, was directed by Richard H. Hedrich. A graduate of Northwestern University, he had a Ph.D. from the University of Maryland and had held administrative positions at the Department of Health, Education and Welfare.

The small staff had the large responsibility of distributing the extremely limited funding for each area. The actual *appropriation* in the federal budget for the first year was only $2.5 million, plus a miniscule $34,308 in unrestricted gifts to the so-called "Treasury Fund." Thus, in fiscal 1966, the staff had total operating funds amounting to $2,534,308. Stevens' successor, Nancy Hanks, stated many years later, "Roger was a genius in starting the Endowment because he did not believe in 'democracy'—that is, giving everybody a little bit of money. Instead, he tried to create an impact where a small sum could make a difference.

You can't do everything at once. Whatever you do, do it well"—a philosophy, she added, that was firmly supported by the Council.[33]

Stevens Analyzes Arts Situation

For the March 12, 1966 issue of *Saturday Review*, Stevens wrote an article called "The State of the Arts: A 1966 Balance Sheet."[34] In it he described a situation in the country for the performing arts where, because of distribution and audience problems, the opportunities for performance were limited to the major cities and a few other tried and true communities with a good track record for supporting professional attractions. The same problem of distribution, he stated, plagued the world of painting and sculpture. He was also concerned about the availability of a discriminating audience for literature, with readers who could make their own judgments rather than accepting parroted attitudes from East Coast critics. He pointed out that, ironically, in the world of the arts failure is never supposed to occur. Only great books, great hits, masterpiece compositions, and stunning art works are supposed to be created. In short, there is no room for risk-taking.

Stevens understood the need for elbow room and risk-taking in the creative process. He also understood the need to use business methods to stimulate audiences. He recognized how federal assistance to state and local arts councils could give them the incentive to expand their resources: how seed money could help arts crops grow. He recognized and deplored the thought of any kind of "official art" and maintained that the only thing that artists and others in the art world seemed to share universally was their complete inability to agree about anything concerning the relative merits of an art work, how it should be presented to the public, or what constituted an appropriate relationship between the private and public sectors for the arts.

Stevens was convinced at this time that the aid of the federal government could be critical in developing new audiences which, in turn, would be sufficient to carry the arts project on local energy in the future. He maintained that, if 10 percent of Americans were stimulated to an active (and one assumes dues-paying and ticket-buying) support, there would be no further need for federal assistance. The important job was building the local support.

While there is a hint in this "balance sheet" of the social action programs of the sixties (part of the operating philosophy of the world at the time the federal arts legislation was passed), the article nevertheless describes the efforts of a practical visionary. Stevens recognized that an extra dimension had been given to his life through the arts and he sought to lay out opportunities for others to have the same enrichment. He cautioned against too much urgency; he insisted on careful selection and high standards; he espoused an approach solidly based on free enterprise in which the arts were given federal attention only when local and private attention and support were also present and active. He knew that the government could not put money in a machine to crank out art for the masses. At best, it could only foster the creative impulse, maintain and increase the cultural resources of the arts, and encourage local support systems. As he said in a speech in March 1966 to the National Electric Sign Convention, "The Council has been charged with the responsibility of building bridges between the federal, state, and other government levels and the community so that high standards of aesthetic consideration flow freely and constantly between them." He added:

> In this connection we are encouraged by the Supreme Court's historic decision in the *Berman vs. Parker* case of 1964. Justice William O. Douglas wrote the opinion and it was one of the Court's unanimous decisions. "It is within the power of the legislature to determine that a community should be beautiful as well as healthy, spacious as well as clean, and well-balanced as well as carefully patrolled."[35]

Initial and Trend-Setting Grants

It is interesting to review some of the projects undertaken in that first hectic year as described in the annual report of the National Council on the Arts of June 1966. Because the report was not sent to the President until six months later, it also reflects developments into the next fiscal year and includes quotations from editorial comments around the country.

Alfred Frankenstein, art editor of the *San Francisco Chronicle*, said, "The Endowment has accomplished infinitely more than anyone dreamed it could accomplish a year ago. . . . the Endowment has instituted no less than 45 projects that were not contemplated a year ago . . . . The breadth of this program is staggering."[36] Howard Taubman, critic-at-large of the *New York Times*, commended Stevens and his advisers on their energy and breadth of vision. "The Endowment has confounded the Cassandras who glumly prophesied that public funds would be spent on cautious principles and unadventurous programs. The reverse had been true . . . . Seldom has a new government program, especially one so beset with possible booby traps, been implemented with so much imagination and dispatch."[37]

The listing in the annual report of these energetic and creative programs makes exciting reading, even when couched in federal office prose. The cast of characters who made up "the fabulous Council," as a staff member later described it, the observers who attended meetings, the comings and goings through every program director's door, the interaction of bright minds, brilliant careers, fame and ego, were like an all-star review of everyone functioning in the arts in the Sixties. Behind every grant were letters, phone calls, office visits, and travel all over the country by program directors for on-site discussions, recommendations, complaints, compliments, howls of joy, bitter criticism, and endless speeches. There were also calls from Congressional offices, subtle and not-so-subtle pressure by constituents, and through it all a steady purpose by Stevens, the Council, and the staff to ensure the right selection of applicants whose work reflected the highest quality possible and whose ideas were truly innovative and creative.

During 1966 new Council members were added: John Steinbeck was appointed to fill the slot opened by David Brinkley's resignation; Richard C. Diebenkorn Jr. and Harper Lee were added when the new legislation of the NFAH Act of 1965 increased the Council membership to 26.

In the short first year of the Endowment's functioning (from September 29, 1965, to June 30, 1966), the Council went right to work to recommend artists and activities for funding and, also, began discussions on a number of ambitious, long-term organizational projects.

Laboratory Theatre Project

Under the general heading of Arts and Education, in cooperation with the U.S. Office of Education (with Kathryn Bloom's imaginative interest), and with the support of state and local school boards, the Council launched an experimental "laboratory theatre" project. A total of $330,000 was committed, to be divided between the two pilot cities of New Orleans, Louisiana, and Providence, Rhode Island. The project, which followed the outlines of an earlier Council study, was to provide these cities with professional theater companies to offer outstanding theater productions—free—to secondary school students during the weekday afternoons and to adults at the weekend performances. The project encompassed some of the favorite ideas of Stevens and the Council: audience building, developing a base for public evaluation and criticism, reaching into the high schools, meshing the efforts of the Arts Endowment and the Office of Education as well as the state and local agencies. In tiny Rhode Island, 40,000 high school students from every section of the state were invited to attend the free performances of the Trinity Square Repertory Company in Providence, directed by Adrian Hall and John McQuiggan. The 1,000-seat theatre was to house Chekhov's *The Three Sisters*, Shakespeare's *A Midsummer Night's Dream*, Shaw's *Saint Joan*, and O'Neill's *Ah, Wilderness!* Senator Claiborne Pell of Rhode Island must have been pleased.

New Orleans expected to attract at least 50,000 high school students from the city and surrounding areas for its productions at the newly-created Repertory Theater. Under the artistic direction of Stuart Vaughan, the playbill included Thomas's *Charlie's Aunt*, Shakespeare's *Romeo and Juliet*, Wilder's *Our Town*, and Sheridan's *The Rivals*. The New Orleans *Times-Picayune* looked forward "with excitement to the start of an experiment with national and local potential."[38]

Ruth Mayleas, the Theatre Program director, recalled the Laboratory Theatre project with mixed feelings. "I think it was a project that really proved you cannot impose theatre from without," she said. "You have to build on a solid base of desire and interest in a given community. But the reason I have mixed feelings is that out of the project came at least one quite extraordinary theatre—Trinity Square. There were many reasons for its success, but the principal reason was the talent and artistic leadership of the director, Adrian Hall." She added that the Laboratory Theatre Project in Providence was built on a very shaky theatrical structure, but it was at least a theatre which existed within the community: that had not been the case with the other two project locations. The New Orleans theatre struggled on for a time after the federal grant assistance was completed and then died. "The third project, the one that was started a year later in Los Angeles, is still in existence as far as I know," Mayleas said, "but along the way it turned into something very different, certainly very valid. It ultimately became the Inner City Cultural Center, largely a minority arts center, which I understand has some excellent programs although the emphasis is not particularly on theatre."

Mayleas thought the Laboratory Theatre project was interesting also because "it showed that there was a great deal of difficulty, both economic and artistic, in developing a theatre whose purpose is educating young people and then trying to make it perform a noneducational role in terms of the adult community. The theatres that have been more successful have been those that started out with adult audiences and then added an educational function with special performances for young people. . . . In a way, the Laboratory Theatre was important because it paved the way for lots of other theatres in this country to begin thinking about instituting special educational programs. By that I don't mean teaching," she explained, "I mean special performances and a cultivation of young people . . . not children's theatre but cultivation of young audiences so they ultimately become adult audiences."[39]

The National Repertory Theatre was one of the major professional companies to incorporate a special student component. The organization was touring classical productions throughout the country and received a $75,000 matching grant to expand its educational program.

Joseph Papp's New York Shakespeare Festival troupe was making headlines during the period in New York City with free professional performances of Shakespeare and other classical playwrights. With an additional $100,000 from the Endowment, the Festival's mobile theatre units were enabled to take plays in Spanish and English to a large number of neighborhoods throughout the city.

This is the first instance of awareness on the part of the Council of the importance of building audiences in less-advantaged areas and of fostering Spanish-language presentations. One can visualize Papp, his shirt collar Byronically open, his verbal verve at its brightest, pressing his case with the Endowment's chairman in Stevens' New York office. "We must do it, it's a way to bring all those people together. They can understand it."[40]

As the fiscal year came to a close there were some unobligated funds. Stevens, working with the Council and the Theater Program director, was able to grant $160,000 to the Carnegie Institute of Technology for the benefit of the American Conservatory Theatre (ACT). Coming at a time of financial crisis, the sum made support possible for the organization's apprentice training program and educational activities. The amount was matched by a Rockefeller Foundation grant and subsequent substantial commitments of aid were received in both Chicago and San Francisco as ACT changed its base of operation.

The American Educational Theatre Association (AETA) received a $7,000 grant to conduct an extensive survey of secondary school theatre throughout the nation. Plans were also in the talking stage for a Music Education project exploring the Kodály method of teaching music to youngsters in the elementary and secondary schools.

In addition to the "Arts and Education" programs, through which the Laboratory Theatre Project, the National Repertory Theatre, and the New York Shakespeare Festival were assisted, the area of drama found other help. A technical assistance grant ($27,824, administered in fiscal year 1967) went to the American National Theatre and Academy to help its program of special services for new and established nonprofit theaters all over the United States, and to open regional offices in Arizona and Florida.

As a way of giving a forum to new American plays, the Council committed $175,000 for a program of public presentation by university and resident professional theaters. This Playwrights Experimental Theatre project actually took place in fiscal 1967 with matching grants of $25,000 each going to the Arena Stage (Washington, D.C.) for *The Great White Hope*, which gave James Earl Jones the opportunity for stardom; the Barter Theatre (Abingdon, Virginia) for *Five in the Afternoon;* Brandeis University (Waltham, Massachusetts) for *Does a Tiger Wear a Necktie?*; the Professional Theatre Program of the University of Michigan (Ann Arbor) for *Amazing Grace;* and the Yale Repertory Theatre (New Haven, Connecticut) for a new adaptation of *Prometheus Bound.*

The Council and Theatre Program director began work on plans for a major program for Resident Professional Theatres to aid in developing their artistic quality by hiring outstanding guest directors and performers and upgrading salaries for permanent members of the companies. By fiscal year 1967, the 33 theaters all over the country were being helped through this program which provided matching grants totaling $1,439,000.[41]

Theatre Program Develops

The funded theatre projects reflected the national interest in the growing nonprofit professional repertory movement, both the so-called resident or regional theaters and the experimental theatres. Ruth Mayleas recalled that one of the first activities of her program area was to develop a panel of peer advisors to ensure that the federal office would be in constant touch with the national developments in the professional nonprofit theater community. Mayleas felt that, although the theatre program originated within the Endowment, in many ways it was a collective program. "It was the product of a lot of listening," she said, recalling the formative early years. "It was a program that said to the theatre world, 'You tell us what you need. We will not structure a very tight program and ask you to conform. We are trying to be responsive within extreme limitations of money . . . . But within these limitations we are trying to answer genuine needs.'" The program addressed issues of artistic growth, of managerial competence, of audience development. But essentially," she explained, "it was concerned less with a narrow project or program definition than with the support of institutions of, we judged, superior quality. It was an institution—rather than project-oriented program and for the most part remained that way. As the program became larger and more sophisticated, there were further breakdowns in categories because there was a need to deal with theaters of certain similarities of budget and type within a particular framework. But the theatre field was viewed as a whole. Even though we had an experimental theater category, a children's theatre category, a large producing company category, these were for administrative ease in handling so that one could look at a given group of theatres with their peers. At the same time our program view addressed the entire non-profit professional theatre community."[42]

Dance Program Begins

The field of professional dance also received positive attention from the new arts agency. On the National Council there was the strong voice of Agnes de Mille to exhort and guide her colleagues on the importance of dance in the pantheon of the performing arts. Almost immediately a Special Advisory Panel of 12 members, representing the broadest aspects of dance expression nationwide, was set up to review requests for assistance from both dancers and dance organizations. The panel was also charged with developing plans and programs to meet some of the urgent current and future needs of a chronically poverty-stricken art field.

In fact, the first official grant-making action of the new Arts Endowment was to respond to a plea from the American Ballet Theatre and its director Lucia Chase. The Council recommended to Roger Stevens that an emergency grant of $100,000 be made. "On December 20, 1965, Vice President Hubert Humphrey presented the first check issued by the Federal Government in direct support of the arts to the president of a ballet theater foundation, assuring the continued operation of one of the country's best existing full-scale dance companies."[43] Suddenly aware of its power, the Council also committed additional funds of $250,000 for the American Ballet Theatre to make nationwide tours in the fall of 1966 and the spring of 1967. These moneys were all in the form of matching grants, as required by law.

That first grant was a dramatic statement about Endowment intentions and was applauded by the press. "The Treasury of the United States has saved a national treasure," wrote Walter Terry in the *New York Herald Tribune*.[44] Clive Barnes of the *New York Times* stated: "The American Ballet Theatre

> made splendid history at the New York State Theatre Tuesday night. It opened its month's New York season before a star-studded, indeed star-spangled, audience headed by Vice-President Humphrey, and with no pain at all became the first American performing arts enterprise to appear with the aid of a Federal grant."[45]

Individual Grants to Artists—Dance

The Council, and especially the artist members, were strongly supportive of individual grants to artists for funding to provide creative men and women with space and time to work directly with his or her art. In dance, the first of these individual grants was awarded to eight of the nation's leading choreographers to "create and produce outstanding works"—Alvin Ailey, Merce Cunningham, Martha Graham, José Limon, Alwin Nikolais, Anna Sokolow, Paul Taylor, and Antony Tudor (who accepted his grant the following year). The immediate results were exciting. Alvin Ailey created "Come and Get the Beauty of It Hot," "Lament," and "Music for Sighs" ($5,000); Merce Cunningham choreographed "Place" ($5,000); Martha Graham did "Cortège of Eagles" and "Dancing Ground" ($39,000); José Limon produced "Psalm" ($23,400); Alwin Nikolais created "Imago" ($5,000); and Paul Taylor "Orbs" ($5,000).[46]

The early dance programs of the Arts Endowment were vigorously supportive of a discipline starved for attention. In 1965, it was estimated that 80 percent of the dance audience was in New York City; gradually, according to Doris Hering, executive director of the National Association of Regional Ballet, that figure turned completely around with the largest dance audience developing outside New York as growth in interest escalated nationally.[47] The Coordinated Residency Touring Program was one of the important reasons for this turnaround. In 1968 the Illinois Arts Council received a matching grant of $25,000 for a pilot project involving four dance companies performing in six cities for eight weeks. The Merce Cunningham, Alwin Nikolais, Paul Taylor, and Glen Tetley companies were selected for the pilot effort and a young dance manager, Charles Reinhart, was given an individual grant of $5,000 to develop several regional circuits based on the project. The idea had been largely developed by June Batten Arey, then head of the Arts Endowment Dance program. In a discussion about the program some years later, Clark Mitze remarked how sorry he was that in the intervening period Arey's innovative role seemed to have been forgotten.

> She was very good. She saw the states as being a really strong point in the growth of dance, and in the developing of a dance touring program. It was a marvelous union. The states really needed something to give them experience. They could take credit for [the project] and at the same time participate and learn.

June Arey also recognized the need of the dance field for lengthened seasons, steadier work, improved touring conditions, with short residencies replacing the hectic and fatiguing one-night stands. In her years as the Dance Program director she devoted herself to trying to find solutions to these needs.

The Coordinated Residency Touring Program enlarged yearly and moved into many regional circuits, encompassing groups of states. Mitze recalled:

> It eventually grew to be a sort of monster, but if they had stuck with June Arey's original plans I think it would have been—would still be—better. But they kept trying to experiment with it. Everybody was so afraid because the federal government was naming a list of companies that could be used. "There you go! The federal government is going to make artistic judgments!"[48]

In an effort to solve this difficulty, the Dance Program guidelines ultimately opened up the list of companies that could be hired through the CRTP; but many of the newly-listed groups were not of the best quality and were not engaged. Disappointments and bitterness began to develop as the decade passed.

For many years the distinguished American dancer Martha Graham had been financially unable to tour her own country, although she and her company had been sent abroad by the State Department to represent America. The Arts Endowment remedied this inversion with a much-acclaimed matching grant of $142,250, which enabled Graham and her troupe to tour the country for the first time in 15 years with eight weeks of performances. Audiences and critics in 32 cities had an opportunity to see the company in "peak performing condition," as Clive Barnes reported from Hartford, Connecticut, where the tour began.

Almost as a footnote to the other dance projects, the Endowment made a grant to the Capitol Ballet Guild of Washington (DC) for $5,000 during the 1966 season. The funding foreshadowed many future grants for arts activities in the capital city, a virtual requirement for an agency located there.

Association of American Dance Companies (AADC) Established

The Council believed the dance field needed special help.[49] In 1966 there were said to be 11 professional ballet companies functioning in America, 40 modern dance companies, and about 200 nonprofessional dance groups. Most of these were existing marginally. A technical assistance grant was made for $5,000 to examine the possibility of developing a national dance association and to plan future support in this area. A National Dance Conference was held in New York City, June 1–3, 1966, cosponsored by the Arts Endowment, the North American Ballet Association, the American Guild for Musical Artists, and the National Association of Regional Ballet. Martha Graham and Sol Hurok addressed the 172 delegates who had come from 24 states and the District of Columbia. The delegates enthusiastically backed the idea of an Association of American Dance Companies (AADC) to act as "a coordinating educational and service organization to promote and encourage the knowledge, appreciation and practice of dance, exclusively through performing and educational activities." The organizational spadework was done by Ralph Black, then general manager of the National Symphony and a founding member of the American Symphony Orchestra League, which provided a model for AADC. Black was given a $5,600 grant to conduct a national survey and organize the conference. In the next year AADC received $25,000 for its annual conference, seminars, training of board members, and a survey of services and ways of improving rehearsal and performance facilities for dance. However, AADC lacked the kind of leadership that had made the American Symphony Orchestra League strong in its field, particularly the organizational talents that its executive director, Helen M. Thompson, had brought to ASOL. In addition, it is fair to say that the two fields are very different and the kind of association that worked for the nation's orchestras may not have been suited to the idiosyncratic problems of the dance. AADC struggled along for years, regularly receiving help from the Arts Endowment, as well as from foundations and corporations, and finally gave up the effort in 1981, having never quite focused its goals.

Costume Design and Folk Art

In the original legislation for the Arts Endowment the term "the arts" was said to include costume and fashion design.[50] Thus, a grant was made to the Metropolitan Museum of Art in New York City to provide a special exhibition in its Costume Wing in the spring of 1967. On display were 100 historical and 65 contemporary costumes reflecting characteristics of the environment. The success of the project was due largely to the staff efforts of Eleanor Pollock, who had been assigned "costume" along with her public information role and who persevered with the help of Council member Eleanor Lambert. The following year a matching grant of $12,500 was made to National Educational Television for two half-hour shows on the American fashion designers Pauline Trigère and Norman Norell, as a part of NET's "Creative Person" series. Although the Trigère program won the prestigious CHRIS award, it appears that Roger Stevens and the Council had not viewed this area of creativity with much enthusiasm and future support was minimal.

Since folk art was also mentioned in the enabling legislation, the Council dutifully discussed it and in the next fiscal year (1967) made a $39,500 matching grant to the National Folk Festival Association for a variety of planning and collecting projects.

Literature Program/Poets in the Schools

During this period, Caroline Kizer held the program desk for "Creative Writing," later designated as Literature.[51] Her vigorous and exuberant championing of the literary arts resulted in many lively projects. One of the most innovative and long-term programs involved matching funds of $46,750 to support a series of pilot projects in Detroit, Pittsburgh, and New York through the Academy of American Poets. The first phase, "Dialogues in the Arts of Poetry," was intended to stimulate teacher interest and improve teaching methods. It got under way in New York first with readings by Denise Levertov, Robert Lowell, Howard Nemerov, Allen Tate, and Robert Penn Warren. The second phase, "Poetry Readings in the Classrooms," was designed to bring younger and lesser-known poets into the high schools to read and discuss their own works with students.

In the 1966–67 school year, the second phase made lively progress when the poet Kenneth Koch began teaching poetry to third, fourth, and fifth grade youngsters in a public school on the lower east side of Manhattan. The project was exciting and successful. Beginning with its second meeting, the National Council on the Arts and Roger Stevens had been seeking ways to work cooperatively with the Office of Education and other federal agencies; the Council and staff quickly picked up the implications of the poetry project to try to push for this cooperative action. Although the Comprehensive Elementary and Secondary Education Act had been passed in 1965, the Office of Education, with bureaucratic deliberateness, did not transfer money into the Arts Endowment until 1969 when $100,000 went to the Central Midwestern Regional Educational Laboratory (CEMREL).

These funds made it possible to place a pilot program for professional visual artists in six secondary schools in California, Colorado, Florida, Minnesota, Missouri, and Pennsylvania. Encouraged by success again, and an eager acceptance by the schools involved, the Office of Education made $900,000 available the next year and the cosponsored (by the Office of Education and the Arts Endowment) Artists-in-the-Schools program was launched. Other disciplines (dance, poetry, music, and theater) were added and the artists were to perform and teach in schools in many parts of the nation, while the grants themselves were to be primarily administered by the state arts agencies and were "designed to train teachers and educate children through actual experience with professional artists working in the schools."[52]

The Arts Council discussed creating a new annual literary anthology of the best American poetry, fiction, essays, and criticism. Editors of leading literary magazines were to be invited to submit the works of three authors published in their magazines the preceding year and a distinguished literary panel was to select the works for inclusion in the anthology.[53] The authors selected were to receive $1,000 each and the editors who had first printed their material were to be given $500. Major American publishing firms were to rotate the opportunity to publish the anthology and 1967 was the target date. It was an innocent effort intended to help America's writers but, down the line a few years, it came close to wrecking the Endowment in the muddy backwaters of so-called freedom of speech.

The Council began to develop a program of grants to individual writers with program director Carolyn Kizer's knowledgeable assistance. By fiscal year 1967, grants-in-aid of up to $10,000 each had been assigned to 22 biographers, journalists, novelists, and poets to complete works in progress or conduct research essential to their continuing productivity. The grants in biography and criticism were given jointly with the National Endowment for the Humanities and the poets in the program were presented in a reading at the Library of Congress. Another opportunity for poets to tour a circuit of five developing southern colleges was arranged in 1968 with the assistance of the Woodrow Wilson Fellowship Foundation.

A new Coordinating Council for Literary Magazines (CCLM) was organized to give support to these struggling publications. By June 1967, matching funds had been raised from The Old Dominion Foundation ($25,000), the Babcock Foundation ($5,000), and United States Steel ($5,000), with the balance of the $50,000 matching money coming from the Institute of Public Affairs in money and services. Grant recipients of the program included *The Kenyon Review*, *Poetry Magazine*, *The Hudson Review*, *Tri-Quarterly*, *Choice*, *Coyote*, *Burning Deck*, *The Chelsea Review*, *December*, *The Virginia Quarterly*, *Audit*, and the *Wormwood Review*.

The Kenneth Patchen Grant

A special individual grant of $10,000 was awarded to poet Kenneth Patchen, who despite a lifetime of agonizing illness and financial reverses had managed to maintain steady artistic productivity. Recommendations to the Endowment for this award came from the Academy of American Poets, *Poetry Magazine*, and the Poetry Center of YM-YWHA in New York, as well as from other organizations and innumerable poets, novelists, editors, and publishers. The grant made it possible for Patchen to change his residence to a climate that, it was hoped, would lessen his continuous pain and allow him to pursue his writing career.

The Radcliffe Institute for Independent Study received a $25,000 grant to help women writers who had domestic responsibilities to find time and other assistance to continue their writing careers. This grant ultimately triggered other support, including a $300,000 gift from the Merrill Trust of Ithaca, New York, which made it possible for the Arts Endowment to terminate future assistance.

International Arts Events Supported

Encouragement of international arts events was one of the early Council goals. As a result, a matching grant was awarded to the Association of Poets, Playwrights, Editors, Essayists, and Novelists (P.E.N.) to host the 34th International P.E.N. Congress in New York City, June 13–18, 1966. More than 800 writers from all parts of the world came to discuss "The Writer as Independent Spirit." To make the visits possible the State Department cooperated with a new policy for blanket visas for the participants.

Musical Beginnings: Some Cacophony

Before the first Music Program director joined the staff in April 1966, the Council had already committed itself, at Isaac Stern's urging, to a Technical Assistance Program and a Composers Assistance Program.[54] The former was established to train administrative personnel for music organizations through seminars conducted by the American Symphony Orchestra League during the summers of 1966 and 1967. The latter program was envisioned in two parts: grants-in-aid to symphony orchestras to encourage commissioning of orchestral works (administered by the American Symphony Orchestra League) and individual copying grants to composers to cover the extremely high copying costs for new music. In the past such copying expenses had often wiped out the value of a commission to a composer. The American Music Center administered this part of the program.

In early 1966 there was also a master chamber orchestra under discussion, to be built around the skills of violinist Alexander Schneider—a long-time member of the Budapest Quartet. This project, before it was laid to rest as infeasible a year later, created incredible pressure and concern from the music world. Schneider was authorized a $31,400 grant to make a national study and to cover the country to seek out able musicians for a small orchestra of virtuoso calibre. The grant letter to him stated: "to develop an organizational structure and personnel for a master chamber orchestra" for which the Council was prepared to commit $400,000. Stern and Schneider devised the name "National Chamber Orchestra Institute" in order to take the project out of the world of commercially-sponsored musical activity and give it its proper educational connotation. Apparently, they also talked with Justice Abe Fortas—a quiet, backstage consultant and himself a violinist—who approved the name. When selected, the chamber orchestra members were expected to tour and perhaps spend two or three days at a given site, offering workshops and lecture-demonstrations.

But conductors and symphony orchestra managers were up in arms. Alan Watrous, manager of the Seattle Symphony Orchestra, wrote:

> True, we are desperately in need of trained orchestra players, particularly in the field of strings; however, the method I understand [that] is being employed is taking established players away who are already . . . with symphonies . . . as well as taking your orchestra on tour in competition with touring orchestras for fees. [It] does not appear to me to be the way of assistance to symphony orchestras.

Watrous added that training players for symphony work could be done better through educational institutions and that the guaranteed salaries being offered were in excess of what many orchestras could afford, thereby attracting personnel away from their present positions. The feeling on the part of symphony management was universal that their best players would leave to join the "government" orchestra.

Schneider reduced the size of the group from 40 to 27; theatre director Ted Mann, who had been hired as manager, quit; the manager of the National Symphony Orchestra in Washington, D.C., was indignant about the name. Schneider interviewed some 500 players around the country and came up with only 12 whom he felt were worthy; the New School for Social Research, which had undertaken to assist the project by assuming sponsorship, reported "incredible opposition" to the whole idea, with the music community solidly against it. Finally, at the May 1967 Council meeting the project was obliquely tabled with the agreement that a need for orchestral training definitely existed and an effort should be made by the Music Panel, staff, and Council to find a solution acceptable to all. Schneider's ultimate funding amounted to only $19,185.

Another music project in the discussion stage was a program for Young Concert Artists to give them an opportunity to develop skills as recitalists through national tours. The Council made an allocation of $310,000 to develop the idea. Young soloists were to be selected by a panel of distinguished musicians and opportunities for seasoning appearances as individual recitalists and/or soloists with orchestras and other music associations were to be sought. The project was to be handled through the Carnegie Hall–*Jeunesses Musicales* agency which had been functioning for several seasons with young American and foreign artists. Again, Council member Isaac Stern, who was president of Carnegie Hall, was involved in this effort to help young artists, along with Carnegie Hall director Julius Bloom.

If the music world had been troubled by the chamber orchestra project, it became hysterical over the Young Artists. The *New York Times* did not help the situation when it published the $310,000 allocation figure as if it were appropriated and already spent in competition with the commercial sales of the artists' managements on 57th Street in New York. But it was not only the commercial managers who were upset. One nonprofit agency for young artists stated: "You have upset the applecart, which foundations shouldn't do. You have probably killed our business." However, the reaction nationally from people interested in booking the artists was positive. There was, nevertheless, a considerable public brouhaha generated by some of the artist management organizations, who felt that the government was essentially poaching on their territory. Chairman Stevens called a meeting of the dissident agents. Letters were written. Quiet, thoughtful discussions were held with Kurt Weinhold at Columbia Artists Management Inc., Herbert Barrett of the Barrett Agency, and others. The project was turned into a feasibility study for the first year and the controversy subsided. The total cost for the study was $17,315.[55]

After this turmoil in music, the Council became more cautious about starting up programs and projects that did not come out of the field and its needs, as expressed in panel meetings, applications, and discussion. Roger Stevens put together a Panel for Music with Aaron Copland as its chairman,* and activities smoothed.

Also discussed in the Council was a program to develop regional opera. During the next year a grant was awarded to the Metropolitan National Company, under the leadership of singer Risë Stevens, for a tour to the Southeast. The project was apparently not favored by Rudolf Bing, the Metropolitan's general manager, and was later discontinued. There was also help given to the San Francisco Opera for the formation of a small flexible ensemble which evolved into the Western Opera Theatre. The latter company had a very successful season in 1967 including a performance in the beleaguered Watts area of Los Angeles—one of the first of many inner-city programs sponsored by the Arts Endowment in its effort to broaden the audience base for the arts all over the country.

*The Music Panel also included Norman Singer, Thomas Willis, Boris Goldovsky, Julius Rudel, William Severns, Allen Sapp, Mario di Bonaventura, Fannie Taylor, Carlos Mosely, Louis Krasner, William Schuman, Maurice Abravanel, Lukas Foss, Gunther Schuller, Rudolf Serkin, Harold Arberg, and Alfred Frankenstein.

The American Film Institute

One of the most ambitious projects of the new agency, reflecting not only Roger Stevens's vision but that of such individuals as George Stevens, Sr. (chairman of the Council Film Committee) and Gregory Peck, was the formulation of a plan to establish an American Film Institute (AFI) similar to those that flourished in other nations.[56] President Johnson had endorsed the proposal for such a new institution at the signing ceremonies at the White House in 1965 when he said, "We will create an American Film Institute, bringing together leading artists of the film industry, outstanding educators, and young men and women who wish to pursue the Twentieth Century art form as their life's work."

To get the plan under way, the Council recommended a grant of $91,000 to the Stanford Research Institute to study how foreign institutes were organized and supported, to examine characteristics of film schools and the use of film in general education in the United States, to assess professional training and opportunities, and to recommend how best to establish a film institute in this country. The study was made and presented to the National Council in February 1967 in an overextended session, but the message was clear and the institute was created in June 1967 as a nongovernment, nonprofit organization to preserve and develop the nation's artistic and cultural resources in film. The Endowment's share in establishing the Film Institute was $1.3 million, matched (after hard work by Roger Stevens) by equal amounts from the Ford Foundation and the member companies of the Motion Picture Association of America. Offices were established in Washington, New York, and Los Angeles under the direction of George Stevens, Jr. and the institute began to concentrate on archives, education, advanced film studies, film production, and research and publication.

Roger Stevens felt that the project never received the money the Stanford Report had stated it should, partly because the industry itself "had not started it [and] never had and never was going to do anything." He also believed, years later, that while his original hopes for the Film Institute had not been entirely fulfilled, the record of accomplishment on the whole was very good.[57] The Film Institute was conceived as the counterpart of other such national film industries in Western democracies. Despite stresses and strains in its early development, it managed to sustain its role as a national service institute by generating interaction between the commercial and independent media and by providing essential archival and preservation services.[58]

During 1969, for example, the annual report states that "the Institute's newly created Center for Advanced Film Studies in Beverly Hills, California, was staffed and equipped; assistance to filmmakers was increased through a total of 62 awards for internships, production, and screenwriting projects; and 3,200 American films which had been made on unstable, short-lived nitrate stock were tracked down, transferred onto acetate stock, and thus saved for permanent preservation in the Library of Congress. A retrospective program of classic films was organized for the Seventh Avenue Film Festival; data were completed (more than 5,000 entries) for the first volume of the Film Institute's American Film Catalogue; the Community Film Workshop Council was established to encourage and coordinate film and television activities in low income areas; and a nationwide education membership campaign was undertaken which enrolled 1,500 individuals and associations by the year's end."[59]

In subsequent years the staff of the Film Institute and the Arts Endowment were often at odds over procedures and budgets, but there is no question that the creation of the AFI was one of the great programming contributions of the Council and Roger Stevens, ensuring the historical preservation of this particular and special art form of the twentieth century.

Housing for Artists

The Council in those first few months was bursting with ideas and the national constituency was eager to put in its requests. In the annual report for fiscal 1966 there were nine pages devoted to "Variety of Art Forms"—most of them cross-disciplinary. For example, there was the proposed Artists' Housing Project to provide studio-living quarters at reasonable rates in which a $100,000 Arts Endowment grant was matched in fiscal 1967 by the J. M. Kaplan Fund Inc. in New York City.[60] The project mushroomed in fiscal 1968 and 1970 with the establishment of the nonprofit Westbeth Corporation which purchased the old Bell Telephone Laboratories in New York City for conversion into America's first national artists' joint living and working center. Westbeth ultimately provided 384 units of studio–living quarters for artists and their families at affordable rents. The complex, located on the Lower West Side, also included film studios, rehearsal rooms, exhibition galleries, sculpture gardens, and adjoining park and playground areas. Clearly, Roger Stevens the real estate man understood the basic need of artists, like the rest of the population, for adequate living and working space. He also sought to find a way for artists to be able to talk and work together in a mutually stimulating setting.

Some years later, Lawrence Halprin, the architect and city planner who had been on the Council when Westbeth was approved, recalled the project with mixed feelings:

> They had a good architect who did the remodeling . . . but it cost an incredible amount of money [not government money]. It produced something which houses even to this day . . . artists and studios and a lot of other things. I think there are 400 artists. They've run into all kinds of problems with it because I think there have been a lot of antagonisms about who got in there and who didn't. . . . A lot of these things end up having the same kind of quality as public housing, which everyone used to feel

> was a wonderful idea; that is, take the poor people and build some housing for them and move them into it and that will solve their problems. But the fact of the matter is, it doesn't. [It creates antagonisms among peers] primarily because the people involved have no say in it. They are taken from somewhere and put into it. It seems to me if you are going to do that kind of thing it would be much better to do what they are doing in housing nowadays, and that is just subsidizing—giving the people the same facilities as everyone else but just subsidizing it. Make it possible for them to be scattered around. . . . I would have taken, say, 50 artists and said "here's $2,000, now go and fix up some studios."[61]

Spreading Resources

In an effort to spread their small resources widely and reach young talent, the Council also authorized the Endowment to make 77 Graduation Awards of $1,000 each to students in the fields of art, literature, music, and architecture.[62]

The Institute of American Indian Arts applied for a grant to support a Festival of the Performing Arts of the American Indian. In June 1966, the Endowment provided a $29,000 matching grant for this festival at the Carter Barron Amphitheatre by 75 young Indian performers from 31 tribes throughout the nation. The outdoor production was cosponsored by the Center for Arts of Indian America, the Institute of Contemporary Arts, and the Bureau of Indian Affairs, plus a heavy barrage of mosquitoes.

The Council members discussed warmly the idea of a Teaching Artists Program of one-year grants of $7,500 to enable men and women in institutions of higher learning to take sabbatical leaves. The concept of the program fitted the pattern suggested by Council member and artist Richard Diebenkorn. He believed that assistance grants to individual artists should be "numerous, not voluminous"—grants should be small but widely disseminated.[63] The program was approved to give 50 novelists, poets, painters, sculptors, and composers the opportunity to take one-year leaves to pursue creative work in the arts during 1966 and 1967.

The men and women on the Council dreamed of support for the arts far beyond the confines of the first modest budgets. One of the projects discussed was an Inter-American Foundation for the Arts, which would develop superior cultural exchange services for artists of the United States and Latin America. The Council envisioned opening up the rich cultures of the two Americas, but the program languished.

An experimental pilot project in Rural Arts was launched with the University of Wisconsin College of Agriculture's Wisconsin Idea Theatre. The project involved an attempt to develop audiences and artists in five rural Wisconsin communities with populations ranging from 1,500 to 10,000 persons. The program continued from fiscal year 1966 into 1968 and 1969, with a total expenditure of $203,767. At a culminating program evening, Lady Bird Johnson came to Spring Green, Wisconsin, joined various university officials for dinner, and sat with the audience for an original theatrical work in a refurbished movie theater.

American Theatre Laboratory

Dancer-choreographer Jerome Robbins was given a $300,000 grant to develop the American Theatre Laboratory, a project enthusiastically supported for its creativity by at least one Council member who called it the "most imaginative, exciting and innovative project passed since formation of the Arts Endowment." Robbins, who had once been called the most gifted of American-born choreographers, was working toward the creation of a new form of lyric theatre in America. His discipline for the company he assembled included daily training in dance, plus speech, diction, or singing. The work involved classical study in Shakespeare, Noh theatre, the Greek dramatists, Synge, Brecht, contemporary writers, and experiments with masks, voice, movement, props, music, lights, and stages. Robbins reported that the experience had been "so fruitful that it is my wish to devote another season to the American Theatre Laboratory."[64]

Architecture and Design Starts Slowly

Architecture and Design had a somewhat slower start as a program than some of the other disciplines.[65] Lawrence Halprin said many years later that he felt that part of the problem lay in lack of staff implementation of the Council programs and projects. The Council approved a contract in 1967 to Robert R. Nathan Associates of Washington, D.C. for $85,085 for a feasibility study about establishing a national institute for design. According to the "History" of the Arts Endowment prepared for the Johnson administration,

> unfortunately, the drafters of the report never fully grasped what the architecture members of the Council were asking, and the final report was not accepted as a blueprint for the proposed Institute as conceived by the Arts Council members.[66]

Halprin recalled "being very annoyed about it, because a lot of money was spent researching this idea."[67] For several years budget cuts and other difficulties forced the idea into abeyance.

There were any number of spot projects undertaken in the Architecture and Design area—student travel, support for research and conferences, studies aimed at improving highway signs, a display of R. Buckminster Fuller's geodesic domes at the Festival of Two Worlds in Spoleto, Italy, and design internships for the

America the Beautiful Fund, a landscape beautification project supported by Lady Bird Johnson.

Visual Arts

The area of the Visual Arts was the province of Henry Geldzahler.[68] From time to time he left New York to preside at his Washington office where his assistant, Devon Meade, followed later by Starke Meyer, was endeavoring to keep the daily flow of grant requests in some sort of order. Geldzahler was ungenerously described in *Art News:* "Nationally known as an enchanting Pop-society celebrity [whose] professional contributions have been, to put it politely, undistinguished."[69] Roger Stevens, however, had been urged to try to obtain Geldzahler's services for the Endowment because of his abilities as an art critic, friend and interpreter of the seminal New York art scene of the Sixties. He knew New York artists and, perhaps more important, he was accepted by those who made up that particular environment. A decade later he became cultural affairs commissioner for New York City.

The first grants in the Visual Arts area began modestly. Matching funds totaling $38,000 were allocated to support American participation in international arts events, specifically the Venice Biennale which was scheduled for September 1966. With this grant, American participation—which had been problematical—was made possible. The exhibition was put together for the American artists by the National Collection of Fine Art of the Smithsonian Institution.

The National Council also made plans for that fiscal year to "initiate a pilot program designed to stimulate public awareness of the visual arts by making facilities of large metropolitan museums available to wider audiences in their communities and outlying areas"—a bureaucratic way of saying that some large museums would be helped to develop some educational programs for students, training programs for teachers, and traveling exhibitions, films, and lecturers.

The Council also put forward plans for several other visual arts projects, some of which came to fruition while some became controversial. The plans provided for $5,000 individual grants to painters and sculptors "in recognition of past contributions"—a Council effort to make up for the long drought of official recognition for America's creative talents. Specifically, these grants were to be used to encourage further efforts by the artists; for the development of original art work in print workshops for exhibition in educational and nonprofit institutions, such as schools and museums; for a survey of community visual arts resources in the country; for a system to make fine reproductions of historical and contemporary drawings available to a wider audience, especially in the schools; and for funds to commission painters to create new prints for distribution in high quality portfolios to schools, libraries, and educational institutions.

Not all of this appealed to all visual arts constituents. In 1967, when the Special Subcommittee on the Arts and Humanities met,[70] mention was made of the $5,000 individual grants for direct assistance which had gone to 60 painters and sculptors (most of whom were men) for a total expenditure of $300,000. At this time, panelists who reviewed and recommended artists for grants were not publicly announced until after the review process was complete. The anonymity was intended to protect the panelists against undue pressure from anxious applicants, but it did not please the arts field and consequently the policy was changed shortly afterwards.

The panelists who had made the grant recommendations for the $5,000 individual awards represented a broad and distinguished group of artists, museum directors, curators, and critics: from the East—Robert Motherwell, painter, New York; Barbara Rose, critic, New York; George Segal, sculptor, New Jersey; from the Midwest—Martin Friedman, director, Walker Art Center, Minneapolis; Edward Henning, curator, Cleveland Museum; Richard Hunt, sculptor, Chicago; and from the West Coast—Walter Hopps, director, Pasadena Art Museum; John Humphrey, curator, San Francisco Museum of Art; John Denman, collector, Seattle. These men and women took their assignment seriously and recommended a carefully-evaluated list of artists, but there were rumblings from the field which erupted in the subcommittee hearings in 1967. Especially distressed were the advocates of "representational" painting.

Senator Claiborne Pell conducted the subcommittee hearings and opened the forum to a discussion of "representational versus abstract types of painting" by Frank Wright, president of the Council of American Artists Societies, Michael Werboff, member of the board of directors of that same council, and Charles Cunningham, director of the Art Institute of Chicago. Wright thanked Senator Pell for the opportunity to bring his organization's point of view to the committee and said that he had already provided, at Roger Stevens' invitation, a position paper on this "rather controversial subject" to the National Council which had met May 12 in Tarrytown, New York. The paper claimed that the Council of American Artists Societies represented "the largest group of practicing artists in the country" and should be invited "to participate in carrying out the purposes of the Act." The group wished to have a voice in making awards or grants-in-aid, selecting American art for foreign exhibition, selecting works of art for government purchase or institutions, evaluating educational institutions in the visual arts field where grants were considered, establishing standards in the visual arts, and measuring public preferences in the visual arts. Wright stated:

> Works of artists already awarded grants include some appalling selections, and only eight out of 60 can be called representational. . . . No one can complain if a painter wants to have a tantrum on canvas . . . it's a free country. . . . But to call the results fine art is something else.

Wright continued in this vein, adding that the fine arts stem from a reverence for life, and the teaching of high standards of craftsmanship involves the teaching of high standards of morality. "The issue before the country is the same as the issue before the civilized world. It is a question of reverence for life versus contempt for life."

Senator Pell thanked Wright for his views and stated that he shared some of his opinion that perhaps there should be more proponents of representational art in the awards list. Pell added, however, that "elements of your statement contained a bit of overstating and editorializing, but that is the privilege of any witness." "All we want is equal time," said Wright.

The next witness was Michael Werboff, an elderly New York portrait painter, who said he was at the hearing to represent the American Artists Professional League of about 900 "dues-paying members." Werboff compared representational and abstract art to the youth of the United States, "the hippies and beatniks and the serious-minded, studious, moral and good members." He felt that "after the creation of the Council [which he had supported] under the protection of the Federal moniker, there is nothing to which the traditional artist can appeal for defense of their rights as contemporary American artists." Werboff went on for considerable time about " 'op,' 'pop' and other kinds of non-art," about "what appears to be a conspiracy to vilificate [sic] and debase the artistic image" of America in international exhibitions, about de Kooning's "monstrous caricatures of womanhood," and "glib gibberish."

> Even the Metropolitan Museum has been invaded. The promoter of it, Mr. Geldzahler, who is a prominent figure in the National Council [sic] and who already was responsible for one scandal in the last biennial in Venice, has now been appointed the head of the Department of American Art of the Metropolitan Museum. It puts the American traditional artists straight into the hands of their worst enemy, artistically speaking.

The hearing concluded with comments by Charles Cunningham, from the Chicago Art Institute, who urged support of Senate Bill 2061 regarding the Arts Endowment appropriation, and who supported the right of an artist to develop his or her own ideas and concepts. He recalled that the English critic, Roger Fry, had made the point that "the only person who is able to determine the success or failure of a work of art is the artist himself because he knows what he has conceived. If an artist is to be ahead of his time, obviously he is going to do something which may not be familiar to the average audience." Werboff then reiterated that they came "as friends, not as enemies," and that he and his colleagues would like to be helpful, that they recognized the difficulties Chairman Stevens faced, but that the Visual Arts department of the agency was understaffed.

There was a brisk discussion on who the members of the selection panel were, with Werboff stating that the American artists had a right to know. Senator Pell stopped the discussion, which had been covered earlier, and said that "there is great merit to the view that since the Council is responsible, criticism should be directed at the Council, not at the panel. I see no harm after the panel has finished its work when they can no longer be exposed to pressure, to letting the names be known. . . . This could be open for discussion. I have not made up my mind on it myself."

As the hearings wound to a close, Roger Stevens submitted an editorial from *Art News* (February 1967) which stated that the first awards to painters and sculptors made by the Council was the "best list of grants (or prizes, or honors, call them what you will) that we have ever seen in the field." The editorial went on to congratulate both Stevens and Geldzahler for obtaining and acting on expert advice. Stevens also submitted a letter from the *Saturday Review* art editor, Katherine Kuh, who praised the fact that the whole country was represented in the awards, not just the New York contingent—"a breath of fresh air." Hilton Kramer, critic from the *New York Times*, also wrote that he felt the list of painters and sculptors was "one of the best-drawn lists of its kind."

As Senator Pell concluded the hearings he thanked all participants and said he hoped that the exchange of opinions had cleared the air, and that "many Americans like myself do appreciate and believe in less abstract art; encouragement should be given to forms of art that have a message or at least that we can comprehend. This as you know is a personal thought of mine." Pell added that a good many points Werboff touched on concerned his views on the general question of modern art, but were not relevant to the particular legislation under consideration. Shortly thereafter, the hearing adjourned.

In the Visual Arts program the Arts Endowment continued to give direct assistance to the artist, covering many different areas of the country. The art critic Thomas B. Hess wrote in a 1967 issue of *Art News* that the awards program

> reveals a sophisticated knowledge on the part of the regional advisory panels which made the recommendations and, even rarer, the facts have been tempered with tact, finesse, and a humane understanding of individual needs. The money has gone to artists at a point in their careers when it can make a financial or psychological difference, possibly a crucial one . . . the whole enterprise is a major contribution to our culture.[71]

Given the social climate of the 1960s, the Visual Arts program, like other program areas of the Arts Endowment, can be said to have steered a fairly consistent course among the shoals of the social action legislation, of the new and acceptable pornography and the flaky philosophies that strewed the period, as well as of the ego trips of the emerging "me" decade.

Another project, begun in 1967 and brought to fruition by 1969, was the "Works of Art in Public Places."[72] This was the dream of Council member René D'Harnoncourt, who first proposed government support for the acquisition of works of contemporary art to be placed in prominent public areas throughout the nation. Matching grants of $45,000 went to Grand Rapids, Michigan, in 1967 and to Seattle, Washington, in 1968 for sculpture projects. Grand Rapids commissioned a stabile from Alexander Calder called "La Grande Vitesse," which was dedicated in June 1969. The presence of the sculpture in his hometown "converted" the future President Gerald Ford to the arts. He reported some years later, "converts, as everyone knows, are the best advocates. . . . It's a great addition to our community."[73]

Further approval was expressed during the following year when the "Black Sun" by Isamu Noguchi was placed in Volunteer Park adjoining the Seattle Museum. The concept of a program that brought together the mayors of the individual cities (through whose offices applications were made to the Endowment and funds handled), the city governments that provided the money for preparing the sites, and the private sector that matched the federal grant was beginning to make political progress. Art works were selected by committees appointed jointly by the cities involved and the Endowment and, in the words of painter Richard Diebenkorn, the community effect was "positive and lasting."[74]

Museum Purchase Plan

Aware that most museums rarely have sufficient funds for purchases of art works and that such purchases are a vital part of the income of the individual artist, the Council began a Museum Purchase Plan in 1968,[75] housed in the Visual Arts area, with a program of $10,000 grants to institutions for buying contemporary art. To stimulate local interest and patronage, each museum receiving the grant had to match it with new money. The idea had come out of a meeting the previous January, planned by the Arts Endowment and hosted by the Metropolitan Museum and its director Thomas Hoving.

Through a series of pilot grants amounting to $341,000 over a three-year period, museums were urged to expand their activities beyond their walls. The Boston Institute of Art set up special educational programs; the Amon Carter Museum of Western Art in Fort Worth established a North Texas Council that reached into the counties; and the Detroit Institute of Art developed a "Project Outreach" that involved the whole state of Michigan and some of its neighbors.

Miscellaneous funding went to print workshops for artists, special exhibitions, study grants, research on the use of new materials, and photographic projects. The Experiments in Art and Technology (E.A.T.), a new service organization, was assisted with a $50,000 matching grant for operating expenses. E.A.T. was designed to promote collaboration among artists, scientists, and engineers on projects involving the artist's use of the new technology.

And the Endowment staff and Council, recognizing the pioneering work in government assistance to the arts in the thirties, made a research grant to Dr. Francis V. O'Connor for the study, "Federal Support for the Visual Arts: The New Deal and Now."

Beginning the Federal–State Partnership Program

In the spring of 1966, action in the area of support to the several state arts agencies was still in the planning stages. The original bill had authorized the Endowment chairman, with the advice of the Federal Council on the Arts and Humanities and the National Council on the Arts, "to establish and carry out a program of grants-in-aid to groups or, in appropriate cases, to individuals," and under a subsection, "to establish and carry out a program of grants-in-aid to assist the several States in supporting existing projects and productions." The state grants were to meet the same standards for the group and individual grants described earlier in the act. The states were charged to "develop projects and productions in the arts in such a manner as will furnish adequate programs, facilities, and services in the arts to all the people and communities in each of the several States."

Funds appropriated were to be equally allotted among the states:

> The amount of each allotment . . . for any fiscal year . . . shall be available to each State, which has a plan approved by the Chairman in effect on the first day of such fiscal year, to pay not more than 50 per centum of the total cost of any project or production . . . and to pay up to 100 per centum of the cost of conducting a study and establishing a State agency.

Funds left over in this category became available to the Arts Endowment for grants-in-aid to groups or individuals.[76]

To receive assistance, therefore, a state had to submit an application for grants prior to the first day of the fiscal year (which was then July 1) accompanied by a plan that the chairman of the Arts Endowment found (*a*) provided for the establishment of a state agency to administer the state plan, (*b*) provided that funds paid to the state would be expended solely on projects and productions approved by the state agency under the same criteria as applied to the federal grants-in-aid, and (*c*) provided for reports from time to time. Such funds were to be equally allotted among the states. Under subsection (h) (2) (B) there was a provision for the first fiscal year through which a state could be assigned funds of not more than $25,000 to conduct a study to plan the development of a state agency and to establish it.

The authorized appropriation for the grants-in-aid to the states was $2,750,000 for each fiscal year until June 30, 1969, when this first authorization would run out. The sums appropriated were to remain available until expended and did not terminate with the end of the fiscal year. However, no funds were authorized for appropriation to the states until the beginning of the fiscal year on July 1, 1966. This extended planning time was critical since the condition of the state arts agencies across the nation was in considerable disarray.

The concept of state agency support was very new for most areas of the country, although decades earlier a few states had recognized the importance of the arts to the total community. Information on these early state efforts varies considerably. In 1899, only three years after becoming a state, Utah created the Utah Art Institute, generally credited with being the "grandfather" organization, or better, "grandmother," since it was undertaken through the request of a woman legislator, Alice Merrill Horne. "There is no evidence that the fine arts received extensive support at that time, and the objectives of the program were not very clear," according to Virginia P. White in *Grants for the Arts*. "The next oldest currently functioning equivalent to a state arts council," she continues, "was established more than a half-century later, not in a state but in one of the special jurisdictions, Puerto Rico. In 1955, the *Instituto de Cultura Puertoriquena* (State Arts Agency) was created." Five years later the New York State Council on the Arts was created with the strong support of Governor Nelson A. Rockefeller.[77]

Charles C. Mark, the first director of the Arts Endowment Office of State and Community Operations, wrote, a decade-and-a-half later:

> The facts are that the Legislative Reference Service of the Library of Congress did a study of governmental support of the arts for Congress. I was employed from July to December of 1964 to further extend and explore the study. States did have support legislation on the statute books, but the councils, or commissions, or institutes had laid [sic] dormant, or practically so for decades.

Mark added that Utah went back to 1899 and Minnesota had something dating from the thirties. "Four states had really active councils before the NEA act passed: New York, California, Missouri, and Illinois. Missouri and Illinois, however, had no funds to speak of then, and were organized with the knowledge that federal legislation was a good possibility."[78]

In *New Dimensions for the Arts*, an Endowment publication for 1971–72, the statement is made that "only 18 councils were in existence before 1965." This statement agrees with the 1966 annual report which says:

> Only 17 states and Puerto Rico had created official state arts agencies or councils before 1965. . . . Nineteen states and the District of Columbia created agencies in 1965, and 14 states and the Virgin Islands and Guam created agencies in 1966. In 29 states the agency was created by the State Legislature. Almost all of the 21 states in which the agency was created by Executive Order will seek legislative endorsement in 1967.[79]

Whatever the actual active number may have been, it is certainly true that the intent of Congress when it enacted the Endowment legislation was to encourage the concept of a state agency with its attendant aspects of local decisionmaking. For this reason it is stipulated in the legislation that part of the Arts Endowment budget should be allocated directly each year to the state arts agencies.

A large National Conference of Governors' Representatives of State Arts Agencies was held at the Ambassador Hotel in Chicago, January 27–29, 1966. At this conference, the first and tentative guidelines of federal grant assistance to the state councils were hammered out.[80] Considerable tension developed when Roger Stevens announced the first grant terms, partly as a result of misunderstandings and power struggles between officials of the Associated Councils for the Arts and the Endowment staff. Clark Mitze, who was at that time director of the Missouri Arts Council and later became director of the Federal-State Program for the Arts Endowment, recalled the meeting. "It was bitterly cold. It was an awful meeting and it took the ACA and the Endowment five years to start speaking to each other again because they got into such a fight." Not an auspicious beginning for a program that was at the heart of the partnership that had to be developed nationally between the federal and state arts agencies and many local arts agencies as well. Mitze added, "Stevens was not happy [with the state program]. It had been thrust on him as a political reality. And he realized they [the state agencies] were giving him problems and not giving him any answers."[81]

The representatives at the conference were trying to develop ideas for special educational services at the community level, community programs to stimulate art appreciation through a variety of tours, exhibitions, master classes and workshops, and technical assistance and advisory programs. Again, according to the 1966 annual report, "The meeting reflected a new respectability for the arts on a grass-roots level and the beginning of a massive, locally supported effort to exploit this responsibility on an official basis." Whoever this nameless and optimistic commentator may have been, it probably was not Roger Stevens, nor Charles Mark, nor the ACA president Howard Adams.

Those states that were sufficiently organized to make application did so at once.

> *Eleven states, the District of Columbia, and Puerto Rico applied for up to $50,000 on a matching basis for programming:* California, Connecticut, Kentucky, Michigan, Missouri, New Jersey, New York, Rhode Island, Virginia, Washington, and West Virginia.
> *Eleven states, Guam, and the Virgin Islands applied for study grants only of up to $25,000:* Indiana, Iowa, Maine, Mississippi, Montana, Nevada, North Dakota, Oregon, South Carolina, South Dakota, and Tennessee.
> *Twenty-eight states applied for combined study and program grants:* Alabama, Alaska, Arizona, Arkansas, Colorado, Delaware, Florida, Georgia, Hawaii, Idaho, Illinois, Kansas, Louisiana, Maryland, Massachusetts, Minnesota, Nebraska, New Hampshire, New Mexico, North Carolina, Ohio, Oklahoma, Pennsylvania, Texas, Utah, Vermont, Wisconsin, and Wyoming.[82]

The budgeting became complicated, but in the annual report for 1967 everything was sorted out:

FEDERAL–STATE PARTNERSHIP PROGRAM

$2,000,000

When the State program was announced in November 1965 to the Governors of all the States and special political jurisdictions, every Governor sent at least one representative, except Guam and American Samoa, to a national meeting called for the purpose of explaining the program. Guam later received instruction and participated.

During the first year of funding, States were eligible for a special nonmatching Federal study grant to examine the cultural needs of the State and establish an official State arts agency. Forty-one States took advantage of this provision. Twenty-eight of these States also applied for $25,000 each on a matching basis to begin programs and projects. Thirteen States decided to enter programming immediately and applied for $50,000 each on a matching basis. Available appropriations were sufficient for grants of $12,053 each, but the study grants remained at $25,000 and full program grants at $50,000. Despite the newness of the program and the limited funds available the first year, 295 projects in all the arts and education were included in the applications. However, the majority of the States spent their energies establishing administrative machinery and approaching legislatures for enabling legislation and appropriations.

By the end of the first year (fiscal year 1967) all of the States, except one, had established official State arts agencies by legislative act and all but three or four were under the direction of full-time administrators under State civil service. On the program side, the majority of the effort went toward bringing the cultural resources within each State to areas previously without such opportunities.

In the second year, every State and jurisdiction except American Samoa applied for some portion of the maximum matching funds of $50,000 each. Seven States did not apply for the full $50,000, though one of these later was appropriated the full amount by its State legislature.[83]

By 1968, $2 million was available to the states. The next year the appropriation was cut back to $1.7 million, thus reducing each state and territorial council share to $30,909. In spite of the reduction, the sums appropriated for the arts by the states and territories from their own constituencies increased more than 30 percent over fiscal 1968 levels to over $6.8 million. State agencies were also beginning to attract higher levels of funding assistance from private sources.[84] The catalytic action of the Arts Endowment was very encouraging to many national arts leaders who had originally felt that federal assistance might upset delicate local balances.

Philip Hanes of Winston-Salem, North Carolina, who was a Council member from 1965 to 1970, expressed this position some years later:

> I was very much in favor of the National Council of the Arts as an advisory organization to the White House. However, I was strongly opposed to the National Endowment since I felt that federal support would dry up support from business and industry. I testified to this effect at the congressional hearings and opposed the National Endowment in the White House on the day that we were being sworn in as members of the First National Council of the Arts.
>
> *I was wrong! Because of the matching grant system of the Endowment, business*

> *support increased dramatically.* Far from disliking federal aid, businesses all over the nation jumped to the fore to be a partner with the government. I think that the National Endowment's small grants have vastly *increased the corporate support* and will continue to do so as long as there is an Endowment.[85]

Thus, the federal–state–local–private partnership began to work. The struggles ahead would often be acrimonious between the federal and state partners. There would be a constant tug of war for ascendancy and frequent disagreements over priorities. However, in 1981, when the whole structure of the Endowment was under review by President Reagan's administration, many of the state directors came to the defense of the agency.

James Backus, the former director of the Maryland State Arts Council, wrote in *American Arts:*

> The role of the Endowment with state arts agencies is a great success story. For all the scrapping they sometimes do, the Endowment and the state agencies rely on and complement each other, and I believe that most state arts agencies would sorely miss the Endowment if it were to be greatly reduced or altered. The Endowment started most state agencies; it has fostered their growth, and many of them still rely on it for much of their program funding. Many would survive very nicely without a National Endowment for the Arts, but many others would not, and therein lies the importance of the federal agency's role vis-à-vis the states.[86]

The Arts Endowment Begins to Take on Character

As mandated by Congress, structured by Council members, nurtured by staff members according to their special concerns, enthusiasms, and understanding of various fields, the programs of the Arts Endowment had begun to take shape during the first fiscal year. There was some special interest pressure from the field, many requests for assistance (often couched in terms as simple as "I'm an artist; send money") but very little sophisticated grantsmanship. The process was new and untried in the arts world. The whole idea of largesse for the arts from Uncle Sam was too fresh, too unbelievable, and too threatening to a segment of the population that had never been helped by the federal government before. Fear of federal censorship was constantly voiced.

Through all these winds of pressures, ideas, fears, and political hesitancy, Roger Stevens guided the infant agency with skill and sensitivity. He developed a remarkably judicious approach to problems for a man with such strong personal convictions. He studied the various arts fields, sought guidance, took advice from the Council and other advisory groups, closeted himself with leaders in every discipline to get their personal input, and steered the agency through its tentative early years with wisdom.

For its fifth meeting, the Council met on May 13–15, 1966, in Tarrytown, New York, to put its *imprimatur* on projects under consideration and to establish a policy that give great strength and flexibility to the members of the Council who were to follow them. In principle, the members decided at that meeting that they, as Council members and frequent participants in the activities being considered for grants-in-aid, would not disqualify themselves from such participation if the activity received Endowment support. They "would be alert to avoid any action which could possibly be interpreted as a use of Council membership to further their own interests or those of an organization with which they are affiliated."[87]

The Tarrytown meetings took place at a former Biddle estate—a luxurious old house-turned-conference center overlooking the Hudson River Valley. Although some additional, rather barracks-like space had been added for sleeping areas and meetings, there were remnants of formal gardens and nineteenth-century park-like vistas, with cement statuary tucked away at the ends of grassy walks. The Council members and the staff enjoyed the old-fashioned, leisurely, friendly atmosphere of the place and found it congenial to work there together. There was little stress between Council members and program staff in the early years—they all sat together around the big conference table and shared what Richard Diebenkorn called "a crackling optimism" about the infinite possibilities for assisting the exploding arts in America. The sun always seemed to shine on meetings in Tarrytown.

The sun kept on shining all through the summer of 1966 in Washington—a blistering hot, humid season, aggravated by an airlines strike which kept the staff (many of whom came from other parts of the country) tied to their GSA desks with only the thrusting presence of the Washington Monument seen from office windows to remind them that the work of that sweltering summer had national impact.

The year 1966 was one of quirky fashion, with youthfully short Mary Quant skirts and textured white stockings considered the ultimate fashion statement. Almost all the program directors were women in their middle years, and all of them were fashion-conscious. In fact, the very bright, very perceptive, and very young women of the assisting staff labeled them "*Les Girls*," after the popular film of that season.

With the programs and projects approved, some of the problems of working within a federal bureaucracy (even a youthfully uncongealed one like the National Foundation for the Arts and the Humanities) began to surface. The two Endowments shared an administrative staff where personnel matters, travel reimbursements, equipment purchases, and grant processing were handled. There was an uneasy relationship among the three areas. The Arts Endowment staff quipped about the Humanities staff, "They think about it; we do it." The shared staff, many of them old-time Washington hands, thought that both the Endowment areas were populated by somewhat inept, naive, and frequently headstrong program directors. The Arts Endowment program directors were considered particularly flighty. They brought bright colors, posters, and artwork to their offices. Unlike a standard federal office with its cubicles-*cum*-maze of corridors and filing cabinets, the space at 1800 G Street was open, airy, friendly. For months the chairman operated out of a huge office with his own extraordinarily efficient secretary, Charlotte Woolard, and the exuberant Council secretary, Luna Diamond, all working together in the same room.

As the staff grew, the Arts Endowment began to evolve a special character as a repository for some very unusual, capable, brilliant, and occasionally distinctly oddball staff members in assisting positions. There was the young woman working at one of the reception desks who was a member of one of the royal families of Europe; there was the dedicated administrative assistant who, rumor said, had been a "bag lady" for the CIA in Paris; there was the secretary who interspersed her supervisor's mail with religious tracts and who was extremely dubious about the arts in the Divine Scheme; and there was a parade of attractive and capable young men and women—black, white, occasionally Oriental—who moved through the Endowment and on to positions of importance in many of the new administrative and service agencies that grew up in the wake of the new emphasis on the arts as a national resource.

"It was the best of times; it was the worst of times." The ferment of the Sixties, with its eagerness to experiment, open doors, try the untried, its exploration of space, its affluence and energy, was felt throughout Washington in the most structured and time-honored agencies. Particularly, it bubbled in the fledgling arts agency with such big dreams and small financial resources. For better or worse, the arts had moved into the public domain, a new field of public concern. As the vernacular of the time described, it was "where the action was," and the arts included a myriad of creative impulses—pop art, op art, dance by chance, the theatre-of-the-absurd, electronic and aleatory music, new architectural concepts, new design. Iconoclastic ideas flourished in movement, stage design, music—where the lighting became part of the music and silences became part of the sound. It was a time of eager freshness and a will to experiment, a time of sharing. The affluent economy, a socially-conscious society, and technological advances joined to create a welcoming climate for new ideas. Society was filled with the kind of people described by composer Milton Babbitt as "appropriate receptors"—people who played music, read, attended theatre, explored television—people who were personally involved. The arts were flourishing. The only cloud in this welcoming climate was the increasing menace of the Vietnam War.

"We Were Invisible"

As one looks over the grants activity in the early years of the Endowment, it becomes apparent that funds dispensed were largely for project grants or grants for specific groups, many of them initiated by Council members. Many grants developed from emergency needs—"like firemen, putting out fires," according to Roger Stevens.[88]

Looking back on this period, Ana Steele felt that dance, theatre, literature, and the visual arts were the first to begin to shape real programs of related activities that could be funded nationwide.

> Early on, there was a group of grants made to individual choreographers, partly because of Agnes de Mille on the Council. That was the beginning. That was the shape of a program, more than a project. And the same thing with theatre, the beginnings of [help] to the nonprofit professional theatre.[89]

Moving into formal programs, away from *ad hoc* projects, was a crucial shift in emphasis, essential for a federal agency, but it took away some of the spontaneity and the sense of pioneering that had characterized the first stimulating Council meetings. The staff slowly began to understand how to get along in Washington, but many of them never quite accepted the system as anything but an irritating, if necessary, impediment to rapid progress.

Ana Steele recalled that the Music office held back on broad program development longer than some of the others for several reasons. One reason was strong Council pressure by member Isaac Stern. Another was because the Ford Foundation had an impending $82 million grant to the symphony orchestras of the nation.

> Mac Lowry [Ford Foundation Vice-President for the Arts and Humanities] almost had a heart attack when we were established because the President mentioned help to symphony orchestras and Mac was about to announce Ford's [80 million dollar] program for them. Why was he worried? We had only $2.5 million those first few months for all the arts. But we did work in music on a project-by-project, group-by-group basis, for quite a while. . . . The first real program in music was the "audience development program," put together by Fannie Taylor, the Music director. And it set quite a marvelous precedent. Sixteen years later we are still fighting over what to do with the sponsors!

Steele recalled the presence of Henry Geldzahler and Carolyn Kizer, both staff program directors with a special concern for the individual artist in the visual arts and literature areas.

> We did incredible things. I suspect that Mr. Stevens rues the day we ever got bigger appropriations because we don't do what we used to when he could put together deals like the Artist Housing Project and the American Film Institute . . . and Jerome Robbin's money for the American Theatre Laboratory.
>
> We were in a position in those days that the Council could sit there and hand Jerome Robbins $290,000 [for the American Theatre Laboratory] because the man's a genius. He wanted to go and work in a laboratory situation with choreographers and actors and dancers and designers and musicians, and he did. . . . It was a lot of money, but the effect on him and on artistic development! It was obviously a major contribution to seeding a lot of good art development that is still being felt. But there is no way today [in 1981] that the National Endowment for the Arts is going to pick up $290,000 and hand it to an artist. That kind of flexibility, that kind of creative energy

> we could use because nobody knew we were around in those days. We were invisible.[90]

Within a few years, Roger Stevens, the Council, and the program directors all recognized that the *ad hoc*, project-by-project response to the field, for all its sparkling vigor, could not be sustained as the agency matured. On May 13, 1968, Stevens sent a memorandum to the program directors concerning preparations for the approaching Council meeting June 14–15 in Tarrytown.

> We have some new ideas for agenda organization in keeping with the discussion at the last meeting. Probably the clearest way to proceed is to describe each step.
> 1. Resubmit your project proposals to the Chairman for approval.
> 2. After projects are approved, reshape them to fit one of the following categories:
>   a. Wider distribution of the arts
>   b. Aid to the individual artist (direct or indirect)
>   c. Aid to artistic institutions
>   d. Research and education
>   e. Aid to State programs
>   f. New national opportunities
>   g. International cooperation
>
> These categories are identical to those submitted to the Congress for our next year's budget. Chuck Mark has developed a fine-honed logic for placing projects and balancing categories, so before you begin writing, please sit down with him for final assignment. If you haven't looked at the FY '69 budget in its final form, you might find it helpful toward learning the new approach.[91]

Increasing Visibility

As the first months of experimental effort passed into the early years of growth, the Arts Endowment became increasingly visible to the general taxpaying public and questions about procedures inevitably arose. The first euphoric ideas about how the agency could help artists became harder to defend against the special interests that began to surface, although on the whole Stevens' custody of the agency was generally trusted by the members of the arts world. He put enormous personal effort into the work, traveling to all but two states to carry his message. In the congressional subcommittee hearings in 1967 he explained that the panels of experts working with the staff and the Council were used "to pick people we think have the most promise" for individual grants.

> We hope we will be fortunate, but I think it would be terribly hard to say that luck is not involved. I also think that the important thing to do for the arts is to make the artist feel wanted, and that he has a place in society, even if our selections do not satisfy everyone.[92]

It was the statement of an honest, dedicated, and totally unbureaucratic leader.

There were staff changes in the next several years as the scattershot programs of 1966 began to take firmer shape. The deputy chairman, Livingston Biddle, left in November 1967 to go to Fordham University to chair its new division of fine arts. He was succeeded by William Cannon. Charles C. Mark moved out of the State and Community Operations (later known as the Federal–State Partnership) and Clark Mitze, a former teacher, musician, and critic who had been director of the Missouri State Arts Council, took over the office. Walter C. Anderson, a concert pianist and professor of music from Antioch College, replaced Fannie Taylor as director of the Music Program. Leonard Randolph, former publicist, critic, foundation executive, and congressional aide, joined the staff as special assistant to the deputy chairman; he later became program director in the Literature area.

"The Art of Making Art"

When the Council met there were always deliberations about what Lawrence Halprin described "as the art of making art, and the craft of performing it." Council members were often divided on the question of whether the performance was a creative or merely re-creative process. But there was never any doubt about the Council's and Roger Stevens' strong support for giving the artist opportunities to create. However, as time passed and the Council members became more experienced at evaluating grant requests, there was a gradual shift from the enthusiasm to make direct grants for creative activity toward providing more indirect opportunities for artists' development. Various programs were arranged for artists to work in the school system, for example. These were basically designed to give support to artists and enable them to function as artists rather than having to support themselves selling gasoline or hamburgers. The programs, however, were also educational, opening opportunities for new ways of learning and new creative response among students.

Audience Development Project

One of these educational innovations was the audience development project which took shape in the Music Program of 1969, and which Ana Steele later recalled as a pace-setter in music. Through this project relatively young or unknown artists receiving bookings sponsored by 58 colleges and universities and a dozen museums throughout the nation. The Association of College and University Concert Managers (later renamed the Association of College, University and Community Arts Administrators) and the Association of American Museums handled the logistics. As a result, thousands of citizens were treated to concerts, often presented in unorthodox settings such as dormitories or patios, with support by matching grants of $1,000 or less from the Endowment. At the California Institute of Technology under the guidance of Jerry Willis, a "confrontation concert" of a string quartet and a jazz quartet was offered. Billed as the

"Grand Encounter," the event turned out to be the most successful concert in five years.[93]

Music Program Grows

The Council had become convinced that, as W. McNeil Lowry of the Ford Foundation had said, the arts "speak more intimately to the young, many times, than even formal education."[94,95] Thus, the Music Program under Walter Anderson's guidance also supported the activities of both the Affiliate Artists and Young Audiences. Affiliate Artists was a young organization that had started in Beloit, Wisconsin. Its purpose was to reach every kind of audience, from blue-collar to academic, and it placed 24 young artists in 15 states for eight-week residencies. During the rest of the year the artists were left free to develop their own careers, with the reassuring sense of stable employment. Young Audiences, a two-decade-old organization devoted to bringing professional performances of chamber music to schools, already had 40 active chapters in 24 states. The Endowment's grant enabled the organization to broaden its work, trying out the results of presentations from kindergarten through the third-grade level, and engaging additional music directors to assist in the training of ensembles. The result in the 1968–69 season was 10,000 concerts in schools throughout the country.

Support for performing groups (which in turn supported artists) seemed essential to the Council members. Although the Endowment funds were limited, it tried to help regional opera groups move toward annual contracts for singers on a salaried basis—an effort to give the gifted American singer an opportunity to work in his own country instead of going abroad (for many years a pattern for young artists). The Seattle Opera Association, the Central Opera Company of Minneapolis, the Western Opera Theater (WOT—a subsidiary of the San Francisco Opera) were all funded modestly. *Newsweek* reported: "To the young American singers, with so few places to develop in the United States, the opportunities of WOT are a godsend."[96] In 1970 the National Opera Institute was created with a matching grant from the L.A.W. Fund, Inc. The New York City Opera Company and its director, Julius Rudel, were enabled to expand their training program for assistant conductors and young singers. The Opera Society of Washington, always an eager presence in the capital city, was also given help. An earlier grant in 1967 had explored and assisted regional opera activity in the southeastern part of the United States. When the Santa Fe Opera lost its building and equipment in a disastrous fire, the Endowment's overnight response with emergency matching assistance helped to encourage donations from private sources which rebuilt the productions.

During this period, the American Symphony Orchestra League was reporting increasing financial pressure on the country's orchestras, in spite of the Ford

Foundation generosity. Roger Stevens, testifying to the subcommittee in 1967, commented on the enormous sums of money the needs of the arts projected. "For example," he said, "the grants from the Ford Foundation totaling approximately $82 million to some 60 of our nation's symphony orchestras have been very helpful but they pertain to only the larger orchestras, and even the orchestras benefited are hard-pressed to obtain the matching funds required."[97]

Although Leonard Bernstein, perhaps reacting to the social turmoil of the Sixties, had once labeled the symphony orchestra a "museum," the Council, like the Ford Foundation, regarded the orchestras as prime national resources for the musical arts in any community. However, the Council was hamstrung by lack of money to make anything but token financial aid possible. In June 1968 it recommended grants of $50,000 each to be given to five orchestras for projects of national and outstanding significance. Atlanta, Boston, Detroit, Minnesota, and the New York Philharmonic ultimately received grants in varying amounts from $15,300 to $50,000 under this program.

One of the first applicants to the Music Program office had been Dr. Herbert Zipper, with his dream of helping community music schools and settlement projects where music could be taught as a means of communication and enrichment for the lives of disadvantaged young city dwellers. In fiscal year 1968 a $24,700 individual grant and a $7,500 matching grant enabled the National Guild of Community Music Schools to establish a permanent national office devoted to stimulating new community schools throughout the country and to providing counseling services. Along with this development went a $25,000 matching grant to the Symphony of the New World, the country's first fully integrated orchestra.

The Music Program also stretched to a wider horizon. A matching grant of $25,000 to the National Music Camp at Interlochen, Michigan, made it possible for the United States to host in 1966 the International Society for Music Education Conference. Two years later the Sixth International Music Council Congress met in New York City and Washington, D.C., with 600 delegates from 50 countries in attendance, the first time the conference had met in America.

There was a small grant of $3,500, matched by the Mellon Fund, for experimental analysis of violin varnish used in old instruments. The grant almost became a *cause célèbre* for wasteful use of federal money because it appeared there had been previous similar studies done. In the Endowment offices for several years afterward, the mention of violin varnish brought rueful smiles.

Music also made the first jazz grant in 1969 to the composer and instrumentalist George Russell of New York City, in recognition of his outstanding contributions to twentieth-century American music. A limited fellowship program to study the Kodály concept of music education in Hungary was undertaken under the direction of Alexander Ringer, professor of musicology at the University of Illinois, as a result of early Council discussions.

The first steps toward creating the *American Music Digest*, under the sponsorship of the Music Critics Association, were taken in 1968 and received grant support in 1969 and 1970. With Gene Bruck as editor, the publication appeared for a few interesting issues, extracting criticism and comment from all over the United States. A strong board of directors included Irving Lowens, *Washington Evening Star;* Albert Bush-Brown, State University of New York at Buffalo; Miles Kastendieck, *Christian Science Monitor;* Raymond Kendall, Young Musicians Foundation; Boris Nelson, *Toledo Blade;* Harold C. Schonberg, *New York Times;* Roger L. Stevens, representing the John F. Kennedy Center for the Performing Arts; and Thomas Willis, of the *Chicago Tribune*. The concept of the digest was to try to broaden and improve national arts criticism and Stevens recalled the project years later as a very good one. "If there's anything in the world that needs help, it's criticism," he said, but the publication was discontinued under the following Endowment leadership.[98]

Public Media Program Takes Shape

In addition to involvement in the American Film Institute, the Public Media area began to take shape with other programs. In the first few years, grants were made to educational television and radio stations for arts programs including WTTW in Chicago; KQED in San Francisco; an Educational Broadcasting Corporation grant of $625,000, of which nearly half was funded by the Bristol-Myers Company; WGBH in Boston; and aid to the National Educational Television NET Playhouse for two major dramatic productions. NET and the American Regional Theatre project received another two-year grant for the filming of four plays for NET Playhouse: *A Celebration for William Jennings Bryan* (Theatre Company of Boston), *The New Theatre for Now* (Center Theatre Group, Los Angeles), *Glory! Hallelujah!* (American Conservatory Theatre, San Francisco); and *Story Theatre* (Yale Repertory Theatre, New Haven). The Endowment had already assisted these companies under the Resident Professional Theatre Program and the staff and Council alike saw these Public Media grants as direct extensions of the benefit of its funding from the regional to the national level—a specific amplification of the impact of the grant. The Rockefeller Foundation provided the necessary matching funds.[99]

Decentralizing American Theatre

By the close of fiscal year 1970 the Theatre Program had developed a vigorous and continuing policy of help with the decentralization of American theatre.[100] A special panel of theatre experts worked with the program director, Ruth Mayleas, to encourage artistic development of these theatres by helping them increase actors' salaries and by assisting them to engage artistic directors, performers, and technical personnel as well as undertake new projects and productions. A continuity of support, not previously available to the American theater as an institution, was gradually taking shape as a result of Endowment funds acting as a catalyst for foundation aid (both national and local), corporation and business support, and help from united arts funds and state arts agencies.

The Theatre Program had launched in 1968 a series of professional experimental theaters and workshops to encourage new playwrights and stimulate new productions. Nationwide, many other performing institutions received assistance in varying amounts of money to be matched by funds raised through the organization's own resources (sometimes new money, sometimes ongoing support, sometimes in-kind). The American National Theatre and Academy (ANTA) and the Endowment set up a contract early in 1969 to accept the donation of the ANTA Theatre building, located in the Broadway theater district of New York City. Under the programming arrangement developed by the ANTA board and funded by the Endowment, professional theatre companies from San Francisco, Stratford (Connecticut), Rochester (Michigan), and Providence (Rhode Island), as well as several experimental groups, were given the opportunity to appear in New York for limited engagements in the 1969–70 season and, not incidentally, to receive reviews from the New York critics.

There were numerous "service to the field" grants. One of the most important was the \$200,000 matching grant in 1967 to the Theatre Development Fund "to stimulate creativity and experimentation in the commercial theatre through development of new audiences and through financial assistance for plays of merit which are unlikely to be produced or are likely to close prematurely without Fund assistance." The grant decision was made with an eye to the future of theater in America and concern about the deepening financial crisis for the performing arts. The grant was made possible by private donations to the Endowment amounting to \$100,000 which were then matched by agency funds.

According to the "History" of the Arts Endowment (housed in the Johnson Library in Austin, Texas), this action of the Council's tenth meeting stirred controversy and problems for months to come:

> Perhaps spurred on by headlines such as "Funds Will Aid Shaky Plays on Broadway," "\$200,000 Fund to Help Sagging Stage Shows," and "Federal Funds to Aid Broadway Laggers," several Congressmen, newspaper people, and private citizens set up a hue and cry that was to reverberate around the Endowment's walls for many a week. Once again, Mr. Stevens was to make those trips to the Hill to explain the full purpose and intent of the grant, and to stress that three major private foundations had made the entire project possible.[101]

The *New York Times* quoted John E. Booth, president of the Theater Development Fund, who said that the basic blueprint called "for the purchase of tickets at box office prices for up to five weeks to plays it regards as meritorious and in need of time to find an audience." The tickets were to be sold at discount prices to selected groups, including students, college faculty, professional people who might be interested but for one reason or another were no longer attending the theatre. Frederick O'Neal, president of Actors Equity Association, hailed the project in the same story. "I think it is a wonderful idea and I hope it works out favorably because any help to the legitimate theater is sorely needed."[102]

Audiences were to be encouraged to return to the live professional theatre; plays of genuine artistic merit were to be given support. The "History" continues:

> There was a certain irony implicit in the attacks, initiated primarily in Congress and, for the first time, with a definite partisan tint: although as *Variety* accurately reported, "the project was primarily inspired and has been largely financed by prominent Republicans," it was Republican Congressmen who found the grant "absolutely ridiculous" and termed it a "prime example of government waste and stupidity."[103]

The timing was bad. The announcement of the grant had gone out just four weeks before the new authorizing legislation was to reach the floor of the House. Months of work in the House Committee on Education and Labor relating to the legislation had preceded the pending floor vote authorizing further funding of programs under the Foundation Act. The "History" explains the situation further:

> What was at issue here was not merely whether the Arts Endowment's programs could continue to exist; for nearly three years, the Arts Council and Endowment had been delving into the entire range of needs in the arts all across the country, and developing limited pilot projects to broaden its own understanding and to test possible solutions to the most pressing problems at hand. At the same time, the Council and the Endowment staff had been keeping an eye on the future, noting the deepening financial crisis facing all of the arts as documented by the Messrs. Baumol and Bowen, two Princeton economists, in *Performing Arts: The Economic Dilemma*. The Council hoped that once its own "trial period" ended, funds would be forthcoming that would enable it to do more than provide stop-gap measures where long-range and substantive support was becoming increasingly essential. A "cultural explosion" had indeed begun in America; it was too early to make a full assessment of this "explosion," but the Council hoped it might be enabled to do more than merely scratch the surface—that the scope and range of its programs could be continued and greatly expanded to meet the expanding need, and to strengthen and support America's growing desire for an active cultural life.
>
> And the Council, it would seem, had good reason to hope: in a very short time and with very limited funds, it had accomplished a great deal in many areas, not the least of them being the stimulation of vast new resources for support of the arts across the Nation.[104]

Reauthorization

The House Committee on Education and Labor understood the accomplishments of the agency as well as the testimony that had been coming to them about the worsening situation for America's artists and arts institutions. The committee reported out H.R. 11308 with a two-year authorization for the Arts Endowment totaling $67.5 million, plus an open-ended authorization to match donations from private sources that might come to the Endowment (as was the case with the Theatre Development Fund, the American Film Institute, and other projects).

But "guns-or-butter" arguments were surfacing. The Vietnamese War had bitten deeply into poverty programs. A *Milwaukee Journal* editorial stated:

> Congress must look to the future. There is more to life than guns or butter or even both: provision must be made for a bit of essential nourishment for the creative spirit, too. The arts and humanities foundation must not be killed off and should get a reasonable funding.[105]

Many Congressmen rose in support of the bill, particularly Frank Thompson, John Brademas, Ogden Reid, and William Moorhead; while the usual attacks came from Congressmen H. R. Gross and Durward G. Hall (R., MO). There were also pleas from Congressman John Anderson of Illinois to establish priorities responsible to pressing needs of American life and to reduce the funding. Others talked about the war which, declared or not, was beginning to consume American attention and resources. The "History" continues:

> Toward the end of the long debate preceding the vote, Representative Mahon (D., TX), Chairman of the House Committee on Appropriations, rose to address the members of the House. Urging "fiscal responsibility," he emphasized that this was the "first key vote of the year on a bill to continue authorization for a going program." He continued: "We are on trial as a nation as to whether or not we have the discipline and the courage and the leadership to pay our way. . . . Today we have a test vote and I hope that we will measure up to the demands of the moment." Taking its cue from Representative Mahon, and making a "test vote" out of the Foundation's continuing funding, the House on that day (February 27th) passed, by a vote of 272 to 123, a radically amended version of H.R. 11308.[106]

Charles Ruttenberg, counsel for the Foundation, explained to the members of the National Council on the Arts at the eleventh Council meeting, April 19–21, 1968, what was going on.

> He reported that the amended version of the bill limited the entire Foundation's authorization to $11.2 million (plus administrative funds and provisions to match gifts), authorized its continuance for only one year (Fiscal 1969) instead of for two, and revoked the Arts Endowment's authority to make individual grants. The first two provisions had resulted from an amendment offered by Representative Ashbrook (R., OH) which had passed the House by a vote of 261 to 130, and the latter provision had resulted from an amendment offered by Representative Steiger (R., WI) which had passed by a vote of 111 to 92. One constructive action taken by the House, in line with the Endowment's request, authorized the special Treasury Fund to match restricted as well as unrestricted gifts, subject to a prior recommendation from the Council on acceptance of the gift.[107]

At this eleventh meeting several matters of policy with long-range importance were discussed. The Council resolved, subject to the enactment of future legislation authorizing the Council to take such action, that it would delegate to the Chairman authority to approve or disapprove requests of $10,000 or less, provided that such action would afterwards be reported to the Council for review.

The Council was gravely concerned about the language in H.R. 11308, revoking the authority to make individual grants, and passed a formal resolution stating that the Council could "not be responsible for the quality of Endowment programs in support of creative artists if the making of such awards in all cases must be delegated to outside institutions or organizations rather than made on the basis of recommendations of the Council and its advisors."[108]

The "History" continued:

> Two weeks later, on May 3, 1968, the Senate Committee on Labor and Public Welfare reported out H.R. 11308; the Committee had revised the language of this bill and had reported it out in lieu of the original Senate bill, S. 2061. And on May 7th, the Senate passed its amended H.R. 11308 by a voice vote. The Senate bill restored a two-year authorization for the Foundation, and the authority of the Arts Endowment to make individual grants. On May 28th, conferees selected by both Houses agreed to file a Conference Report, having settled their disagreements in conference. That report (H.Rept. 1511), recommending a two-year authorization and the authority to award grants to individuals of "exceptional talent," was agreed to by the Senate on May 29th and the House on June 5th.
>
> On June 18, 1968, President Johnson signed Public Law 90-348 (H.R. 11308). The Law authorized appropriations for Fiscal Years 1969 and 1970: for the Arts Endowment, a total of $12.5 million for programs and $4.5 million for the State arts agencies. The bill also authorized funds to match both restricted and unrestricted donations in Fiscal 1969 and 1970 not to exceed a total for both Endowments of $13.5 million for both years. (The total two-year authorization for the entire Foundation was $47.5 million—a far cry from the $135 million originally recommended by the House Committee on Education and Labor, but nevertheless an improvement over the House of Representatives' original $11.2 million, plus gift funds, one-year authorization.) Of course, although the new Public Law authorized $6 million for Arts programs and $2 million for the States for Fiscal 1969, plus some portion of $13.5 million to match donations, an appropriation still had to be obtained before the Council could know exactly what funds would be available for Fiscal 1969 programs.[109]

The ultimate appropriation for fiscal 1969 amounted to $3,700,000 for grant programs, $1,700,000 for state assistance, and $2,356,875 in federal funds to match donations.

Cooling the Inner Cities

The turbulent Sixties saw not only demonstrations against the Vietnam War but inner-city race riots, which began in New York City and other large cities in

1964 and spread the next year into larger disruptions, especially in the Watts section of Los Angeles.[110] According to the *New York Times,* many black leaders had abandoned the nonviolent tactics of the Rev. Dr. Martin Luther King, Jr. and the riots grew in intensity. "In two years alone—1967 and 1968—large portions of more than 200 cities were destroyed, 125 people were killed, 7,000 were injured, and more than 40,000 arrested."[111]

President Johnson, Vice President Humphrey, senators and congressmen were casting about in every direction to find panaceas. The President's Council on Youth Opportunity had been created and it was suggested that, with the help of the Endowment, inner city arts programs be set up in 1968 to try to prevent the cities from simply blowing up. Vice-President Humphrey worked closely with Roger Stevens to implement this idea. As a result, the Council recommended grants to 16 of the nation's largest cities (Atlanta, Baltimore, Boston, Buffalo, Chicago, Cleveland, Detroit, Los Angeles, Milwaukee, Minneapolis, Newark, New York, Philadelphia, San Francisco, St. Louis, and Washington). Because there were no specific funds provided, Stevens had previously written the chairmen of the Senate and House Appropriations subcommittees asking approval to transfer some left-over Arts Endowment program funds to the Inner City project. He had received approval from the House Subcommittee, "and not having received any reply from the Senate Subcommittee, and therefore assuming that the Subcommittee did not disapprove the plan," he asked for the Council recommendation. Five weeks after Stevens submitted his letter, a reply came back from the Senate Subcommittee—objecting to the proposal!

"And suddenly, there was Roger, stuck," recalled the Federal-State Program Director Clark Mitze many years later. "He had to put on a benefit for the U.S. government! It was in the Pierre Hotel. I was sitting in his office when he called up [a producer] . . . and said that he was putting down ten tables or something like that at $1,000 a table. I think they must have raised $200,000 . . . . He called in a lot of chips for that one."[112]

The "History" also records the story of "these financial difficulties":

> A benefit to raise the necessary funds for the program was to be held for the Endowment in New York City. The benefit, entitled "A Salute to H.R. 11308, As Amended" was . . . held June 26th; aided by Mr. Stevens, all the costs of the benefit were covered: the program was designed and donated by artist Robert Indiana; the room and refreshments were paid for by a private foundation; and the entertainment was provided free of cost through the American Federation of Musicians. Thus, when the Endowment raised $200,000 in private donations including the benefit, every dollar was available for matching by the Treasury Fund, freeing $400,000 for these programs. Each city in turn matched these funds on a two-for-one basis; thus, $200,000 in Federal funds resulted in $1.2 million being available for arts projects in the Nation's inner cities.[113]

Availability of funds was one thing; program was another. The Johnson

Foundation in Racine, Wisconsin, held a conference May 8–9 concerning plans for the summer venture. The cities participating in the project had agreed that the federal arts money would be used for projects of artistic quality. Workshops that might discover and develop talent and that could have a permanent value were encouraged.

Clark Mitze recalls the scene at the Frank Lloyd Wright-designed headquarters for the Johnson Foundation—a serene meeting place, far removed from the stresses of the hot inner-city streets:

> That's where I first met Katherine Dunham [Dunham was one of the first black dancers in Hollywood, and later in East St. Louis developed a remarkable program in the arts for inner city youngsters]. It was one of those strange things. Everyone would get up and say something about what they would be doing. . . . A gal from New York, I've forgotten her name, said "Oh, fun city, it's going to be great! They're going to be painting the stoops, and they're going to be out in the streets, and they're going to be singing, and it's going to be just fun in fun city." And the young lady from Los Angeles said, "well, not only that, but our symphony is going to play a concert in Watts, and the union has agreed to let them do it." And it went on, about three more like this. And Katherine Dunham got up and looked around for about five seconds of silence, and said, "I've never heard so much stuff from so many phoneys in my life." And then the program began.[114]

There were other less dramatic programs aimed at improving the quality of life in the inner cities. An emergency grant of $3,500 went to the Elma Lewis School of Fine Arts in Boston in 1967 to help this outstanding school keep its doors open in a time of financial trouble. The school developed into the National Center of Afro-American Artists.

Also in fiscal year 1967 a matching grant of $24,500 went to the Harlem School of the Arts to help support dance, art, music, and theater programs for disadvantaged young people. The program was under the supervision of Dorothy Maynor, a well-known black soprano who had retired from the concert stage. The project went so well that in 1969 another matching grant of $32,700 was provided.[115]

Obviously, there was a need for a defined program area within the Arts Endowment structure to handle these programs aimed at community stimulation. At the thirteenth Council meeting (Nov. 21–22, 1968), it was discussed at length and the Council passed a resolution requesting aid for projects with sociological and educational components from the Office of Economic Opportunity. However, not until October 1970 did the National Council on the Arts recommend establishing the Expansion Arts Program "to help the growing numbers of professionally directed community arts groups with activities involving ethnic and rural minorities whose cultures have been inadequately supported in the past."[116]

The President Hosts a Dinner

As the Lyndon Johnson years drew to a close, President and Mrs. Johnson hosted a dinner to honor the members of the National Council on the Arts. There were the usual introductions and recollections. Roger Stevens introduced the President:

> Mr. President, Mrs. Johnson, members of the Arts Council, distinguished guests:
>
> I am pleased to have this occasion to introduce the President to the members of the National Council on the Arts, because it gives me a moment to say publicly what many of us have expressed privately in the past few years.
>
> Without President Johnson's firm and unwavering support, we would not have an Arts Council today.
>
> Three years ago last summer, I remember sitting all day in the House Gallery during a session of the 89th Congress. The Democratic leadership was attempting to extract seven bills from the House Committee on Rules. There was quite a pull and haul, and the opposition used every stalling tactic in the book. Late that night, it appeared as if they would only be able to get the first three of the seven bills out of Rules. The bill on the establishment of the National Foundation on the Arts and the Humanities was number four.
>
> I am told by reliable friends that, as we sat there facing what appeared to be the doom of the arts bill, word came from the White House that the leadership was to get that fourth bill out of the Rules Committee if they had to keep the House in session half the night.
>
> So I think it would be well for the artistic community to remember that none of the programs initiated over the past few years by our Council would have been possible if it had not been for the personal efforts of the President. If you will review the many other accomplishments of his Administration during these years, it is quite evident that, as I have said on other occasions, President Johnson has done more for the arts than any other President in the history of the United States.
>
> We all know that the arts are, if anything, controversial. But through all these years, the President has left us alone to make our own decisions. He has offered us only encouragement and complete support. Because of this, I believe we can say today that the artistic world no longer fears, as some did at the beginning, that the heavy hand of government will somehow interfere in the freedom of the arts. Let us hope that fear has been firmly set aside.
>
> During all these years, there was one evening here at the White House I shall remember especially. I was talking quietly with the President when he introduced me to someone saying, "This is my friend Roger Stevens, who causes me no trouble and gives me great pleasure." That was the kindest thing said to me in all my days here in Washington, and I think the President knows how much it meant to me, personally.
>
> This evening, therefore, I have the distinct honor of introducing to you a man who, during his term of office, to use your own words, Mr. President, far from ever having caused us any trouble, has given the members of the National Council on the Arts a great deal of pleasure. I am very proud to have served him, and to have known him.
>
> Ladies and gentlemen, the President of the United States.[117]

Final Months

Roger Stevens was served by three deputy chairmen. Livingston L. Biddle was the first, remaining until November 1967, followed by William B. Cannon. Then Douglas G. MacAgy (a Canadian citizen who had to become naturalized for the job) joined the staff and remained through the next several years as deputy chairman and acting chairman of the Endowment and the Council. After Nancy Hanks' appointment to head the agency, he became program director for National Exhibitions.

The final few months of Stevens' chairmanship began to unwind. Richard Nixon was President, and there seemed no possibility of a leading Democratic fund-raiser like Stevens being reappointed, although a number of prominent Republicans who were interested in the arts were urging the President to do so.

Howard Taubman of the *New York Times* sought out Stevens in January to get his assessment of his four-year stewardship of the arts agency. Stevens spoke first about several major projects: the conversion of the Bell Telephone Laboratories in lower Manhattan into studio and living quarters for artists; the American Film Institute; three laboratory theaters supported by the Endowment in cooperation with the Office of Education in Providence, New Orleans, and Los Angeles. Stevens then went on to mention some of the "less showy achievements": individual grants to composers, painters, sculptors, writers, and choreographers ranging from $1,000 to $10,000, usually about $5,000 per person. "It wasn't the money alone that mattered," he said. "It was recognition. It showed that the country cared." He added, "We've killed the bugaboo of government control of the arts. The Endowment has worked with Democrats and Republicans and can continue to do so."[118]

In spite of his success and the trust of many Republicans, Stevens' appointment ran its course to March 11, 1969. He resigned (or was told to clear his desk) and was not reappointed, although later there were numerous rumors flying about that the White House staff would have liked to have had him remain.

The newspaper reports of the period are interesting. *Variety* said tersely that Stevens had gone out of office and Douglas MacAgy, deputy, was taking over as acting chairman. "It is believed that a number of fat-cat Republicans, including Huntington Hartford, have been openly after the job."[119]

The *Milwaukee Journal* reported:

> Less than 24 hours after they fired him, the Republicans were admitting they had made a mistake. . . . The Nixon people called here [the Endowment office] because they were worried about what the press was saying. [Charles C.] Mark said, "Mind you, they were not worried about the Endowment. They told us to assure the press that they were looking hard for a replacement."[120]

Newsweek commented:

> So far, several New York Republicans have turned down the job. The latest one to give a definite no is reportedly Metropolitan Museum director Thomas Hoving.[121]

Meantime, the operations of the National Council and the Arts Endowment had to continue. The Council met May 22–23, 1969, at Le Chantecler in St. Adele-en-Haut, Quebec, the only time the Council ever met outside the United States, probably as a result of the ex-Canadian acting chairman's desire to build international bridges.

MacAgy reported that successful efforts were being made by the White House to fill the position of chairman. The budgetary situation for fiscal 1970, beginning July 1, was not yet clear since Congress was reluctant to appropriate funds for an agency without a chairman. MacAgy also reported on staff changes. Clark Mitze, director of the States program, was acting deputy chairman. Charles C. Mark and Henry Geldzahler had both resigned. Carolyn Kizer and David Stewart had dropped their program director roles to become consultants. There were also some new appointments: James K. Guthrie, planning and analysis; John Hoare Kerr, education program; Brian O'Doherty, visual arts; and James Thomas, grants office.

There were two Council resignations. Minoru Yamasaki, a member of the Council since 1965, resigned in January. Richard Diebenkorn, feeling he had fulfilled his mission and not being comfortable in the existing political climate, resigned in March, shortly after Stevens. Some months later, in October, Helen Hayes also resigned.

At the Quebec meeting the feeling that the chairmanship appointment was settled had been so solid that Morton (Buster) May from St. Louis was actually announced as the incoming but part-time chairman, while John MacFadyen, the New York architect and former executive director of the New York State Arts Council, was to be his full-time and powerful deputy. Unfortunately, that arrangement did not please the Hill. Senator Claiborne Pell from Rhode Island and Rep. John Brademas of Indiana both spoke against a half-time chairman.[122]

There were other names floating in the air: Claire Booth Luce, John D. Rockefeller III, Dorothy (Buffy) Chandler from Los Angeles, John Walker, George Irwin, Shirley Temple Black. In all, the speculation was that at least 50 names were considered for the post that needed "a political virgin who can produce political results,"[123] according to one anonymous senator. The vacancy was becoming critical since the legislation for both the Arts and Humanities Endowments was due to expire June 30, 1970. Barnaby Keeney, on a different appointment schedule from Stevens', was still chairman of the National Council and National Endowment for the Humanities, but his agency was equally affected by the legislation deadline.

All through this period Nancy Hanks' name floated in and out of discussions and occasionally hit the papers. On August 22, 1969, Howard Taubman broke the surprising news in the *New York Times* that "the long search for a new chairman of the National Arts Council is apparently coming to an end. The indications are that Michael Straight, 53, writer and philanthropist, will be named to the post by President Nixon."[124]

Straight was a friend of Leonard Garment, the President's civil-rights and arts adviser. Garment, a musician and a law partner of Nixon, was carrying most of the burden of the search for a new chairman and was even occasionally mentioned for the post himself.

However, the news did not sit well with Senator Jacob Javits of New York, whose own candidate, John Walker, had been turned down by the White House. He was especially aggrieved that Straight was not a Republican.[125] One of the stories circulating in Washington at the time was "Do you mean to tell us that you've fired a Democrat, you've searched for seven months, and the best you can come up with is another Democrat?"

Suddenly, the problem was settled. In the *New York Times* of September 3, 1969, Nan Robertson wrote from Washington: "President Nixon has selected Nancy Hanks, a 41-year-old executive of the Rockefeller Brothers Fund in New York, to be the new chairman of the National Council on the Arts."[126] It was just in the nick of time. The new budget for the fiscal year ending June 30, 1971, had to be ready by September 30 if the agency and its growing strength were to be maintained.

Reference Notes

1. "Government and the Arts: How Much to Whom?," *Newsweek* (July 18, 1966), p. 59.
2. E. J. Kahn, Jr., "Closings and Openings," *The New Yorker*, 29 (February 20, 1954), pp. 41*ff.*
3. T. Prideaux, "The Man Behind Washington's Kennedy Center," *Smithsonian*, 9 (January 1979), pp. 56*ff.*
4. D. Norton-Taylor, "Roger Stevens, A Performing Art," *Fortune*, 73 (March 1966), p. 151.
5. "Producer," *The New Yorker* (October 9, 1954), pp. 28–29.
6. "Stage-Struck Shrewdie," *Time*, 72 (October 20, 1958).
7. *Variety*, May 25, 1955.
8. Press release, November 1956, The Playwright's Company Papers (Archives, Wisconsin State Historical Society, Madison, Wisc.).
9. *Fortune* (March 1966), p. 151.
10. *The New Yorker* (February 20, 1954), pp. 41*ff.*
11. *New York Times*, October 20, 1958.
12. Quotations and information about Stevens's speech to the Platform Committee were found in Remarks of Roger L. Stevens, Special Assistant to the President on the Arts, before the Platform Committee of the Democratic National Convention, Atlantic City, N.J., August 20, 1964.
13. National Council on the Arts, "The First Annual Report of the National Council on the Arts 1964–1965" (Washington: unpublished report to the President of the United States, 1965), p. 11.

14. *Ibid.*, p. 12.
15. *Ibid.*, p. 53.
16. *Ibid.*, pp. 12, 51.
17. *Fortune* (March 1966), p. 152.
18. National Council, "Annual Report 1964–1965," pp. 12–14.
19. National Endowment for the Arts (NEA), "The National Council on the Arts and the National Endowment for the Arts During the Administration of President Lyndon B. Johnson: The History," Vol. I (Unpublished document available from the Lyndon B. Johnson Library, Austin, Texas, 1968), pp. 14–15.
20. National Council, "Annual Report 1964–1965," pp. 14–15.
21. *Ibid.*, pp. 16–19.
22. G. T. Seaborg, "The Sciences, the Humanities, and the Federal Government," *American Education*, 2 (September 1966), pp. 8–11.
23. National Council, "Annual Report 1964–1965," p. 20.
24. Quotations and information on the White House reception were taken from H. Taylor, "The Arts in America," *The Colorado Quarterly*, 14 (2) (Autumn 1965), pp. 101–104.
25. Lady Bird Johnson, *A White House Diary* (New York: Holt, Rinehart, and Winston, 1970), p. 287.
26. Quotations and information about the second Council meeting were taken from National Council, "Annual Report 1964–1965," pp. 21–36.
27. *Ibid.*, pp. 37–42.
28. Rockefeller Panel Report, *The Performing Arts: Problems and Prospects* (New York: McGraw-Hill, 1965), p. ix.
29. L. L. Biddle, Taped interview, Washington: December 22, 1980.
30. Press statement by R. L. Stevens, for release Friday, October 8, 1965.
31. National Endowment for the Arts (NEA), *Annual Report 1966* (Washington: U.S. Government Printing Office, 1966), p. 7.
32. Information on program staff was taken from *Ibid.*, pp. 82–85.
33. N. Hanks, taped interview, Washington, D.C., January 28, 1980.
34. R. L. Stevens, "The State of the Arts: A 1966 Balance Sheet," *Saturday Review*, 49 (March 12, 1966), pp. 24–25.
35. R. L. Stevens's address to the National Electric Sign Association, Annual Convention, Miami, Fla., March 15, 1966.
36. A. Frankenstein, *San Francisco Chronicle*, October 23, 1966.
37. H. Taubman, *New York Times*, September 1, 1966.
38. NEA, *Annual Report 1966*, pp. 26–32.
39. R. Mayleas, taped interview, New York City, December 19, 1981.
40. F. Taylor, personal reminiscence.
41. NEA, *Annual Report 1966*, pp. 49–50; and National Council on the Arts and National Endowment for the Arts, *The First Five Years, 1966–1970*, "Theatre Programs" (Washington: U.S. Government Printing Office, 1970), pp. 1–7.
42. Mayleas interview.
43. NEA, *Annual Report 1966*, p. 39.
44. W. Terry, *New York Herald-Tribune*, February 13, 1966.
45. C. Barnes, *New York Times*, January 20, 1966.
46. *The First Five Years*, "Dance Programs," pp. 1–8.
47. D. Hering, Executive Director, National Association of Regional Ballet, personal communication, June 8, 1981.
48. C. Mitze, taped interview, Chicago, Ill., June 29, 1981.
49. Quotations and information were taken from NEA, *Annual Report 1966*, pp. 44–46.
50. Information was taken from *Ibid.*, pp. 34, 51.

51. Information was found in *Ibid.*, pp. 35–37.
52. National Endowment for the Arts (NEA), *Artists in Schools* (Washington: U.S. Government Printing Office, 1973), pp. 22–23.
53. Information on literary activities was taken from National Endowment for the Arts (NEA), *Annual Report 1967* (Washington: U.S. Government Printing Office, 1967), pp. 32–37; and *The First Five Years*, "Literature Program," pp. 1–7.
54. Quotations and information on the Music Program were taken from NEA, *Annual Report 1966*, pp. 52–54.
55. F. Taylor, Music Office memoranda and personal reminiscences of 1966–1967.
56. General information was taken from NEA, *Annual Report 1966*, pp. 55–56; and *The First Five Years*, "Public Media," p. 1.
57. R. L. Stevens, taped interview, Washington, D.C., January 30, 1980.
58. "Briefing Book on the National Endowment for the Arts—Media Arts" (Washington: Unpublished report for the Presidential Task Force on the Arts and Humanities, June 1981), p. 2.
59. National Endowment for the Arts (NEA), *Annual Report 1969* (Washington: U.S. Government Printing Office, 1969), p. 31.
60. General information was taken from NEA, *Annual Report 1966*, p. 58.
61. L. Halprin, taped interview, San Francisco, Calif., September 18, 1981.
62. General information was taken from NEA, *Annual Report 1966*, pp. 58–63.
63. R. Diebenkorn, telephone interview, November 5, 1981.
64. NEA, *Annual Report 1967*, p. 46.
65. General information was taken from *The First Five Years*, "Architecture, Planning and Design Programs," pp. 1–4.
66. NEA, "The History," p. 81.
67. L. Halprin, interview.
68. General information was taken from *The First Five Years*, "Visual Arts," pp. 1–7.
69. T. B. Hess, "All's Well That Ends Well," *Art News* (February 1967), editorial.
70. Quotations and information on the subcommittee hearings were taken from *Hearings Before the Special Subcommittee on Arts and Humanities of the Committee on Labor and Public Welfare, United States Senate, 90th Congress, 1st sess., on S. 2061*, August 15–16, 1967 (Washington: U.S. Government Printing Office, 1967), pp. 425–453.
71. Hess, *Art News*.
72. *The First Five Years*, "Visual Arts," p. 6.
73. "Ford: A Convert to the Arts," *Washington Star-News*, September 5, 1974.
74. R. Diebenkorn, interview.
75. Information was taken from *The First Five Years*, "Visual Arts," pp. 1–7.
76. *National Foundation for the Arts and Humanities Act of 1965*, Public Law 209, 89th Cong. (Washington: U.S. Government Printing Office, 1965), sec. 5.
77. V. White, *Grants for the Arts* (New York: Plenum, 1980), pp. 123–124.
78. C. C. Mark, *Arts Reporting Service*, 246 (July 7, 1970).
79. NEA, *Annual Report 1966*, p. 73.
80. Ibid., p. 79.
81. C. Mitze, interview.
82. NEA, *Annual Report 1966*, p. 74.
83. NEA, *Annual Report 1967*, p. 21.
84. NEA, *Annual Report 1969*, p. 41.
85. R. P. Hanes, personal communication, June 23, 1981.
86. J. Backas, "In Defense of the National Endowment for the Arts," *American Arts*, 12 (5) (September 1981).
87. Minutes of the National Council on the Arts Meeting, Tarrytown, N.Y., May 13–15, 1966.

88. R. L. Stevens, interview.
89. A. Steele, taped interview, Washington, D.C., August 4, 1981.
90. *Ibid.*
91. National Endowment for the Arts, Office memorandum, May 13, 1969.
92. *Senate Hearings*, p. 370.
93. NEA, *Annual Report 1969*, p. 27.
94. General information on the Music Program was taken from *The First Five Years*, "Music Programs," pp. 1–10.
95. *Senate Hearings*, p. 395.
96. *Newsweek* (February 24, 1969).
97. *Senate Hearings*, p. 351.
98. *American Musical Digest*, 1 (2) (November 1969), p. 2.
99. *The First Five Years*, "Public Media Programs," pp. 1–3.
100. General information was taken from *Ibid.*, "Theatre Program," pp. 1–8.
101. NEA, "The History," p. 73.
102. L. B. Funke, "Subsidy Plan Is Devised," *New York Times*, January 29, 1968.
103. NEA, "The History," p. 73.
104. *Ibid.*, p. 75.
105. *Milwaukee Journal*, November 25, 1967, editorial.
106. NEA, "The History," p. 77.
107. *Ibid.*, p. 78.
108. Proceedings of the National Council on the Arts, Eleventh Meeting, Tarrytown, N.Y., April 19–21, 1968.
109. NEA, "The History," pp. 84–85.
110. General information was taken from *Ibid.*, p. 87.
111. *New York Times*, July 23, 1981.
112. C. Mitze, interview.
113. NEA, "The History," pp. 84–85.
114. C. Mitze, interview.
115. NEA, *Annual Report 1967*, pp. 31–32; and *Annual Report 1969*, p. 19.
116. National Endowment for the Arts, *New Dimensions for the Arts 1971–1972* (Washington: U.S. Government Printing Office, 1972), p. 29.
117. National Endowment for the Arts (NEA), "The National Council on the Arts and the National Endowment for the Arts During the Administration of President Lyndon B. Johnson: Supplement, Vol. II" (Unpublished document, available from the Lyndon B. Johnson Library, Austin, Texas, 1969), pp. 6–7.
118. H. Taubman, "Subsidies for Culture," *New York Times*, January 11, 1969.
119. *Variety*, March 12, 1969.
120. *Milwaukee Journal*, March 30, 1969.
121. *Newsweek* (May 5, 1969).
122. M. Straight, *Twigs for the Eagle's Nest* (New York: Devon Press, 1979), p. 17.
123. R. L. Coe, "The Politics of Art on Capitol Hill," *Washington Post*, July 17, 1969.
124. *New York Times*, August 22, 1969.
125. Straight, p. 19.
126. *New York Times*, September 3, 1969.

4

The Nancy Hanks Years

> With the help of the National Endowment for the Arts, the cultural life of this country has the opportunity to shift from a state of paradox to one of vigorous fulfillment.
> —Nancy Hanks, *Annual Report 1974*

The first decade of the National Endowment for the Arts breaks naturally into two divisions under its successive chairmen. If the first period was exciting, innovative, without a discernible pattern, often narrowly focused but full of promise, the second period began to fulfil the promise, develop patterns, and broaden the commitment to the world of the arts.

Under the sure and persuasive leadership of Nancy Hanks, Congress started to give real financial support to the agency. Funding increased and major programs of assistance to arts organizations were undertaken. Applications proliferated and the staff to handle the work of the agency expanded also. New programs were devised, bringing new dimensions to the impact of the Endowment on the nation's cultural activities.

Hanks Assumes Chairmanship

Nancy Hanks had been nominated as chairman for the Arts Endowment and the National Council by President Richard M. Nixon on September 3, 1969. A month later, October 6, she was sworn into office. The deputy chairman, Michael Straight, was appointed on November 20, 1969. Together they made a memorable team for the next eight years in Washington.

The new chairman was born in Miami Beach, Florida, on December 31, 1927. She was the daughter of a Texas lawyer, Bryan Cayce Hanks, and his wife, Virginia Wooding Hanks. Bryan Hanks was a member of the Florida and New

York bar and a prominent Florida utilities executive. He moved his family to Montclair, New Jersey, when Nancy was only 10, but her Southern accent remained on call. In fact, her ability to move easily into regional accents became one of her great assets as the ultimate persuader for the arts. Nancy was educated at Duke University and graduated magna cum laude in 1949 with an A.B. degree. She was a member of Phi Beta Kappa, Phi Kappa Delta, and Kappa Alpha Theta. During the summer of 1946 she attended the University of Colorado and spent the summer of 1948 at Oxford University.

In 1951 she came to Washington and found a staff job in the Office of Defense Mobilization and there sometime later met Nelson Rockefeller, beginning an association with the Rockefeller family that was to continue for many years. When Nelson Rockefeller became chairman of the President's Advisory Committee on Government Organization in 1953, Nancy was a member of his staff. The next year she was an assistant to him as Undersecretary of the Department of Health, Education and Welfare. She worked as his special assistant in 1955 when he was Special Assistant in the Special Projects Office of the White House. From 1956 to 1959 she continued as his assistant and from 1959 to 1969 was an associate of his brothers, Laurance S. Rockefeller and John D. Rockefeller III. During this period she became executive secretary for the Special Studies Project, the Rockefeller Brothers Fund, and the project coordinator for a landmark publication, *The Performing Arts: Problems and Prospects.*[1]

"The Rockefeller Report," as it was immediately tagged, was based on a series of research papers; on lengthy discussions with some 40 experts in the arts, government, education, management, and labor; on subcommittee studies of special aspects of the problems encountered; on a survey of 100 corporations; and on a survey of 75 officials of philanthropic institutions and performing arts organizations who gave their thoughts about foundation programs. Eight states and nearly 50 municipalities were also queried about their support for the arts in their areas.

As chairman of the project, John D. Rockefeller III stated in his foreword to this report that it was intended as a challenge and not an answer.

> Only in our time have we begun to recognize the arts as a community concern to be placed alongside our long-accepted responsibilities for libraries, museums, hospitals, and schools. . . .
>
> If the arts are vital to a mature civilization, how do they best flourish? What organizations are needed to nourish them? How are they to be supported and maintained? Questions such as these, especially when applied to the performing arts, need public discussion and are worthy of thoughtful inquiry and debate. . . .
>
> From the beginning, the panel had particularly in mind a study that would be useful to those responsible for the direction and management of performing arts and institutions. We also wanted to be helpful to foundation and corporate executives who are considering support for the arts. We hoped, too, that the study might be of value to

> local, state, and federal officials as the arts become increasingly important to the well-being and happiness of the people. And finally we wished to serve private citizens who are working to enhance the quality of life in their communities.[2]

All these are noble aims, sounding perhaps more like a last gasp of the Kennedy romanticism of the early sixties than the pragmatism of the Johnson "Great Society." Nevertheless, half a decade later under a Republican administration, they became the cornerstone of Nancy Hanks' philosophy of action when she moved into the chairmanship of the Arts Endowment.

The study discussed the increased cultural interests in the country among the members of an ever more affluent society, an interest that was bringing with it a financial crisis as the gap between earned income and costs of operation widened yearly. The report pointed out that "the private donor—the individual, the foundation, the corporation—has the major responsibility for insuring the survival and growth of the performing arts organizations,"[3] since the earned income at the box office and from other sources was not sufficient to make the nonprofit performing arts organization self-sustaining. The study urged corporate support of the arts as good business practice and maintained that a healthy cultural life in a community is a major strength. It pointed out the long and distinguished history of the charitable foundations of America and deplored the fact that while education, scientific research, and welfare were all handsomely supported, the arts rarely received attention. Finally, the panel study explored the need for government aid to the arts and concluded that "while private support should remain dominant, the federal government—together with state and local governments—should give strong support to the arts, including the performing arts, by appropriate recognition of their importance."[4]

In 1966 another study with hard statistics on *Performing Arts: The Economic Dilemma* was published by the Twentieth Century Fund. It was the product of research by two Princeton University economics professors, William J. Baumol and William G. Bowen, and statistically reinforced the trends described in the Rockefeller Panel Report.

The two studies were blueprints for Nancy Hanks' leadership of the Arts Endowment. While some critics claimed that reliance in the Panel Report on studies, surveys, and the judgment of panels reflected the Rockefeller approach to problems (touch all bases and run around a lot), the system nevertheless became the pattern for effective accomplishment in the next eight years. Combined with the subtle persuasiveness of broad geographical and social outreach programs, the Endowment programs created the climate for a period of remarkable cultural growth.

The transition for the National Endowment for the Arts from the era of Roger Stevens to that of Nancy Hanks was not without pain. Council member Lawrence Halprin, who ultimately became a strong supporter for Hanks, said,

"Roger was a hard act to follow. Nancy made a very slow start . . . . I thought at the beginning she did not have a handle on it."[5]

Karel Yasko, assistant commissioner for design for the Public Buildings Service of the General Services Administration, in warm reminiscences about the period recalled that "the staff members . . . dragged their feet . . . when she got appointed. It was really a no-confidence situation, but it wasn't long before they were in awe of what she was able to do."[6]

One Senator is rumored to have said that Nancy Hanks was the best appointment Nixon ever made. She was honest and straightforward, very intelligent, and compulsively hard-working. In the early years of her tenure, she was considered to be a skilled administrator and, when the staff had accepted her, its members were generally devoted. Hanks radiated charm and good sense in a time of national uproar. She saw the arts in America as a resource to knit the country together. As she sat through endless panel meetings, month in and month out, quietly working at the needlepoint in her lap, she absorbed, evaluated, and organized needs and problems—and potential solutions. Roger Stevens had told her that the panel meetings were important and to be sure to attend them "or they will run away with the Endowment."[7] She found them illuminating and helpful in setting goals and priorities. She also traveled from one end of the country to the other, giving speeches, cutting ribbons, examining local arts activities from kindergarten classrooms to artists' studios to old-age recreational programs. Accessible, enthusiastic, energetic, not in the least bohemian or avant-garde, she came to platforms, meetings, and legislative sessions with the presence of a capable League of Women Voters matron, friendly and informed.

Deputy Chairman Michael Straight

Throughout these productive years, the deputy chairman, Michael Whitney Straight, was a strong and sure presence for the staff and the chairman.

Straight was born in Southhampton, New York, September 1, 1916, the son of Willard Straight, a J. P. Morgan partner and founder of the *New Republic* magazine. His mother was Dorothy Payne Whitney, who founded Dartington Hall in Devon, England, and was a philanthropist in both the United States and Great Britain. He was educated at Dartington Hall and the London School of Economics where he took triple first-class honors, and at Cambridge University.[8]

As a young man, Straight was a writer and researcher for the cabinet of Franklin Delano Roosevelt from 1937 to 1940. He was an economist for the Department of State and from 1941 to 1943 was the Washington editor for the *New Republic*. During World War II he joined the Air Force and piloted B-17s. After the war he became the national editor and publisher for the *New Republic*, from 1946 to 1956, and published several books: *Make This the Last War* (1943), *Trial by Television* (1954), *Carrington* (1960), *A Very Small Remnant* (1964), and one performed play, *Caravaggio*.[9]

Straight was president of the Whitney Foundation, New York. As an art collector he had made contributions to the White House, the National Collection of Fine Art, the Cleveland Museum, and Cornell University (where his father's name as a philanthropist was perpetuated in Willard Straight Hall). He was also national chairman of the American Veterans Committee and president of Amnesty International.

Variously referred to by press and friends as the "resident Brahmin" or the "patrician presence," Michael Straight carried with him not only his family connections and easy access to the nation's most powerful individuals and institutions, but a strong sense of propriety as well. He was watchful of any policies that might be interpreted as politically partisan and he was never convinced that individual grants to artists were appropriate for federal largesse.

Leonard Garment's Support

Straight had a much-needed ally in Leonard Garment, who had become special counsel to President Nixon and the White House advisor for civil rights and cultural affairs. Garment was an oddity in that regimented administration. For one thing, he was a musician. He played the clarinet and had worked his way through law school playing in the Woody Herman band. He was an associate of the New York law firm of Nixon, Mudge, Rose, Guthrie, Alexander, and Mitchell. Like Straight, he was a liberal and a Democrat.[10] Garment was also the vital conduit to the President, which the young agency continued to need since it no longer benefited from Roger Stevens' dual appointment as special assistant to the President and chairman of the Council and the Endowment.

A *Public Image*

Hanks was shortly joined by an assistant in the public relations area (although it was never spelled out that way in official reports). Florence Lowe was a long-time Washington correspondent and television producer. She had been a *Variety* reporter and worked for the *Philadelphia Daily News*, *TV Guide*, and other New England and Pennsylvania papers. She had been accredited to political conventions since 1948 and had a wide acquaintance in Washington.

No artist herself, Florence Lowe was a sculptor of public images. She worked diligently to develop the image of Nancy Hanks into the great lady of the arts. Whenever Hanks went on a trip, Lowe was with her as aide and confidante, and impresario of the public view. She worked on Hanks' schedules, supported her on the long flights and tedious airport waits, stirred up the local press and arranged interviews in the newspapers and on television. She was determined to make Nancy Hanks' name a household word, recognizable as the quintessential twentieth-century protagonist for the arts.

Not a press release left Mrs. Lowe's office that did not carry Nancy Hanks' name in its lead. Where other agencies in the federal government put their press emphasis on the agency itself, the National Endowment for the Arts was upstaged by the chairman. The publicity was not particularly offensive and, by and large, the National Council for the Arts and the staff of the Endowment were not concerned. It was understood that the chairman was doing an incredible promotion and service job for the arts throughout the United States and individual recognition of Hanks in the public eye was not only deserved but probably easier for the general public to understand and support than the complicated alphabetical and legislative name confusions of the federal government.

A "cult of personality" developed but it was offset most of the time by the chairman's own charm and willingness to praise the work of her staff, the panels, and the star-studded National Council, which went a long way toward assuaging any possibility of hurt feelings.

The Early Partnership

As Nancy Hanks and Michael Straight worked together in the early years of their partnership, it became evident that they differed in many substantive ways. Straight was a Democrat, Hanks a Republican. She zeroed onto problems that needed (and could possibly find) solutions. She looked for workable arrangements whereby the artists and their institutions and managers could coexist productively with legislators, bureaucrats, and the political realities of federal funding. Straight, on the other hand, was the philosopher searching for principles. He understood the misgivings of artists who "from Shelley to Sartre . . . had been conditioned to see the state as an enemy."[11]

In an article in the *New York Times*, Straight explored the problem. Using the example of the support of John Adams in 1780, who had predicted in a letter to his wife from France that one of the results of the American Revolution would be that their grandchildren would have the right to a developed cultural life, Straight countered with the attitude of great-grandchild, Henry Adams, who dismissed the precepts of his forebear as being an ill preparation for life. What this indicated, according to Straight, was that the arts which had stood at the center of American society in the period of the Revolution had been thrust to the perimeter. Why did John Adams' dream turn sour, he asked. The reason seemed plain.

> Here, as in Europe and in classical Greece, standards and styles in the arts were set by an elite. That elite lost its monopoly on political power with the advent of social democratization that evolved under Andrew Jackson. The majority of citizens, to

> whom that power passed, then dismissed esthetics as the pastime of an outmoded aristocracy; they did not grasp what Adams knew—that the arts are a means of human fulfillment, open to all.[12]

Straight pointed out that throughout much of our history the country has paid the price of its alienation between society and its artists. The results, he felt, have been what the city planner, Carl Feiss, described as "the Century of Non-Design." Both artists and society have suffered by their separation. There as been little connection or communication between the audience and the artist. "The incoherence and aimlessness that still infest the visual arts derive, I believe, from the long-standing lack of a vital communication between the artist and the society in which he lives and works."[13]

Together, Nancy Hanks and Michael Straight searched for solutions to problems and for a grand design, each with his or her own bias. Although Hanks was sometimes accused of political pragmatism and "band-aiding" where a transfusion was needed, she herself made a distinction. She pointed out that any arts administrator in her kind of job needed to be looking ahead at least five years, and she described working with legislators as a *politicalizing* (rather than a *politicizing*). "We have had to work very hard to have legislators know what's going on in the arts. Most of them didn't know anything about the arts, that's why they weren't coming up with any money. Is that politicizing the arts? Not at all. It's *politicalizing*—and maybe my word isn't right—but it's bringing the arts of politics into the funding of the creative arts."[14]

One of the first crises the new chairman and her deputy had to face was office space. The lease had run out at the offices at 1800 G Street, NW. The General Services Administration had a new head, Robert L. Kunzig, who had been administrative assistant to Senator Hugh Scott from Pennsylvania. Kunzig did not appear to be interested in the arts; even though Nancy Hanks had been appointed by President Nixon and had been photographed with him with public accolades about "a woman in government," Kunzig made the selection of her offices a difficult matter.[15]

The problem was solved with offices on the ground floor of the General Services Building, where the agency remained until it ran out of space again. After considerable further skirmishing with GSA, Hanks agreed to take quarters in the Shoreham Building at 806 15th Street, although the building had to be thoroughly overhauled before the growing agency could be transferred into what ultimately became attractive offices.

Expanding the Budget

When Hanks entered the chairmanship in the fall of 1969, she inherited a program that was sound, "conceived and carried out in accordance with the objectives set forth by Congress in the National Foundation for the Arts and the

Humanities Act," as the *1969 Annual Report* stated. Nevertheless, the programs were, in general, still basically scattered projects lacking cohesive thrust, due in great measure to the small amount of money which had been available to Roger Stevens and his Council. Hanks recognized that the only way the agency could develop a program with breadth and continuity which could really serve the nation's artists and arts institutions would be through a greatly expanded budget. Stevens had tried to get Congress to increase funding. His program funds in fiscal year 1968 amounted to \$4.5 million (plus \$2 million for the state agency bloc grants and \$74,291 in Treasury funds to match private donations). In fiscal 1969 Congress had cut the agency back to \$3.7 million with only \$1.7 million for the state agencies, but because of Stevens' aggressive fund-raising a total of \$1,262,473 in Treasury funds was budgeted. In fiscal 1970—the year Hanks took office—the agency was operating on program funds of \$4,250,000, a sum Stevens had managed to wrest for it as a last-ditch effort of his chairmanship. The state bloc grant was back up to \$2 million and Treasury funds to match private donations also equaled \$2 million.[16]

Increased funding was imperative. In addition, the agency was up for reauthorization, since legislation creating the National Foundation for the Arts and the Humanities was due to run out at midnight, June 30, 1970. With the training she had obtained in her years in Rockefeller offices, Hanks went to work to prove the significant importance of the agency as a patron for the arts and its need for adequate funding to support that importance. Statistics were needed and, fortunately, some were available.

The Belmont Report

President Johnson had initiated the first project to help the documentation. In a letter in 1967 to Dr. S. Dillon Ripley, chairman of the Federal Council on the Arts and the Humanities (and secretary of the Smithsonian Institution), Johnson addressed the situation in America's 5,000 museums, which he called "among our most precious cultural and educational resources . . . contributing immeasurably to the enrichment of the nation's life and to educational advancement at every level." He pointed out in the letter that attendance had already passed 300 million visitors a year and that in many places "inadequate museum budgets and facilities are under severe strain." He recognized that in the future these public institutions would be "expected to reach and serve additional millions." He cited accelerated research programs that would also cause more and more scholars to seek information in museum collections. He felt that museums should have the "wherewithal to work effectively, especially to promote the increase and diffusion of knowledge among men."

"For this reason," Johnson's letter continued, "I am requesting the Federal

Council on the Arts and Humanities to study throughly the status of American museums and report to me. What is their present condition? What are the unmet needs of America's museums? What is their relation to other educational and cultural institutions? I hope that the Council will recommend ways to support and strengthen our museums. . . . The Federal Council is the appropriate body to consider the status of our museums. Its member agencies should provide all possible help to the Council as it performs its work."[17]

This was a tall order for an organization that existed on paper and had no staff. The Federal Council turned to the Association of American Museums for aid and, in November 1967, the association began its work with funds supplied by five member agencies of the Federal Council. A small group of museum directors were selected, along with several nonmuseum persons (one of whom was Nancy Hanks), and a writer. The group, chaired by E. Leland Webber, director of the Field Museum of Natural History in Chicago, turned to Roger Stevens for counsel. It also asked Barnaby Keeney, chairman of the National Endowment for the Humanities, for a grant to make publication possible. Because the conferees met for two lengthy sessions at Belmont, a Maryland country estate, the resulting report was named "The Belmont Report."

On November 25, 1968, Roger Stevens, who had succeeded Dillon Ripley as chairman of the Federal Council, sent a summary of the Council's view to President Johnson, along with the Belmont Report itself.

> It is the view of this Council that the report documents the broad scope of museum services and makes it abundantly clear that the nation's museums play an authentic and major role in the nation's cultural and intellectual life. The report makes clear, too, that a pervasive and insistent financial crisis confronts these institutions.
>
> A strong case can be made for federal support. It is in the national interest to protect our cultural heritage as other countries have effectively done for many years. Collectively the nation's museums preserve, exhibit, and interpret the irreplaceable treasures of America, and of man. Together with schools and libraries they represent the communities—and the nation's—resources for educating tomorrow's citizens. If the present financial dilemma were not a source of serious concern, these functions of museums alone would commend a sustained federal interest to a nation increasingly concerned with the quality of our national life.
>
> Faced, as are all of America's cultural institutions, with a demand for greater service to their community and nation and experiencing a relative decrease in traditional sources of funds, it is apparent on the basis of information presently available that additional resources will be required to meet these expanding demands, or in some cases, to prevent further reduction in existing services.
>
> But a reduction of museum services at the very time when millions of Americans are looking eagerly to them—and to other cultural institutions—to give added dimension and meaning to their lives must not come about through inaction or inadvertence. Steps can be taken now to meet specific serious needs. Further steps should be taken in the near future to insure continuing support which will provide federal resources while encouraging increased support from traditional sources.[18]

Thanks to the Belmont Report, the financial situation of the nation's museums was well-documented. But as 1969 moved into 1970 the financial problems of other arts organizations began to increase rapidly as well. Services offered and costs incurred were expanding faster than the earned income and contributions. Financial pressures increased. By the end of 1969 representatives of 77 symphony orchestras met in New York to examine the situation, in which expenses of principal orchestras were said to have doubled in the past five years. The conference was chaired by Amyas Ames, president of the New York Philharmonic. Ames brought figures to the platform indicating that "although the 88 major and metropolitan orchestras had increased their earned income by 20 percent in the 1968–69 season, and had doubled the sums raised from private contributors over the past five years, they had ended the season with a net cash loss of $5 million. He estimated that the aggregate net cash losses of the 88 orchestras would rise to $8.5 million in the 1970–71 season. The conference acknowledged the gravity of the situation and, by a unanimous vote, called on the Federal Government for substantial support."[19]

The stage was set for Nancy Hanks to move in with her effective political skills and her understanding of the uses of documentation to achieve major goals. The days of the *ad hoc* projects at the Arts Endowment were numbered and program area by program area the agency began to organize itself by goals and priorities—a change not always well-understood by the program directors themselves.

The Support of the President

The *1969 Annual Report* points out in the chairman's foreward that, "while the material conditions of artists in general improved in 1969, the financial prospects of arts institutions did not." Costs were rising and financial pressures mounted. By the end of the year the new chairman felt that the question of the government's support of the arts was becoming urgent. No doubt with the encouragement of Leonard Garment, President Nixon was persuaded to include a statement about the arts in his Special Message to Congress of December 10.

> The attention and support we give the arts and the humanities, especially as they affect our young people, represent a vital part of our commitment to enhancing the quality of life for all Americans. The full richness of this nation's cultural life need not be the province of relatively few citizens centered in a few cities; on the contrary, the trend toward a wider appreciation of the arts and a greater interest in the humanities should be strongly encouraged, and the diverse culture of every region and community should be explored.[20]

Thus, the chairman had the mandate she was seeking: regional development, diversity, a broadening of the base. The next step had to be an increased budget in order to develop the mandate with any success.

The President expanded the theme further:

> There is a growing need for Federal stimulus and assistance—growing because of

> the acute financial crisis in which many of our privately-supported cultural institutions now find themselves, and growing also because of the expanding opportunity that derives from higher educational levels, increased leisure and greater awareness of the cultural life. We are now able to use the nation's cultural resources in new ways—ways that can enrich the lives of more people in more communities than has ever before been possible.
>
> Need and opportunity combine, therefore, to present the Federal government with an obligation to help broaden the base of our cultural legacy—not to make it fit some common denominator of official sanction, but rather to make its diversity and insight more readily accessible to millions of people everywhere.
>
> Therefore, I ask the Congress to extend the legislation creating the National Foundation on the Arts and Humanities beyond its termination date of June 30, 1970, for an additional three years.
>
> Further, I propose that the Congress approve $40,000,000 in new funds for the National Foundation in fiscal 1971 to be available from public and private sources.
>
> Few investments we could make would give us so great a return in terms of human understanding, human satisfaction and the intangible but essential qualities of grace, beauty and spiritual fulfillment.[21]

The text of the President's message created an unprecedented response from the national arts constituency. It was a response triggered in large part by the state arts agencies who alerted their own supporters, and by symphony orchestra associations who urged their patrons to write their congressmen. Letters and telegrams poured into the White House applauding the message in one of the first major manifestations of the enormous support for the arts that existed in America which, up to that time, had not really been tapped as a political consideration. During the Hanks years it became almost an organized lobby, to the point that by the end of her second term the *Washington Post* was reporting that even such a strong arts supporter as Representative John Brademas (D.,IN) was "expressing concern that the Endowment was forming a national base for a bureaucratic empire."[22]

In 1970, however, there were no such concerns. The problem at hand was the reauthorization of the agency and the passage of an adequate budget. Since the support for the President's message had resulted in a favorable press for the incumbent administration, it might have remained there with no further effort on the part of Nixon's staff, who felt that the statement had served its purpose. But Nancy Hanks had a goal. She and her deputy, Michael Straight, felt themselves part of a national movement and they worked with missionary zeal to convince Congress that the young agency merited continued and increasing support. Day after day they went up the Hill, called on congressmen, were rebuffed, ignored, sometimes humiliated. Michael Straight bought a box at the Kennedy Center, and Tuesday after Tuesday during the season he invited two congressmen and their wives to dinner at his home, followed by a concert at the Center.[23]

There were some problems. One of the more celebrated resulted from *The American Literary Anthology*, a project developed in the Literature Program in the early years of the agency. The anthologies reprinted the "best writing appearing in American literary magazines of limited circulation." Independent juries made the selections; major publishing houses carried publishing costs; authors received $500. The first volume, published by Farrar, Straus & Giroux in 1968, appeared on the public shelves with little fanfare and no incident. The second, published by Random House in 1969, contained an example of the post-World War II poetry experiment known as "concrete poetry," a kind of word art in which the visual image is as important as the words. The selection, "lighght" was by Aram Saroyan, reprinted from a concrete poetry issue of *The Chicago Review*.

Representative William Scherle, an Iowa Republican, read the poem and found it just what he needed to spearhead an attack on the Arts Endowment. Without troubling to examine the reasons for or merits of this particular art expression, he launched his attack. "If my kid came home from school spelling like that, I would have stood him in the corner with a dunce cap." He calculated that the $750 paid out amounted to $107 per letter which the taxpayers had to underwrite, ignoring the fact that an artist worker was being paid for his imagination and his special skill.[24]

In spite of such attacks, the chairman and her deputy worked their way through office after office on the Hill with persuasion, facts, charm, and perseverance, as well as help from the redoubtable Julia Butler Hanson (D., WA), who was chairman of the Appropriations Subcommittee on the Interior, where the Endowment's budget was assigned, and from other staunch supporters in Congress. The word went out around the country that the Arts Endowment needed indication of national support. Local arts agencies saw to it that fliers about the Endowment were placed on the seats of practically every theater and concert hall in the country. Thousands of letters—mail bags full—poured into Congress within the next several weeks.

Reauthorization

On June 30 the bill went to the House floor, while teams from both the Arts and Humanities Endowments sat tensely in the gallery watching the comings and goings below, keeping an eye on the floor leader, readying themselves to call in their friends when a vote was anticipated. Finally the time came; the vote was in; the tally made: 262 for the bill and 78 against.[25]

Thus, the agency was authorized for another three years and, for fiscal year 1971, its budget had been almost doubled. Nancy Hanks and her staff had won a crucial political battle. From then on her chairman's role as protagonist and "personable persuader" for the arts was never seriously challenged.[26]

While the public commotion over "lighght" was being aired in Congress and the press, another potentially more devastating problem surfaced in the agency office. Editor George Plimpton and his colleague Peter Ardery were at work on the third edition of *The American Literary Anthology*. As reauthorization time was approaching, it occurred to Michael Straight that a look at the galleys of Number Three might be worthwhile—since forewarned could be forearmed. A set of galleys was located.[27]

Among other items that had been selected for the new anthology was a story called "The Hairy Table," a description of erotic exploits in a bookstore in Manhattan. The exploits were described with vivid detail, including one episode in which the man telling the tale comes up with the idea of mimeographing poetry in the midst of a sexual encounter.

> I reached under her belly to the squack, and what an idea escaped the boundary of my polemic gush brain! To frig and to publish! Hands trembling, I slashed her with the pud, one hand cranking the mimeo, the other steadying the orgasm donut. And the paper was fed through, printing the second edition of "The Toe-Queen Poems" kuh-plak kuh-plak kuh-plak kuh-plak, faster and faster. . . .[28]

Nancy Hanks was no prude. She proved over and over again during her tenure that she completely understood and approved of Section 4(c) of the Foundation Act which stated:

> In the administration of this Act no department, agency, officer, or employee of the United States shall exercise any direction, supervision, or control over the policy determination, personnel, or curriculum, or the administration or operation of any school or other non-Federal agency, institution, organization, or association.

The mandate for freedom of expression was clear; however, the language did not mention censorship of the work of individuals—always a highly sensitive area. And the grant for *The American Literary Anthology* was an individual one to George Plimpton. Thus, on procedural grounds, and procedural only, Hanks felt she was entitled to intervene. According to the *Washington Post*, she and Straight phoned Plimpton and urged him to take "The Hairy Table" out of the anthology. It was discovered that the story had been low on the lists of the two judges who had picked it, and Plimpton himself had not read it before the inclusion. But, as editor, he refused. Plimpton was quoted as saying, "Nancy said it would cost the Endowment millions, cut it to ribbons. I sympathized with her position, but I told her that she just couldn't do it. Then she said she would have to stop publication of the anthology. I told her a storm would break out. But she said she had to think of the Endowment, that this thing could kill it!"

The storm never did break out. Instead, at a meeting in Manhattan, it simply fizzled out. Hanks told Plimpton that she was cutting off the anthology project after the third volume, one edition sooner than originally planned. That meant he would have to seek money elsewhere for a fourth volume that was already in the works. Plimpton decided to take "The Hairy Table" out of the government-sponsored book and include it in the privately printed one. So,

"The Hairy Table" never appeared in the Endowment book and the episode ended.[29]

The delicate balance between artistic integrity and political good sense was maintained and the threat of censorship abated. The concept of individual assistance to artists remained intact, but there was a change. Grants began to move to artists to give them future time and opportunity to work; no longer were cash awards made for past work. The right of an artist of proven ability to accept an individual grant and move ahead to create the work of art he or she envisioned—whether poem, sculpture, theatre piece—was thereby freed of any judgmental decisions by the Endowment staff, panels, or Council.

With the agency authorized for the next three years and the budget voted, the new team settled into action.

Changing Staff

There were some key staff changes by January 1971. An executive officer, Charles Kirk, was added, and a special assistant to the chairman, Douglas Richards, was named. Florence Lowe became assistant to the chairman. The Architecture Planning, and Design slot was open for a period since the next director, Bill N. Lacy, former dean of the University of Tennessee School of Architecture, did not join the staff until mid-1971. Alece Morgan performed the interim assistance duties. June Batten Arey was still program director for Dance; she was replaced in late 1971 by Don S. Anderson, who had been associated with the Repertory Dance Theater of Utah. John Hoare Kerr remained at the Education program desk and Stephanie Singer continued as his able assistant. Leonard Randolph had moved from assistant director of State and Community Operations to program director for Literature, replacing Carolyn Kizer. Walter F. Anderson continued as Music director with Ralph Rizzolo as assistant director, and the special talents of Marjory Hanson. Douglas G. MacAgy, who had gallantly tried to hold the agency together after Stevens' tenure, was variously described as "Special Exhibitions" director and later "National Exhibitions" director; before the year was out he had died. Chloe Aaron replaced David Stewart in the Public Media Program. Clark Mitze remained director of State and Community Operations (later called Federal-State Partnership) with the aid of David Sennema, who had been executive director of the South Carolina Arts Commission, and the fiercely loyal Joanne Perlstein. Ruth Mayleas continued as Theatre Program director (a post she ultimately held longer than any other staff director). Brian O'Doherty, former editor of *Art in America* magazine and an M.D. from Dublin's University College, headed the Visual Arts Program, while Starke Meyer and Julia Moore assisted both him and the incoming Museum Program director, Thomas Leavitt. Later, Starke Meyer went to the White House as assistant for cultural affairs, working with Leonard Garment. Ana

Steele shifted directing titles from Special Research Projects to Office of Research. Madelyn Mailman, who had been working with Steele, was joined by Anne Clark, making a troika of formidable accuracy for information. Charles B. Ruttenberg was succeeded as legal consultant by Lawrence L. Reger, who soon took over the new Office of Planning and Management, while Robert Wade became general counsel. Luna Diamond continued her dedicated and exuberant tenure as secretary to the National Council on the Arts. For the shared staff of the two Endowments—Arts and Humanities—Paul P. Berman remained director of administration, Joyce Freeland, financial manager, David C. Johnstone, personnel officer, James Thomas, grants officer, and Aida Schoenfeld, projects coordinator. Marjorielane Menke and Beth Alexiou were loyal secretaries to the chairman and deputy chairman.

In the ensuing months, other able and dedicated staff members joined the agency: Kirsten Beck and Diane Lansing as staff assistants; Bennett Schiff as consultant to the chairman; Edward Wolfe as administrative officer; Chris Morrison as librarian; and Bettiann Dickerman as correspondence supervisor.

On the whole, it was a remarkable staff that picked up on the enthusiasm of the chairman and the Council and began to implement the agency's newly-articulated goals.

Council Defines Goals

In her foreword statement for the *1970 Annual Report*, Nancy Hanks wrote:

> With the support of Congress, the Endowment and its advisory body, the National Council on the Arts, set three goals for the next three years: to encourage broad dissemination of the best of American arts across the country; to work toward solutions of some of the core problems that plague arts institutions in their efforts to provide greater public services; and to provide support that encourages creativity among our most gifted artists and advances the quality of life in our nation.[30]

She pointed out in her report that in at least two areas the year 1970 had seen notable progress toward these goals with support of education in the arts and of the nation's symphony orchestras.

In fiscal 1970 there had been a sharp rise in education funding through a transfer of $900,000 from the Office of Education, following the $100,000 transfer of the previous year. The funds opened the door to a vigorous Artists-in-the-Schools program, coinciding with the peak elementary school enrollment, which in the opinion of Nancy Hanks and others became one of the Endowment's best endeavors. Artists-in-the-Schools offered financial assistance to artists, broad national ingress into some of the smallest communities in the nation, opportunity to interest children in the arts while they were still young enough to accept and enjoy them without negative peer pressure, involvement with the local and state arts and education groups and, in the long run, became a political tool of great strength when dealing with Congress.

In the 1969–70 season, the leading symphony orchestras were playing 70 percent of their concerts for a general public or for educational purposes. This was a dramatic change from the performance schedules of a few years before, according to the chairman's report. "The image of the orchestra's audience as an elite and affluent group is simply not valid." The Endowment, which had previously had no substantive program of institutional assistance for symphony orchestras, now opened one under which 73 orchestras in 38 states received grants for the 1970–71 season.

In the early Seventies, when Hanks and her agency undertook to make an impact on the country through the arts, society was fragmented. The nation was affluent, but inflation was beginning to affect the country as it gradually changed from a world of abundance to a world of shortages. (Indeed, permanent inflation may well have been the most influential factor of the decade.) The nation was torn apart by the war in Vietnam. Protests, marches, bombings, and other violence were still the order of the day. People continued the Sixties trend of speaking out and making opinions heard. But now, instead of sit-ins and placards, neighborhood associations began to grow; special interest groups and national drives for new causes proliferated. It was a perfect climate for the growth of the Arts Endowment with its new dedication to reaching out to all parts of society with the arts.

One of the major influences of the period was the ubiquitous presence of television. The chairman and the National Council were aware of this and encouraged the Public Media Program to expand its grants to filmmakers and to organizations (especially the Corporation for Public Broadcasting) for programming concerned with the arts—dance, poetry, theatre, and music. Assistance was given to the U.S.A. Film Festival in Dallas in 1972. The American Film Institute was expanding vigorously. It established an Institute Theatre at the National Gallery in January 1970 to serve as a showcase for classic films as well as contemporary works.

> The response to the film series was enormous—4,000 members enrolled within five weeks of its public announcement, and membership had to be suspended until the Institute could provide larger facilities. As a result of the tremendous demand, the AFI Theatre established a full-time operation in the fall of 1970 in a new 800-seat, fully-equipped theatre in Washington's L'Enfant Plaza.[31]

In the Literature Program the Coordinating Council of Literary Magazines (CCLM), established in 1966 with a matching $50,000 grant to the National Institute of Public Affairs, was functioning well, representing all of the major and many of the smaller literary magazines in the country. As an independent organization, the CCLM not only made grants through its own grants committee, but to magazines judged as "serious, energetic, exploratory" and showing a "minimal professional level of competence." The CCLM also organized conferences, workshops, college contests, and other projects intended to improve the "content, production and distribution of non-commercial literary magazines."[32] It functioned as a buffer between artists and the Endowment—an outside organization making its own decisions on how to spend the annual grant money. How the funds were dispensed (as long as CCLM's own guidelines were preserved) was strictly a matter for internal monitoring and neither the National Council nor the Endowment staff had any involvement. In addition, the reading audience of the CCLM was small—not the mass audience that had been contemplated for the ill-fated *Anthology*.

New Dimensions

In the introduction to *New Dimensions for the Arts*, the statement was made that "the period between July 1, 1970, and June 30, 1972, known in government parlance as fiscal 1971 and fiscal 1972, will undoubtedly be judged in the future reckoning of the arts in America as among the most significant in their history."

> These two years were important not only in terms of the increased and broad-based financial support for the country's artists and arts institutions, but this period also marked a turning point in public, and therefore governmental, attitudes toward the involvement of the arts in our society and the importance of the arts to the total fabric which clothes a civilization.[33]

Nancy Hanks recognized that this change in public attitude was reflected in the positive reactions she and Michael Straight received from the Hill. The stunning budget victory of 1971, when funds nearly doubled to reach more than $15 million, was repeated the next year when the final budget reached $29,750,000. The institutionalizing of patronage for the arts through a combination of government funding, private enterprise, and philanthropy—rather than random patronage dependent on some personal interest or whim—was beginning to take solid form. The function of the Arts Endowment as a pump-primer to pull money from the private sector was becoming clearly defined.

In 1968 a kind of liaison group, the Business Committee for the Arts (BCA), had been formed with Goldwin A. McLellan as president and a distinguished membership from the corporate sector. McLellan wrote that when the BCA was formed

> its members were convinced the most persuasive arguments for increasing business support for the arts by the business sector were actual examples of business involvement. Some businesses had been participating in arts programs, but effective channels through which other companies might profit from their experience were not available.

The BCA undertook an extensive communication program and began to disseminate its lists and examples widely. McLellan continued:

> Financial contributions head the list, but there are also examples of the contribution of marketing skills for use in audience development; assistance in improving arts organizations' administrative and fiscal practices; the donation of equipment and space, including the loan of computer services; help in development and promotion of programs that will reach new or broader publics . . . the list can be stretched as far as the proven ingenuity of American business.[34]

Foundations, too, in the early Seventies were extending their support of the arts and the humanities.

Public Opinion Surveyed

The National Research Center for the Arts, an affiliate of Louis Harris Associates, put out a survey of public opinion for the Associated Councils of the Arts, funded by Philip Morris, Incorporated.[35] Digested into a report, it became the handbook for every speaker and fund-raiser for the arts for several years to come with its surprising figures about the relationship of the arts to public attitudes and opinions.

In the survey introduction, John Hightower, then president of the Associated Councils of the Arts that commissioned the study, wrote:

> Regardless of the measurement of dollars, there is overwhelming evidence of public recognition that qualities which elude the gross national product are qualities the arts possess . . . . The solution to the world's ills may no more lie with greater activity in the arts than it does with an ever-increasing gross national product. But the American public is aware that at least some of the elusive, less tangible qualities of making life worth living can be found in the arts.

The survey cited some interesting statistics:

- 71% of the adult public—103.3 million people—had attended at least one live performance of theatre, dance, or music, or one museum during the 12 months preceding the survey:
- 56%—81.5 million Americans—had gone to a history museum, historic building or site.
- 49%—71.3 million Americans—had gone to a science or natural history museum.
- 48%—69.8 million Americans—had gone to an art museum.
- 32%—46.6 million Americans—had gone to a theatre.
- 27%—39.3 million Americans—had gone to a live concert or opera.
- 8%—11.6 million Americans—had gone to a live ballet or modern dance performance.

The survey looked further into these attendance patterns and discovered that there was a significant drop in attendance at cultural events among Americans 65 and over—perhaps pointing to a potential senior citizen market that had been overlooked.

Education, income, and place of residence were cited as among the important determinants of attendance at cultural events, but sex and race were not as important as other socio-economic factors. Forty-five percent of the respondents felt they were more interested in the arts and culture than their parents had been—perhaps an echo of John Adams' long-ago prediction about the importance of the arts to the lives of his grandchildren.

A remarkable 89 percent of the population felt it was important "to the quality of life in the community to have facilities like museums, theatres, and concert halls"; and another 80 percent felt that such facilities were important to the financial well-being of the community. Many people (half the public, or 72.7 million Americans) felt there were not enough "places for cultural events—places such as theatres, concert halls and museums in the community where they live."

The public was divided in its perception of the financial situation in most cultural organizations and certainly uninformed about the real economic situation facing most of the country's institutions in a time of rising costs and threatening recession. However, 38 percent felt that cultural organizations should receive direct government funds, 34 percent were for letting the organizations pay their own way, and 14 percent took to the fence.

Greater support for the idea of government funding came from urban areas, the Northeast and Mid-Atlantic states, and the West, from people under 50 (and especially the very young), those with incomes over $10,000, the college-educated, men, nonwhites, and those cultural attenders who fell into the frequent and moderately frequent categories. In no group was a majority opposed to supporting the arts with government funding; and, in fact, there was a remarkable willingness to provide personal, individual assistance.

It would be difficult to say whether the survey results indicated that the message the Arts Endowment had been sending out about cultural activities was making headway in the country, or whether the attitudes reflected the general public feeling of the Sixties and early Seventies that most of the ills of society could be addressed through taxation and the application of federal programs. Probably both conditions obtained. In any case, there was scarcely a publication or speech from the Arts Endowment in the next few years that did not point to the willingness of some 93.1 million Americans to pay an additional $5 annually if the taxation would go to maintaining and operating "cultural facilities such as theatre, music, and art exhibitions."

There were other statistics generated during the early seventies about the state of the arts. In the 1970 census, the number of writers, artists, and entertainers in the labor force amounted to 797,574 people. In 1975, the Bureau of Labor Statistics reported 1,055,000 in this category, "reflecting a compounded annual growth rate of 4.7 percent. At this rate of growth, the labor force of artists would double in a period of about 12.5 years." In the Arts Endowment's own research papers in 1975, professional, technical, and kindred workers are listed as 3.2 percent unemployed while writers, artists, and entertainers—as an occupational group—had an unemployment rate twice as high, at 7.4 percent.[36]

Nancy Hanks was a strong believer in getting the data needed to support her statements about the needs of the arts and sought information from all sources. Following this federal example, the general arts field was also beginning to recognize the need for solid data. As support for the major cultural institutions shifted from private donations from the country's wealthiest and most civic-minded citizens to foundation grants and public moneys, the need for these economic data became more and more important to validate requests.

Cooperation and New Efforts

There were other changes occurring in the cultural community as well. As the chairman wrote in an article for *Museum News*,

> Among the most significant changes during the past four or five years has been the strong development of a spirit of cooperation within the cultural community . . . . Our cultural institutions are faced with problems caused by growing public interest and demand on the one side, and by rising costs on the other. These problems have never existed before, or, more accurately, have never existed in such dimension . . . . The need for cooperation may, in the long run, be more significant than the undoubtedly important question of economics and finance. Growing alliances at the state and local levels among all the cultural institutions are a healthy trend and one of great importance for the future of the arts in this country.[37]

In the first two years of the seventies, the Arts Endowment used its significant budget increases to expand many of its programs to levels that could become meaningful and also begin some new, challenging efforts of a kind not heretofore seen in American government. *New Dimensions* lists:

- A major program of assistance to the nation's symphony orchestras, launched with $3 million in grants in fiscal 1971, rising to over $4 million in fiscal 1972.
- A $1 million pilot program in fiscal 1971 to aid museums, followed by a $4 million program of assistance the next year.
- Creation of the Expansion Arts Program to assist and encourage community-based activities—arts at the "grass roots" level—ranging from the folk heritage of Appalachia, the diverse Indian legacy and the culture of the Spanish-speaking Americans, to the vital arts of the inner city.
- Initiation of a pilot program in fiscal 1972 to enable the large professional dance companies of the country to bring their performances to cities around the nation.

- Creation of a new program in Public Media to assist television, radio, and film programming in the arts; regional film centers, film preservation, upgrading of film education, and increased opportunities for young artists.
- Extension of programs of support to individual artists: choreographers, writers, painters, poets, sculptors, photographers, jazz musicians, playwrights, and art critics.
- Establishment of a new program area for Architecture and Environmental Arts, reflecting the increasing concern for our physical environment.
- Expansion of the Artists-in-Schools Program, enabling 635 painters, sculptors, poets, filmmakers, dancers, and craftsmen to engage school children in all 50 states and five special jurisdictions in exciting new learning experiences. (The program enlists the cooperative efforts of the Endowment, the Office of Education, the Bureau of Indian Affairs, the state arts councils, schools, students, and, of course, the individual artists.)
- Development of a jazz program, from a pilot effort of $20,000 in fiscal 1970, to $250,000 in fiscal 1972.
- A major program of assistance to the nation's opera companies, for improving artistic and administrative standards, increasing the audience for opera, and providing expanded career opportunities for young American artists.
- Substantially increased assistance to resident professional theatres across the country for production of new plays, staff development, extended educational and community services, and audience development.

As the programs grew, the goals of the National Council were sharpened. *New Dimensions* defined them.:

> *Availability of the Arts:* making our cultural resources more available to all people throughout the country.
>
> *Cultural Resources Development:* strengthening our major cultural institutions so they can more adequately serve the people.
>
> *Advancement of our Cultural Legacy:* preserving our heritage and enhancing future creative development.[38]

President Nixon Speaks

One of the stunning accomplishments of the Hanks, Straight, and Garment team was the public support of President Nixon for the arts. Whatever political reasons he may have had, the fact remains that he gave strong assistance when it was needed. On May 26, 1971, he addressed the Associated Councils of the Arts af the Mayflower Hotel in Washington—the first time a President of the United States had appeared personally at a national arts organization gathering—and made a much-quoted comment: "We could be the richest nation in the world, the most powerful nation in the world, the freest nation in the world—but only if the arts are alive and flourishing can we experience the true meaning of freedom, and know the full glory of the human spirit." Nixon went on to say:

> We all no doubt remember the debates that went on for many years over government involvement in the arts—the feeling of some that it was a frivolous waste of the taxpayers' money, the concern of others that government support might lead to government control, or to a drying-up of the private funds on which ultimately the arts depend.
>
> The important thing now is that the government has accepted support of the arts as one of its responsibilities—not only on the federal level, but on the state and local levels as well. And, increasingly, governments at all levels see this not only as a responsibility but also as an opportunity—for there is growing recognition that few investments in the quality of life in America pay off so handsomely as the money spent to stimulate the arts.

And the capstone of the speech:

> So, in urging greater support for the arts, I do it not only because the arts need help. I do it also because the nation needs what the arts—and only the arts—can give.
>
> That is why I urge the Congress to provide full funding for this year's authorization for the Arts and Humanities Endowments—funding that would raise each to $30 million, more than three times the level of two years ago.[39]

Although the President's suggested funding levels were not reached in fiscal 1972, the support sent shock waves around Washington. Obviously, the little agency that no one took very seriously had some powerful friends.

On another occasion President Nixon stated that "the considerable growth of the state arts council movement is a proud phenomenon in American life."[40] Indeed, the growth of the state agencies had been phenomenal, spurred on by the lure of federal money and fitting comfortably into the national special interest groups proliferating on all sides. By 1972 official state arts agencies were operating in all 50 states, plus the District of Columbia, American Samoa, Guam, the Virgin Islands, and Puerto Rico.

Appropriations had grown, too. In 1966, the Associated Councils for the Arts compiled figures for the first time on state funding and reported a total of $2.66 million. Five years later, in 1971, the support had grown to $6.79 million plus the New York State appropriation of $20 million—which was more than the whole federal funding. In 1972 state appropriations rose again to $7.64 million, excluding the New York appropriation of $14.42 million, which had been slashed.

The growth of the state legislative funds was the intent of Congress when it stipulated in the original Endowment legislation that a certain portion of the Endowment's budget was to be allocated each year to the official arts agencies of each state and special jurisdiction. This bloc grant amounted to $75,377 per agency in fiscal 1971 and increased to $101,320 the next year. A statutory requirement restricted both American Samoa and Guam to $65,000 each in both fiscal years.[41]

Throughout the nation there were exciting projects developing in the various states as a result of the growth of the arts funds. Unique, however, was the concept of the Michigan Artrain which had been dreamed up by E. Ray Scott, executive director of the Michigan Arts Council and Mrs. William Milliken, wife of the governor of the state.[42] They had seen how successful an automotive art-van in a remote area of the state could be and originated the idea of a traveling art experience by train. They sought and received state legislative support and help from the National Endowment for the Arts to plan and set up the project.

Artrain was housed in three once-abandoned Pullman cars and an old baggage car donated by the railroads. A power-generating car was on loan from the Michigan National Guard and an aged red caboose was fitted up to serve as office and staff lounge for the seven young staff members traveling with the train. Railroads provided free transportation, hitching the Artrain from stop to stop, and the Southern Growth Policies Board picked up part of the tab with the assistance of the Endowment.

The Artrain exhibition was housed in the redesigned Pullman cars through which visitors wound their way at eight-minute intervals among sculpture, paintings, graphics, prints, pottery, jewelry, photography, slides, films, and sculpture with lights. A potter, sculptor, and a silversmith traveled with the train in its first years and later a printmaker joined the staff. Demonstrations were given in the baggage car "studio" and in many towns local artists and craftsmen came alongside to exhibit works.

In 1971 Artrain toured 20 Michigan cities and towns between May and December and was seen by 110,114 people who signed themselves into the exhibition. Later, Artrain stretched its influence as a gallery and workshop on rails into parts of the Rocky Mountain area and a southeastern tour of Georgia, Florida, Alabama, Mississippi, Tennessee, and North Carolina. In the little town of Parrott, Georgia, Governor and Mrs. Jimmy Carter were on hand to cut the ribbon.

Artrain may not have been high art but it was a great catalyst. As it continued to chug its way around other parts of the country, Michigan explored its impact on its own communities where the train had stopped.

> It found that a coming visit of the Artrain often inspired local communities to help existing local organizations and encouraged new sponsorships. In turn, these stimulated regional interest, drew school groups to the Artrain, set up arts-related lectures or screenings, and most important, put together local support sources for the arts. The Michigan Council for the Arts now finds that 12 new community councils have resulted from Artrain visits; at least seven Michigan art shows are now annual events because of the Artrain visit; a major new art center has been established in St. Joseph as a result of the enthusiasm created in the community; and at least five other post-Artrain communities are developing plans for their own art centers.[43]

There were, inevitably, some criticisms of the project. Occasionally the advance team was said to be not "sensitive" enough to local feelings. Sometimes the Artrain staff seemed weary of its task and sometimes the local tour guides seemed inadequately trained. Often there were complaints that the tour was too structured and too rushed through the gallery cars and that there was no follow-up after the train pulled out of the community. But the positive reactions far outweighed others and the Michigan Artrain was one of the successful state-federal collaborations.

Late Summer Report, 1972

Things were going well throughout the agency and the enlarged budget made possible many new and expanded programs. The Chairman decided to take note of the agency's activities and changing Council and staff members in a special memorandum to the members of the National Council on the Arts. (See Figure 1.)

More Staff Appointments

As the programs enlarged and pressures grew, additional staff members joined the Arts Endowment and some changes were made. Don S. Anderson replaced June Arey as director of the Dance Program. John Clark came to the chairman's office as executive staff assistant. John Spencer replaced Thomas Leavitt as the Museum Program director, and Gordon Braithwaite joined Vantile Whitfield as assistant director for Expansion Arts.

Managerial Instincts of Politicians

During her years in office Nancy Hanks was awarded a number of honorary degrees from various universities. The University of Michigan citation read: "Miss Hanks, whose task it is to dispense to the fine arts the monies appropriated to them by the federal government, must mediate between the libertarian instincts of artists and the managerial instincts of politicians."[44]

The "managerial instincts" were well-served by the program developed to upgrade the quality of design in the federal government. It began with a directive from President Nixon (which was probably conceived by Nancy Hanks and Leonard Garment) to the heads of all executive departments and agencies to look over their work and determine how and where arts and artists could benefit government programs and how, in turn, the programs could help the art world.

The National Council on the Arts reviewed the responses to the survey and made recommendations. Lawrence Halprin and Charles Eames were especially supportive. Both had felt the Endowment's own publications were extremely

National Council on the Arts

National Endowment for the Arts

WASHINGTON, D.C. 20506

August 21, 1972

MEMORANDUM

To: The National Council on the Arts

From: Nancy Hanks

Subject: Late Summer Report, 1972

Remiss

As a means of keeping current and former Council members, and panel chairmen, up to date on goings-on at the Endowment, we instituted in 1970 monthly informal reports, which became periodic reports, which became spasmodic, which became non-existent. Sorry about that! Going to start again.

Retiring and New Council Members

As you know, the following terms are up September 3: Charlton Heston, Marian Anderson, Virginia Gerity, Helen Hayes, Lawrence Halprin, Jimilu Mason, Donald Weismann, and Nancy White.

New Council appointees announced by the President on August 17 are:

Rosalind Russell Brisson, of Beverly Hills, California, stage and motion picture actress, Trustee of Motion Picture Relief Fund.

Henry J. Cauthen, of Columbia, South Carolina, General Manager of the South Carolina Educational Television Network and President of the Southern Educational Communications Association.

Clint Eastwood, of Sherman Oaks, California, motion picture actor, producer and director.

Figure 1

Memo
Summer Report '72 -2- August 21, 1972

Judith Jamison, of New York, New York, principal dancer, Alvin Ailey American Dance Theatre; formerly with American Ballet Theatre and the Harkness Ballet.

James D. Robertson, of San Francisco, California, partner in the firm of Goldman, Sachs & Co., Director and Treasurer of the San Francisco Opera Association, Trustee and Executive Board Member of the San Francisco Conservatory of Music, and Governor of the San Francisco Symphony.

Billy Taylor, of Riverdale, New York, jazz pianist; musical director of the David Frost Show, Member of the Board of Governors of the Newport Jazz Festival, member of the Harlem Cultural Council, and member of the Special Advisory Committee on Jazz at the Lincoln Center.

Eudora Welty, of Jackson, Mississippi, novelist; author of a number of novels, including Losing Battles and The Optimist's Daughter; Honorary Consultant in American Letters, the Library of Congress.

James Wyeth, of Chadds Ford, Pennsylvania; painter and member of Postal Service Stamps Council; designer of 1971 Christman stamp (Partridge in a Pear Tree); son of Andrew Wyeth.

Relatively New Staff Members and Consultants

Norman L. Fagan replaced Doug Richards as Director of Performing Arts and Public Media on July first. Norm previously served as Director of Education for the Kennedy Center and before that as Executive Director of the West Virginia Arts and Humanities Council. Doug has returned to Phoenix and established an arts consulting firm. In addition to other contracts, he will from time to time assist the Endowment, particularly in regard to state arts councils and orchestras. You will recall the successful survey of the Southeast orchestras made last year. Selected orchestras in the West will be included in the next phase.

Fannie Taylor, who at one time served as Director for Music at the Endowment, has returned to head the new office of Program Information. This office has been established in response to the growing need for more printed material, films and publications concerning the programs

Memo
Summer Report '72 -3- August 21, 1972

and goals of the Endowment. High on her priority list (and it's a long one) will be a two-year review (1971 and 1972). We decided this would be better than printing two annual reports. Fannie is on leave from the University of Wisconsin at Madison.

Jerome Perlmutter, Chief of the State Department's Publishing and Reproduction Services, will be on loan to us beginning September 1, to coordinate efforts of the Federal agencies to improve the quality of graphics. This is one part of the President's program on Design that we are carrying forward. Notes on other developments follow.

Progress on Design

Planning for the Federal Design Assembly, which is scheduled for Spring 1973, is moving forward apace under Lani Lattin's deft pushing. The planning task force is headed by J. Carter Brown, and includes federal design experts and outside professionals like Ivan Chermayeff and Richard Wurman. Bill Lacy has his first consultant on board to plan for the "Guiding Principles for Federal Architecture" study. And, to complete the Design package, we have been meeting with the Civil Service Commission (with the strong personal interest of the Commissioner) on the review of employment practices of the federal government that affect design.

Almost forgot: Arthur Sampson, Acting Administrator of GSA, has reinstated the one-half of one percent for arts in the new federal buildings that will be contracted for in the next go-round. Doesn't sound like much of a percentage BUT could total $3,750,000!

Speaking of Money

As you will recall, the President requested $39,000,000 for the Arts Endowment. After House-Senate-Conference action, we ended up with $38,200,000. We will sorely miss the $800,000, but there was a strong continued endorsement of our programs and there were many statements on the floor and in conference applauding the Endowment.

Memo
Summer Report '72 -4- August 21, 1972

The Council has been constantly pushing the philosophy that we use monies to encourage other monies and effort and that the Council also direct its attention to using its impact in ways other than grants. (The leadership taken in Design, and the resulting actions by other government agencies, is one example.) Therefore, I thought -- to cheer you -- that I would quote from the Washington Post, August 17, in an article about converting old railroad stations for cultural activities. The article referred to some of the small grants we and the America the Beautiful Fund (which we partly finance) have made. The writer noted: "The sums are trifling, but the prestige of the National Endowment is not, and recognition by either the fund or the Endowment is considered a great spur to community action."

Nancy Hanks

pedestrian for an organization devoted to the arts. Here was an opportunity to locate an emphasis on design in the places where the power would be exercised to make the emphasis work—a development of the earlier concept of the Institute of Design, first approved under Roger Stevens' chairmanship but never implemented.[45]

Federal Design Improvement Program

The President took the opportunity to make a positive statement without investing particular time or expense and released a new directive which established the Federal Design Improvement Program.

> FROM THE WHITE HOUSE
>
> Washington, D.C.
> May 16, 1972
>
> One year ago I asked the heads of 63 Federal agencies to determine ways by which their agencies could more vigorously assist the arts and, in turn, how the arts might be used to enhance their programs. The response to that request has been gratifying, calling fresh attention to the importance of the arts in the daily operations of Government and leading to the development of several recommendations by the National Endowment for the Arts.
>
> Today, based upon this first set of recommendations by the Endowment, I am pleased to announce that we shall move forward on three fronts:
>
> • First, I am asking the Federal Council on the Arts and Humanities to sponsor an annual Design Assembly for Federal administrators and artists.
>
> • Second, I am asking the National Endowment for the Arts to appoint a special

> ad hoc task force committee to review and expand the publication, *Guiding Principles for Federal Architecture*; this document was first printed in 1962 and set forth broad aesthetic recommendations of considerable value. I am also asking the National Endowment to recommend a program for including art works in new Federal buildings.
>
> • Third, I am taking a series of actions to improve Federal graphics and publications. The National Endowment will now be responsible for coordinating the efforts of the executive agencies to upgrade their graphics. I am also requesting Federal agency heads to make a comprehensive review of their own graphics and production, and I am asking the Civil Service Commission to review existing procedures for employing artists, architects and designers for Federal service. The Commission is also to evaluate the need for expert rating panels to review credentials and portfolios of applicants for such jobs, as is done in other professional areas.
>
> The people of this country are increasingly concerned—and properly so—with the physical appearance of their communities. There should be no doubt that the Federal Government has an appropriate and critical role to play in encouraging better design, and I am hopeful that the actions announced today will enable the Government to reflect new standards of excellence in all of its design endeavors.
>
> Richard Nixon[46]

While some of this program was never really implemented, within the Endowment itself great strides were made. The Architecture + Environmental Arts program area under the direction of Bill N. Lacy and Robert McNulty, and with vigorous help from Council members in the field, encompassed the federal design program. The Federal Design Assembly began to take shape with Lani Lattin directing. Jerome Perlmutter, chief of publishing for the Department of State, had joined the Endowment as federal graphics coordinator. Within the arts agency and other federal offices, the design of stationery, annual reports, posters, graphs, and so forth began to take on a modern look, and the familiar logo of an eagle in a half circle was added to official Arts Endowment documents.

The Federal Design Improvement Program spearheaded other developments as well as the changes in graphics, according to the *1974 Annual Report*. A report, *Federal Architecture: A Framework for Debate*, created discussions on the problems of improving federal architecture; *Excellence Attracts Excellence* resulted in the assignment of a staff member at the Civil Service Commission to coordinate federal recruitment and training of design professionals; the General Services Administration added interior design to its program of placing fine art in public buildings; and a new program was started to turn over federal buildings of historic quality to state or local agencies to be renovated for local use or cultural activities.[47]

The First Federal Design Assembly was scheduled for April 2, 1973, and was to include administrators from all federal agencies, state governors, and "a small group of leading designers of everything from postage stamps to freeways."

> The assembly, in fact, is only a prelude to some fairly solid and well-funded staff work that is already under way. The April meeting is to sanction that work, as it were. Its purpose is to start convincing the bureaucrats that "design is necessary because it serves human needs."[48]

A publication called *The Design Necessity* was prepared for the assembly and described as a "casebook" of federally-initiated projects by designers Ivan Chermayeff, Richard Saul Wurman, Ralph Caplan, Peter Bradford, and Jane Clark. It opened with a "Theme Statement":

> The First Federal Design Assembly was devoted to an examination of "the design necessity." The Assembly program discussed the necessity of design in visual communications, in interiors and industrial design, in architecture, and in the landscaped environment. Design was considered as an instrument of organization, a medium for persuasion, a means of relating objects to people, a method for improving safety and efficiency, and a way of coping with the complexity of contemporary Federal agency assignments.
>
> The Assembly's emphasis, then, was on design *performance* in response to human needs. Moreover, the emphasis was on *demonstrable* design performance. The Assembly program, the book called *The Design Necessity*, an exhibit and a short film all document the following points.
>
> 1. That there are sound, proven criteria to be applied in judging design effectiveness.
> 2. That design is an urgent requirement, not a cosmetic addition.
> 3. That design can save money.
> 4. That design can save time.
> 5. That design enhances communication between people.
> 6. That design simplifies use, simplifies manufacture, simplifies maintenance.
> 7. That the design necessity is recognizably present in projects ranging in scale and complexity from a postage stamp to a national highway system.
> 8. That the absence of design is a hazardous kind of design. *Not* to design is to suffer the costly consequences of design by default.
> 9. That, on any given project, designers and Government officials are committed to the same basic goal: performance.
> 10. That effective design of public services is itself an essential public service.
>
> Criteria for the design necessity are illustrated, in both the book and the exhibit, by case studies of Federally sponsored projects that work because they were designed to work. The case studies deal with significant aspects of design not visible on the surface, and discuss how problems were solved.
>
> The aim of the First Federal Design Assembly was to present a clear and compelling view of design as a process. For in Government today that process is crucial.[49]

The wide interest in the federal design program also accounted for a new publication, *Federal Design Matters*, started in January 1974. The newsletter was intended to come out periodically and cover both design news for federal agencies and related material from private American and foreign sources. The whole design program was a good example of Nancy Hanks' success in public office based on her ability to take existing programs, activities, and assignments and, by bringing them together, create new alignments and new impetus.

In the early seventies the climate for the arts was conducive to political approval and also for general growth. Museum attendance was expanding incredibly, even though many museums were beginning to ask for "donations" at the door. Annual concert attendance had reached 12 million people. The dance audience was said to have increased 600 percent since the signing of the original bill for the Arts Endowment in 1965. A Gallup poll in January 1972 looked at college student attitudes toward the arts and concluded that 76 percent of the young people contacted felt that the arts should play a more important role in the daily lives of Americans.[50] Deputy chairman Michael Straight even commented to the *Washington Post* in a flight of Whitmanesque fancy, "I look forward to the day when the working man comes home, opens a can of beer, turns on the television, and watches the Metropolitan."[51]

Establishing Expansion Arts

Throughout the first five years of the Endowment's activity there had been continuing efforts to reach the figurative working man with his can of beer. "Cultural enrichment" was often discussed in the National Council and in program offices and ways of exposing poor and usually nonwhite youngsters to the so-called enrichment of Western middle-class cultural traditions were explored. There had been an early grant to the National Guild of Community Music Schools to enable them to set up a permanent office to help start new community schools throughout the country and provide help where these institutions already existed. Dr. Herbert Zipper, who headed the effort, was convinced that only through such schools would the potential musicians among the disadvantaged black population be able to get training in the string instrument area. "It will help solve the shortage of string players," he said repeatedly.[52]

But more than the shortage of string players for major establishment orchestras was at stake. There were new community arts programs of all kinds developing—painting, dance, literature, photography, drama groups, workshops and get-togethers by filmmakers and sculptors—often occurring in areas heretofore considered totally inappropriate for any cultural activity. It was the era of the storefront studio, the coffeehouses, street activities. Suddenly churches, abandoned schools, and dusty train stations and firehouses—all the leftover inner city residue of the middle-class move to the suburbs—became centers for a population searching for new creative outlets, new personal and community expression—not sociological "band-aids."

Junius Eddy of the Ford Foundation described this new social development of the sixties in an article for *Public Administration Review:*

> As the blacks, the Puerto Ricans, and the Mexican-Americans, particularly, began to seek out the roots of an ethnic or racial heritage which the dominant society had systematically ignored or denigrated, the nature of the community-based arts

> movement began to change. The arts became an obvious and powerful vehicle in this cultural renaissance, a vehicle through which minority-group artist-leaders could begin to voice the social and economic concerns of their communities, to asset a new-found historical identity, and to reflect the new sense of ethnic pride and awareness they believe is essential to their survival in white America.[53]

There had been an effort in 1967 by the New York State Council on the Arts to address this sense of ethnic pride and awareness with a $300,000 grant for a so-called Ghetto Arts Program, a sum representing 20 percent of the total state arts budget that year. It was an effort on the part of the council to provide "what the ghetto community wanted rather than what we, as an outside agency, decided it should have," explained the council director, John B. Hightower.[54]

In 1968, with Treasury grant funds, the President's Council on Youth Opportunity had made more than $400,000 available to 16 cities for summer workshop programs in the arts under professional direction. Nancy Hanks later recalled this program as the real beginning of what became the Expansion Arts program for the Arts Endowment. "I reminded Roger [Stevens] of this fact," she said many years later. Reconstructing her conversation with him, she said,

> You will recall, Roger, that you, personally, put on a huge benefit in New York City because you had promised federal money and could not get it. So we all had to gather together and put our private dollars in so that you could do the program in 1968 when we had the riots in our cities. You had promised the President that you would do something for the young. "Oh," he said, "was that really the beginning of the Expansion Arts program?" I said, "Of course it was, because you developed in that program the understanding of professional artists and what they could do for their communities!"[55]

It took Hanks two years to persuade Vantile Whitfield to join the Endowment staff as director of the new Expansion Arts office. Whitfield, a Howard University graduate, was a West Coast theater and television director, one-time probation counselor for Los Angeles County Juvenile Detention, teacher of play production, set designer, co-founder of the American Theater of Being, and artistic director of the Performing Arts Society of Los Angeles at the time he finally agreed to come to Washington.

The National Council had recommended establishing a "community arts" program in October 1970 and Whitfield arrived in Washington to begin his task in April of 1971. He announced to the chairman that he wanted to call the program "Expansion Arts" because he felt that nobody really knew what the phrase meant. "We did not know what the program might develop into ourselves," Hanks said, adding that Whitfield believed that they could be expanding both the vision of the professional artist and the receptivity of the community. She felt that Whitfield was looking toward the expansion of both sides into a really creative partnership that had much to do with the arts and he believed it would take about five years to accomplish. In this length of time they thought they would be able to sort out which groups had become truly professional and had had an opportunity to grow. At that point the intention was to move the theater projects into the Endowment's Theatre program, and dance into Dance, and music into Music.[56]

In its original concept, therefore, the Expansion Arts program was supposed to be short-lived. Hanks recalled,

> And then we ran into a few little problems. The biggest was the recession—1973, 1974. We had been working very hard to develop increased private monies for these groups, and it was difficult to get private money into groups that were mostly minority oriented, and mostly lasting only four or five years. Which is all right, I think . . . . However, the local money that moved into the groups was either private or from the cities, never from the state arts agencies or other state funds. Vantile would just go round and round with the state arts councils and they would not put any money into these groups, which incidentally were largely minority and very talented, but they weren't part of the establishment. A very bad situation.[57]

The funding, therefore, came basically from the federal government, matched by the cities themselves, with perhaps about 15 percent of private money. With the recession closing down on the availability of this private money and city money also cut back, the federal assistance had to stay in the game. The Expansion Arts program began to work on its weeding-out process (some of the groups were basically demonstration groups), but the envisioned moving of new but stable organizations into the Arts Endowment theatre, dance, or music program areas did not happen and the Expansion Arts program continued to operate separately. Some of the grantees did grow spectacularly, such as Harlem School of the Arts, where the dance company under Arthur Mitchell achieved a performance level that was sometimes compared to the American Ballet Theatre.

The concept of Expansion Arts was targeted to the times. Within a year the fiscal 1971 budget of $307,000 had more than tripled to cover its five categories: instruction and training, arts exposure programs, neighborhood arts services, community cultural centers, and special summer projects. Rural areas, Mexican-American theater, Puerto Rican traveling theatre in New York, prisons, graffiti alternatives, workshops for careers in the arts, assistance to well-established institutions like Chicago's Urban Gateways, the Henry Street Settlement in New York, and the Elma Lewis School of Fine Arts in Roxbury, Massachusetts, were all part of the expanding package in its first year of operation.

Expanding Aid to Individual Artists

The increased budget allowed for other growth. The 1973 *Annual Report* pointed out the expanding assistance to individual artists.

> Of the total funding nearly $4 million went to individual assistance, over and above the many Endowment programs that indirectly helped the individual such as

> Works of Art in Public Places, Visual Arts in the Performing Arts, the Museum Purchase Plan, workshops, Artists-in-Schools, and other artists' residencies. The direct assistance included fellowships in almost all art forms, training programs in many professions, and opportunities for experimentation through workshops, experimental groups, and a variety of short-term activities.[58]

Nancy Hanks was steadfast in her support of the individual artists in spite of the pitfalls of such help, both politically and in terms of artists' personalities. She understood the value of steady, ongoing support and, in a speech to the Associated Councils for the Arts, spelled out her concerns, theories, and enthusiasm for support on a federal level. She looked back at earlier federal history.

> If time permitted I'd like to review the Federal Government's almost accidental experience in supporting individual artists through its massive employment programs of the 1930s. Suffice it to say that blanket aid to individual artists—almost without regard to quality—directly led to New York City becoming the world art capital it is today. Job programs enabled Mark Rothko, Willem de Kooning, Jackson Pollock and many others to survive the Depression while practicing their art and developing as painters.
>
> Writers like Kenneth Rexroth, Saul Bellow, Ralph Ellison, Richard Wright, John Cheever and Conrad Aiken were also assisted. Uncle Sam, theatrical producer pro tem, presented Clifford Odets, John Houseman, Orson Welles and many more in plays by Clifford Odets, Shakespeare and Gilbert & Sullivan. But, like the brief federal patronage of the 19th century, this aid was an exception to the rule that prevailed for the better part of two centuries.

Hanks reported that "the spectrum of individuals who receive support is very broad but not all-inclusive," but stated that it was necessary to face up to a nebulous problem that "the aggregate effect of grants to individual artists is almost impossible to quantify." There was no consensus in America that artists should be accorded the same kind of help as scientists, because the nation needed their products. Creating that consensus was the challenge.

> We must also convince them of the truth underlying the statement that for an artist to create what society needs, he or she must be given the opportunity to try—which means the slim chance to succeed or the more likely chance of falling short of the mark. That is the gamble of backing pure creativity.
>
> There is yet another snag: what about the artist who receives no-strings-attached support and creates a work that triggers controversy? . . .
>
> Our critics and supporters need to understand that no single work—brilliant, bad or simply controversial, can be allowed to eclipse the broad purpose of fellowships. The programs cannot be tested against the criteria of instant success—or failure. The concept of encouraging individual creativity is the goal.
>
> But these problems can be solved—and are being solved—with good policies, effective procedures, professional expertise, a bit of courage, and a more than considerable amount of determination. I am convinced that with the help of foundations, arts councils and other organizations there can be a mosaic of support for individual, independent artists.
>
> Finally, I am convinced that such a mosaic of support must be created if the

> nation's cultural resources are to continue growing. I say that because of my conviction that *the cornerstone of any culture is the nurtured talent of its creative artists*, its individual creators. As Rudolf Serkin said, "A great symphony orchestra is an instrument made up of one hundred individual artists, directed by an individual artist, and playing music composed by an individual artist—even sometimes a live one." We must all find ways to support those live ones.[59]

Coordinated Residency Touring Program

Ever since its inception in the 1967–68 season, the Coordinated Residency Touring Program (CRTP) for dance had been increasingly successful. The first project had been a $25,000 matching grant to the Illinois Arts Council to involve four dance companies in an eight-week tour of six cities. The project went straight to the heart of the problem of dance as a performing art in the United States. There were brilliant young American dancers; there were a few companies to use their talents; there were occasional performances in New York City, often of a "studio" kind; there was almost no touring opportunity even for the best-known, "name" companies—and certainly none for unknown groups; most dancers were living marginally for the duration of what was, at best, a short professional career. The CRTP developed regional circuits of local sponsors through the cooperation of state arts agencies. Each local sponsor was required to engage at least two companies for half-a-week or more, during which time the dance company provided a variety of services, not only in performance but with master classes, workshops, lecture-demonstrations, and other related activities such as music and design workshops. The program grew steadily and, by its sixth season in 1973, it encompassed about 150 communities in 40 states and was involving 50 American dance companies.[60]

The "City" Programs in Architecture

In the Architecture+Environmental Arts program a national research effort, entitled "City Edges," was designated as a Bicentennial program by the National Council on the Arts. City Edges was announced as a new program by a handsome poster in browns and blues, featuring portions of maps which merged Los Angeles, San Diego, Chicago, St. Louis, Washington, D.C., Philadelphia, St. Paul and Minneapolis, Boston, New York, and other cities. The City Edges were defined as rivers, canals, lakes, oceans, freeways, streets, railways, urban transit corridors, forests, hillsides, mountains, valleys, city limits, zoning enclaves, economic and/or racial enclaves. "In ancient cities," the poster stated, "fortification walls established the limits of growth. The location and shape of our own cities were dictated by frontier towns located on rivers or at the intersection of overland trails. These city edges still exist. Some are old edges, neglected too long. Some are new edges growing out of contemporary needs and functions."[61]

The concept was imaginative and the activities of the program office were praised by Ada Louise Huxtable in the *New York Times* as "unusual . . . under any auspices or conditions, but under the weighty bureaucracy of administrative Washington . . . nothing less than miraculous for their creative and pertinent professionalism."[62]

Under this initial theme concept, 37 projects for redesign and planning of boundary areas were authorized. In an Architecture+Environmental Arts report, Nancy Hanks was quoted: "We felt that if we dramatized a single theme of widespread importance, then earmarked a substantial number of our funding dollars to implement it, we would stimulate some fresh thinking."

The report continues.

> Among the examples of "fresh thinking" rewarded with grants were a plan to study how development was eroding the "natural edges" of the Pine Barrens wilderness area in south central New Jersey; design of safe and functional pedestrian paths to protect citizens of Cambridge, Massachusetts, from the "time edge" of darkness in the city; and an investigation of how one of the least appreciated urban spaces—rooftops—could be used for cultural and recreational facilities.[63]

The program was so successful that another effort at "fresh thinking" was undertaken and the national theme moved from the outer edges to special settings within a city which provided distinctive character and identity. Ada Louise Huxtable had asked, "How does a city face what is really a massive socioesthetic catastrophe? How does it keep its individual quality and style against the onslaught of scaleless, quality-less, value-destroying, speculative construction that produces pedestrian lookalikes and disaffected citizens without pride of place or community? . . . How do you help cities to think about the problem and to devise answers; ways to exercise the 'city options' of style, quality and continuity that make a satisfying and identifiable place to live?"[64]

Out of such concerns "City Options" developed and became the largest of the environmental theme programs. More than 600 grant applications were received and a total of $3 million was distributed among 143 projects that included the following: a design of the immediate areas around the 40 stations being planned for the new Washington, D.C., subway system; a plan to preserve the character of Auburn Avenue in Atlanta, Georgia—the historic center for black culture and business; the development of a cultural, recreational, and commercial complex on the old Idaho Territorial Penitentiary property—a Boise landmark on the outskirts of town; and a plan to preserve the old Jamaica Avenue Elevated in New York City in an effort to tie together business and residential sections of Jamaica in the borough of Queens.[65]

City Options engendered broad interest from communities that saw it as a Bicentennial project which could affect the future environment. While only about 20 percent of the requests could be assisted with federal arts funds, "the local enthusiasm for these plans for community futures was so intense that in many cases good proposals found independent funding—an example of the Arts Endowment acting as a catalyst to create new partnerships between the public and private sector."[66]

Later on, there was a third national theme program—"Cityscale"—based on the belief that design of the small elements within communities, the signs, the plantings, the small parks, the lighting, street furniture, and paving, are important if a town or city is to be a liveable, human place. One of the projects funded under this program was the New Orleans "Fountains for the City," a study of water as a design element for improving the character of the Louis Armstrong Park project adjacent to the Old French Quarter.[67]

Council member Lawrence Halprin stated some years later that in the "City" programs,

> We were becoming more and more aware that the way to handle the environment was not through individual projects here and there, but to try to get those cities interested in their environment. It included the participation on the part of the city council people, the mayors, and others. What we were doing was saying, "Okay, we'll give you some grants and we'll help you along, but then you'll have to take some responsibility for what you do in your city yourself."

He added that there was one final program called City Spirit, which really exemplified that idea. "All of these seemed to me made a big impact."[68]

The Bicentennial

All through this period the pending bicentennial celebration of the United States had been looming large in Washington cocktail parties, if not in much hard planning. Perhaps the trauma of Watergate had soured the bicentennial celebration of the virtues of America. Whatever the reasons, the federal organization seemed always uncoordinated and really did not get under way until too late to be nationally effective. However, within the Council and among Endowment staff, discussions concerning the coordination of these intiatives began early, since many fell logically into the cultural realm. The Council appointed a Bicentennial Committee among its members, chaired by Robert Wise, the film producer and director. The committee recommended grants which would total approximately $13 million for projects for artists and cultural organizations that had a Bicentennial relationship. Such programs were concerned with recognizing and preserving the nation's cultural heritage, celebrating creativity in American life of the day, and expanding the cultural horizons for future generations. It was a broad brushstroke that emphasized the programming of the arts on television and the use of film in a cooperative program with the states to portray the cultural life of the country. Special development grants for the states were also established to hire staff to help the Bicentennial Committee plan a new approach to linking the arts to the people where they actually live—in their neighborhoods, towns, rural areas, regions. Out of this approach grew the concept of City Spirit.

Obviously, many of the ongoing programs of the Endowment fitted comfortably into the Bicentennial patterns. As the Chairman's statement in the *Annual Report 1974* stated:

- the jazz/folk ethnic music program was enlarged
- more than 100 composers, librettists and translators were given fellowships
- special grants were made to two groups of symphony orchestras to commission new works, each of which will be premiered by one of the orchestras, followed by performances eventually by every orchestra in each group
- a pilot series of summer "tour-events" was initiated in several sites through the country with community arts groups invited to take part in a three or four day festival
- projects in museum renovation and conservation were given special consideration reflecting the long look at our heritage which the bicentennial encourages
- many of the projects for special museum exhibitions and catalogues will be part of bicentennial activities. Already about 100 exhibitions are being supported, ranging from historical perspectives on folk arts and crafts to exploration of the art and architecture of the present day.[69]

Triennial Authorization

The authorizing legislation for the National Foundation for the Arts and the Humanities was due to expire June 30, 1973. Once again the agency would be up for review and the previous six months were a time of justification, hearings, and considerable backstage jockeying in Congress, where Representative Julia Butler Hansen of Washington—the 16th-ranking Democrat on the House Appropriations Committee—was vigorously counterattacking President Nixon's effort to hold spending to $250 billion in fiscal 1973. Representative Hansen was feuding with Secretary of Agriculture Earl Butz, the cabinet member in charge of natural resources, who had been involved in the impounding of forest service funds. Mrs. Hansen felt that the whole business was detrimental. She threatened to appropriate no money at all for fiscal year 1974, until all the 1973 funds appropriated by Congress but impounded by the President were released for spending.[70]

For the Arts Endowment, however, the joint Senate-House budget hearings on the Foundation in March, co-chaired by Senator Claiborne Pell (D.,RI) and Representative John Brademas (D.,IN), were fundamentally pleasant. *Newsweek* reviewed them:

> In a rare change of pace, Capitol Hill is currently witnessing some happy hearings. Testimony on behalf of a budget boost for the National Endowment for the Arts is not only getting a warm reception from Congress (including once-hostile conservatives), but the Nixon administration is actually requesting Congress to double current Federal spending on the arts from $38 million in fiscal '73 to $80 million in fiscal '74. Though much of the public remains unaware of it, the Federal government, in a break with long tradition, has become a grand patron of the arts.[71]

Ironically, the strong White House support concerned both Pell and Brademas. They pressed Nancy Hanks at the hearings firmly but apologetically on her increased budget in relation to what Brademas called "savage slashes" in health, welfare and domestic services. She fielded the questions with veteran composure. "It is not within my competence to determine whether existing social programs are reaching people they are intended for," she stated. "I can assure you Endowment grants are reaching people and the money is well spent."

Brademas and Pell were also apprehensive about the political implications of the Endowment's estimated allotment of $30 million for bicentennial programming, fearing that the White House might find political uses for the programs. "I don't want to see politics at either end of Pennsylvania Avenue in using arts funds," Brademas said.

Senator Pell also questioned whether Chairman Hanks might be left "fairly unprotected" from White House pressure if the current limitation on the chairman-authorized grants were to be raised from $10,000 to $25,000, as the Council was suggesting. He feared that it might free additional unsupervised funds for Bicentennial or potentially political program spending. In reply, Hanks stressed that the request to raise the chairman's funding level was administrative, to free the National Council on the Arts for more policy-making discussion time. She added that, in fact, the connection of the increased funding ceiling with Bicentennial programming had never crossed her mind.

The political irony of the situation of Pell and Brademas questioning the extent of the added funding for the Arts Endowment impressed the reporters of the period because the two men were the principal sponsors of the bill to extent the authorization of the National Foundation for the Arts and the Humanities for the next three years, with a funding authorization exceeding the administration request.[72]

The hearings to extend the authorization of the agency continued for several days, with a star-studded list of artists and arts administrators appearing in support of their various areas.

Council member Beverly Sills reported that operas were performing before standing-room-only audiences and still operating on a deficit. Without federal aid, she felt, opera in America would collapse. "With the tax structure as it is, the day of the dowager and her pearls single-strandedly supporting an opera company is over."

Representative Brademas asked Kurt Adler, general director of the San Francisco Opera Association, if his organization received any aid from the state of California. When Adler replied that regretfully it did not, Brademas called it scandalous. "Yours is considered the richest state and you have a performer for governor [Ronald Reagan]. I have a hard time understanding why there is so little sensitivity, so little political leadership in the state to help the arts."

The venerable former New York representative, Emanuel Cellar, came out of retirement to pay tribute to opera at the hearings. "In a way, I was weaned on music and opera," he said, and added he had attended the Metropolitan Opera in New York for several decades. He felt the national priorities were illogical. "We pledge $1 billion to protect investors against losses from Wall Street purchases. But we are niggardly when it comes to supporting the art forms."[73]

Joseph Papp, producer of the New York Shakespeare Company, testified in favor of the bill's extention and added that he felt that certain "landmark theaters" should be subsidized on a continuing basis by the government. He specifically suggested that Washington's Arena Stage, New York's Negro Ensemble Company, New York's Lincoln Center Theater, and the Tyrone Guthrie Theater in Minneapolis should be funded.

Robert Hooks, director and producer of the Black Repertory and the Last Colony Theater in Washington, spoke as one of the black artists who, he felt, "have been largely ignored and excluded. There's never been an honest attempt to enter blacks truly into the mainstream of TV, films, theatre. The black artist is often in the corner and has no real outlet. The National Endowment," he pointed out, "came to the rescue of many black artists' attempts to do something worthwhile. Their help has been generous but limited and I've always felt they wanted to help more than they were able to."

Playwright Edward Albee felt that the theatre tastes of the country are still formed by what happens in commerical theatre. "Commercial theatre needs subsidy," he said. Thomas Fichandler at Washington's Arena Stage felt that his theatre "might well cease to exist" if there were not significant help from the Arts Endowment.[74]

Film actor Charlton Heston, a former member of the National Council, asked for increased funds for both the Arts Endowment and the American Film Institute, of which he was board chairman. "Of all the arts, the one most significantly of our time and our nation is film," he stated. He was concerned that the federal allotment for the Film Institute was dropping from what had been 10 percent of the Endowment moneys in 1968–70 to 6.8 percent for 1972. George Stevens Jr., director of the American Film Institute, and Jack Valenti, president of the Motion Picture Association of America, also urged more generous funding.

But film critic Pauline Kael warned against putting "all our eggs in one basket" because she felt that "the old Hollywood system of movie-making is dead." However, her enthusiasm for the current season was unbounded and she was certain an aesthetic revolution lay ahead.[75]

Senator Pell asked his routine question on how the decision on grants to painters and sculptors were divided between abstraction and realism. Brian O'Doherty, program director for the visual arts, gave a masterful response:

> Gradations in realism: 12 grants to the "frankly realistic" school in which there is "no doubt" of what is being seen; 14 grants to "recognizable subject matter" with modifications of fantasy and wit; four grants to "metaphorical," "elusive," "very indirect" interpretations; and nine grants to subject matter from everyday life—like ropes, street salvage, nails and the like.

O'Doherty added that the giving of 39 grants out of 65 to these modes of painting and sculpture was a reflection of the revival of realistic styles.[76]

At the final meeting of the House Select Subcommitte on Education, chaired by Brademas and held in New York City at the New York Cultural Center, three national leaders in the funding for the arts were heard from.

W. McNeil Lowry, vice president for the humanities and the arts for the Ford Foundation, spoke about the Ford study scheduled for fall release which would indicate that expenditures for the country's performing arts institutions had risen more than two-thirds in the six years leading to 1970–71, with more increases predicted. "The question is, how long private sources can and will continue [their support] at this rate."

G. A. McLellan, president of the Business Committee for the Arts, praised the Arts Endowment matching fund provisions which he felt stimulated support. Amyas Ames, chairman of Lincoln Center for the Performing Arts and of Partnership for the Arts (a national fund-raising lobby), said the Partnership was one of the first organizations to propose a $200 million annual federal budget for the arts by 1976. He deplored the nation's double standard that always seemed to find extra funds for highways, fighter planes and moonshots; "but," he added, "we do not want the government to take over the arts, we do not want bureaucracy to deprive us of excellence."[77]

Five or six weeks later, Senator William Proxmire of Wisconsin introduced an amendment to S.795, the bill being sponsored by Senators Pell and Javits to authorize the funding for the next three years of the Arts Endowment: $80 million for fiscal 1974, $140 million for fiscal 1975, and $200 million for the Bicentennial year of 1976. Senator Proxmire took issue with this funding. He claimed that the amount was too much money, given too fast to be spent efficiently. He felt that such abundance would produce stale, sterile, and second-rate art; and he felt that there was a "great danger" that "we will get a government takeover of the arts in this country. That means the dead hand of government and the dead hand of censorship over art."[78] Harold C. Schonberg in the *New York Times* characterized this reasoning as nonsense and proceeded to attack Proxmire's arguments.

> In reality, S.795 is not a giveaway. It is, rather, a pump-priming project intended to keep a certain sector of American industry going—and the word "industry" is used advisedly . . . . Let others talk about art; I'm talking about economics. For the sum total of the American cultural apparatus is, in dollars and cents, a damn sight more valuable than the total assets of many corporations that the Government rushes to bail out when they have mismanaged themselves and then come whining to Papa for help. Waving the banner of free enterprise, of course. Write your congressman and senators. Try to get the Proxmire amendment knocked back to the Middle Ages, where it belongs.[79]

Other voices were heard supporting the agency. One was that of Michigan's Representative Gerald R. Ford, the House minority leader, who had originally opposed the creation of the Foundation in 1965. He became converted, he confessed, when his hometown of Grand Rapids purchased an Alexander Calder sculpture with the help of a matching grant from the Arts Endowment. The piece was installed downtown in an urban renewal area. He commented:

> At the time I did not know what a Calder was. I doubt if many people here do today. It was somewhat shocking to a lot of our people out home. I must say that I did not really understand, and I do not today, what Mr. Calder was trying to tell us. But I can assure the members that Calder in the center of the city, in an urban redevelopment area, has really helped to regenerate a city . . . . The federal arts and humanities program was a participant and it was a good investment both locally and federally.[80]

When the vote came, two crippling amendments were rejected and the authorization for $145 million for fiscal 1974 was voted 309 to 63. The vote came the day after the President had called for a renewed battle against inflation and other vital programs were being cut back. It was a victory that would have to be fought again when the arts came up for actual appropriation—indeed, the ultimate total for the Foundation was reached at $111,775,000, with $60,775,000 of that sum for the arts. But in April 1973 the congressional and national support filled the members of the staff and the National Council with confidence that their efforts were bearing a positive return.

Another Office Move

"For the fourth time in the past six years, we are moving!" began a memorandum from the Chairman to the Arts Endowment staff on August 25, 1973. The move was scheduled to take place over Labor Day weekend. No one was particularly happy about the shift to the McPherson building. The Shoreham offices had been an attractive space, if very confining, in an old buiding with some atmosphere. The new quarters offered "standard government" space with fluorescent lighting and little atmosphere. "We have attempted to take this type of space and make it congenial without spending much money because we don't know how long we'll be there. (Long enough to unpack, however!)," the memo continued.

Another problem developed in the McPherson building before the Endowment staff could settle in. The special prosecutor for the Watergate hearings, Leon Jaworski, and his staff were suddenly added to the bureaucratic broth of Washington. Space for their offices was carved out of the allocated space for the Arts Endowment, squeezing what had been barely adequate footage into totally inadequate quarters for the agency. None of the program office units could be left behind in the Shoreham building because the expanding Humanities Endowment had already spoken for the office areas. For months to come it was a difficult work situation, not alleviated until the agency was able to move into the several floors of sunny new office space in Columbia Plaza.

Nancy Hanks Reappointed to Chairmanship

On September 14, 1973, President Nixon reappointed Nancy Hanks as chairman of the National Endowment for the Arts. The President signed the reappointment certificate in a short ceremony in the White House Oval Office while various members of the Council, then in session in Washington, looked on. The spectators included Rosalind Russell, Billy Taylor, Jamie Wyeth, and Robert Merrill. President Nixon pointed out in his announcement of the appointment that in the past four years the Endowment had proved convincingly its capacity to serve the nation, and a "firm partnership" had been created between the Endowment and cultural organizations in the country. He took amused note of the fact that funding for the agency had increased by 900 percent since 1970 and said to Miss Hanks, "That's why we are reappointing you here. I don't want anything else increased by that amount!"[81]

The budget at that date was before the conference committee, endeavoring to adjust the President's request for $72.5 million for the Arts Endowment with the House authorization of $65.8 million and the Senate authorization of $53.7 million. Ultimately the authorization for fiscal 1974 was set at $60,775,000, almost twice that of the preceding year.

With the chairman reaffirmed, the National Council members went back into session at the September 1973 meeting and came up with a number of new initiatives and ways of taking new leadership. One of these was the unanimously adopted resolution that attention be given by the Endowment to encourage institutions to make their cultural activities accessible to the physically handicapped—an initiative that was developing throughout the federal funding at the time, although the Council pointed out that it reflected one of the agency's main goals to make the arts more available to more Americans.[82] Council member Jamie Wyeth introduced the resolution with the explanation that he knew the problem well because his wife was obliged to use crutches.

Obscenity Ruling

At that same September 1973 meeting, the Council, operating as one member put it "as the country's conscience on the arts," called on artists and arts groups to take an active role in any response to the recent Supreme Court decision on obscenity at the local level, and to make certain that "valid artistic and creative freedoms are not restricted or curtailed."[83] The obscenity decision, issued in June by the Supreme Court, essentially left judgment on what constituted obscenity to community standards, thereby establishing a principle of local option. Some of the members of the National Council were concerned about the decision and its effect on local creativity, but how to handle this concern posed problems. The general counsel, Robert Wade, was quoted. "The council doesn't want to be put in the position of defending obscenity. It does want to issue a statement without delay to express its concern for the possible effects at a local level on artistic creativity and freedom."

The Council directed the Endowment staff (principally deputy Michael Straight and counsel Robert Wade) to redraft more concisely the statement originally proposed at the previous July Council meeting held in Denver, where film producer Robert Wise had suggested the need for the resolution. Wise agreed that he, like most others in the arts, had been concerned with the Supreme Court decision:

> Not as a member of the arts council but as president of the Directors' Guild of America. I am helping to form committees on both coasts to look at it and see how we can get a clarification. The Supreme Court's ruling could create a chaotic and explosive situation. It has already been inhibiting to the movie arts. It could affect all media.

Another council member, Attorney Charles McWhorter, cometimes known as one of President Nixon's "unofficial lieutenants," also urged the Council at the open session to take new leadership in the arts. He was quoted in the *Washington Post* as saying, "I would like the bad guys in the country to be afraid to do anything they shouldn't in the arts because they know the Endowment wouldn't let them get by with it." McWhorter, on weekdays, went about his business in pinstripe suits. At Council meetings he frequently appeared in serapes and beads, the only Council member in a decade who ever appeared in costume.

The new leadership role that McWhorter and the Council were advocating also urged the initiation of programs, the offering of technical assistance, and the expression of opinions on artistic matters. Nancy Hanks agreed to try to produce an agenda that might provide such leadership but warned the Council that it was a departure from the agency's established, responsive partnership role, could cause controversy, and might make it necessary to enlarge the staff.

The agency itself was becoming increasingly more visible to the artists and arts organizations of the nation and its work was exploding. Phone calls, letters, and applications poured in, many of them showing a good understanding of the effort to build a partnership between the federal agency and the local and state organizations. Applications more than doubled from 6,000 to 14,000. In the Office of Program Information at the end of June 1974, 1,800 phone calls a month were being logged in and about 360 letters of inquiry. A new "Guide to Programs" was developed. An information folder was prepared about the Arts Endowment called *What It Is—What It Does*. The folder was translated first into Spanish and later into French, German, and Japanese for use with foreign visitors and for overseas information packets. The *Annual Reports*, largely edited by Ann Guthrie, were increasing in complexity and new efforts had to be made each year to keep them manageable in size.[84]

Museum Report

Following up on the earlier work of the *Belmont Report*, the National Council had directed the Endowment staff to commission a study from the National Research Center for the Arts on the financial state of American museums. The results were documented in a major survey report, a publication called *Museums USA*, and a summary pamphlet released in November 1973 entitled *Museums USA: Highlights*. More than 1,800 art, science, and history museums were reviewed and the results provided a solid basis for the developing Museum Program within the Endowment.[85]

There were other initiatives during this burgeoning period of the early Seventies, when enthusiasm for the arts, awareness of the environment, and concern for human needs was being met by the implementing tool of an increased federal budget. For example, a Folk Arts program headed by Alan Jabbour was begun to assist living American traditional arts, while the support for crafts projects and for craftsmen was expanded, under Sandra Zimmerman and, later, Elena Canavier.

The national energy crisis of the winter of 1973–74 impacted on the Endowment, too. The Chairman assigned the director of Special Projects, Stephen Sell, to the job of coordinating energy policy matters and working with the Federal Energy Office. (Later, Larry Reger took on the task.) The effort was to help resolve crucial questions for arts institutions, particularly those concerned with transporting students to cultural educational programs.

The Council discussed a related energy problem—the use of existing heated and lighted spaces for performing arts groups of small size. The idea was that such groups could appear more widely in parks, factories, hospitals, shopping malls, churches, community centers, and similar areas where people are already congregating during both day and evening hours. It was an idea that Affiliate Artists had launched successfully some years before and the energy utilization component gave it new appeal.

The Staff Expands

Increasing budgets and new national pressures for assistance made it necessary to expand the program staff in the early seventies. Assistant directors were appointed to several program offices, with David Ryan coming to the Museum Program, David Hawkinson to Special Projects, Richard Koshalek (and, later, Roy Knight) to Visual Arts, and Donald Dillon and Phillip Hyde to the Federal–State Partnership Program. William Weld was appointed Bicentennial coordinator, followed later by Carl Stover. In the office of Performing Arts and Public Media, Polly Buck replaced Norman Fagan. Joseph Krakora followed Don S. Anderson in the Dance Program.

Challenge Grants Develop

For about two years the Chairman, with Larry Reger and other staff members, plus Council members and advisors around the country, had been working on the idea of a special challenge grant to major cultural institutions to start them thinking in longer terms than the yearly budget. The concept was based on the Treasury grant program of private matching funds, engendered by the grant from the Endowment. The private funds were expected to greatly exceed the federal input whose chief function was always catalytic. Application information put out by the Arts Endowment emphasized that the challenge grant program was "to secure new and increased sources of continuing income."[86]

The concept of the Ford Foundation cash reserve fund had been a start in this general direction for beleaguered cultural institutions of the early Seventies and had been designed to help such institutions build long-term endowments and substantially raise their capital for permanent, ongoing activity. With the advent of the Endowment's challenge grant program, there was additional reason for well-developed cultural institutions of the nation to take advantage of this kind of financial opportunity.

In recalling the evolution of the challenge grant program some years later, Nancy Hanks said, "I'm very proud of it. There is no way in the world a challenge grant program would have been suitable in 1965 when Roger started the Endowment or in 1969 when I came in." She explained that few institutions had had the courage to think beyond the budget problems of the current years or at best the next year's performances. Their pressing needs had always been for current support and development, a continuing treadmill.

By the early Seventies, Hanks and her advisors felt, however, that some of the major cultural institutions had reached a point of organizational maturity, "where they could start thinking of themselves as stable institutions in a community, like hospitals and universities." The program Hanks and her advisors provided "worked out far better than many people thought it would," but, she said, "I never had any question. I thought that if people were challenged to give to their institutions for a longer period than one year that they would." It was an old fund-raising concept, but new for the Endowment.

As always, Nancy Hanks did her homework well, and went about convincing the people she needed for help about the workability of the program before announcing it. "Vice-President Rockefeller picked it up in five minutes and he saw President Ford the next day. In effect, President Ford told him, 'Now, you're only going to be in town a short while. This is good; this is exactly the kind of thing I would like to see done!' And therefore it went through the administration in a matter of a few days."

Hanks and her staff had also been working on the idea with members of Congress and their aides.

> Congressional associates took a great deal of credit for it, as indeed they should, because they got it through [Congress]. To me, that was an interesting aspect of the Endowment and showed how the process worked. We had gotten to a particular point where an idea that couldn't have done anything years before was workable. It was a *beauty* of a program. The purpose was to say to a community, "This institution is as important as any other stable institution you've got, and by gum, you've got to march up and meet it by challenge."[87]

In the 1973–74 season, covered by the 1974 *Annual Report*, individual and private foundation support was increasing nationally in spite of inflation and tight money. The Treasury Fund was matched that fiscal year by private sector donations of $6.5 million and racked up the largest number of individual donations received to date—19,165 out of a total of 19,950.[88]

In the late winter of 1974 the challenge grant concept, still in its evolutionary stages, received its first dramatic test when the Metropolitan Opera turned to the Arts Endowment for special assistance. "For progress, not for bailing out," as Schuyler Chapin, the general manager, explained it.

The National Council authorized a $1 million grant for a two-year period to be matched by an equal sum in private contributions. Nancy Hanks and Schuyler Chapin went on the air for the Saturday afternoon "Met" radio broadcast of *The Barber of Seville* in March to announce the grant and call for contributions to boost the opera's fund drive, which was already under way.[89]

Their plea for assistance touched a national chord. Money poured in from more than 21,000 individuals, ranging from a few dollars to thousands, in a heartwarming expression of interest and concern for one of the nation's great cultural institutions. Every state and three of the special jurisdictions was represented in the gifts, and the combined generosity amounted to over $1,100,000, more than matching the challenge.[90] The success of the venture prompted Hanks to stress again her oft-stated principle of action that the way to strengthen cultural institutions is to broaden the base of support at the grass-roots level, a kind of support which government should encourage, but always as a "junior partner." Years before, Arthur Goldberg had urged this cooperative sharing of responsibility at the time of the settlement of the 1961 Metropolitan Opera strike.

In her broadcast statement, Nancy Hanks reminded the estimated seven million listeners that "if they have only a dollar to send, that dollar is as important as someone else's $10,000 or $100,000.[91]

Schuyler Chapin commented years later that "the first million dollar challenge grant to the Metropolitan Opera . . . was of major importance . . . . [It] had a tremendous impact both on the Metropolitan's fund-raising ability and, I believe, was equally helpful to the Endowment in demonstrating a national constituency for overall arts support."[92]

Shortly after the Metropolitan Opera challenge announcement, Nancy Hanks became seriously ill and was out of the office for an extended period, recovering at the Harkness Pavilion in New York where Duke Ellington, another Council member, was hospitalized on the same floor.

Because it was time again for subcommittee hearings in Congress on the Endowment budget, deputy chairman Michael Straight and other staff members had to carry the campaign. But Congress was very supportive. Senator Alan Bible from Nevada commented to Straight at the conclusion of the hearings, "Urge her to get back, pounding on our doors. We'll be here. She'll probably take advantage of her absence and want twice as much!" [93] The enthusiastic congressional support continued. For the fiscal year 1975 (authorized in 1974), program funds of $67,260,000 were approved, which included at least 20 percent for the state arts agencies and regional groups, plus funds to match private donations in the amount of $7.5 million. The total for the year came to $74,750,000.

Growth Brings Problems

The growing burden of applications, public recognition, and public demands on the time of the staff began to take a toll from the creative and freewheeling agency. Staff members were still coming in on Saturdays and working late at night, but there seemed to be less opportunity to deal with applications and problems in a human way as the application pressures grew. In the early years of the Endowment there had been a feeling among staff members that somehow they were different from other federal employees, not really a part of a rolled-out, cookie-cutter bureaucratic staff, carrying out guidelines and processing authorizations. For a long time, the homogenizing effect of the federal government was kept at arm's length. Brian O'Doherty wore his fringed jacket to work and continued his painting career; Leonard Randolph wrote notes of personal encouragement to poets and worried over the survival problems of small presses in the country. Walter Anderson maintained his office piano and played for staff get-togethers. Ruth Mayleas lived in New York and commuted back and forth to Washington, rather than living in the capital. When the National Council came to town, the Council's secretary, Luna Diamond, at the Chairman's behest, put together a rush of luncheons, cocktail parties, dinners, and special programs at the John F. Kennedy Center or the Corcoran Gallery, or the Phillips Collection. The Council members had barely time enough to glance through the three-inch thick Council books, sipping a cup of coffee which Mrs. Diamond also provided along with enormous good will, before they were rushed into discussion and action around the Council room table in the downstairs meeting room of the Shoreham building, or at one of the hotel conference rooms. The Council was always presented with a bounty of achievements to savor. The arts in America were flourishing and the catalytic influence of the Endowment was having a national impact.

In a prepared statement for the 1974 subcommittee hearings, Hanks had written:

> The National Endowment for the Arts—and the arts themselves—are caught up today in a paradox. How we handle it—we, the Endowment, the arts community, and the country at large—will greatly affect the creative life of our children and their children. The paradox is that the arts are at the same time threatened and flourishing in America.
>
> We must be concerned that so many of our people lack opportunity for enriching experience in the arts; that so many talented artists must choose between using their talents and supporting their families; that so many of our great orchestras, dance, opera and theatre companies and museums live on the edge of financial insolvency from year to year; that, for a variety of basically economic reasons, the humanizing effects of the arts do not reach far enough into areas of our national life where they are needed and wanted.
>
> The other side of the paradox is that, in so many ways, the arts are advancing brilliantly in this country today. American creativity in dance, music, theatre, painting, sculpture, photography, film, crafts, literature, and architecture is recognized around the world. And, despite continuing obstacles, the arts are being more broadly shared by more Americans every year. Individual creativity is high on our national scale of values, and the arts are being seen not as a frill but as an essential element in the truly good life.[94]

All of this expansion and good will created new problems, however. When Nancy Hanks returned to Washington after her illness, she was faced with almost uncontrollable growth, proliferating projects, enlarged budgets, and increasing demands. She tried to respond to the agency's new needs by hiring additional staff to carry the burden of increasing bureacracy but her lack of experience in dealing with a large staff became evident. In many ways the attempts were frustrating for all. Government grantsmanship problems grew exponentially. The efforts of bureacratic managers to line up the program directors in some sort of uniform approach to the problems were resented and resisted—especially by men and women who had been part of the agency since its early years and had helped give it the creative vigor that was now contributing to its problems. Some program directors objected to a layer of management interposed between them and the chairman and longed for the more elastic days of the past when programming decisions did not depend on administrative guidelines. And the new management staff members found that, in actuality, little real power was given them. It remained firmly with the chairman and a handful of close associates who still devoted frantic extra efforts in the early mornings, nights, and weekends to the daily tasks.

Watergate Surprises

In Washington, the summer of 1974 was a daily headline revelation, as the findings of the Watergate investigation took over every other activity. However, the Arts Endowment was not greatly affected, although one of the revelations glanced off the agency. It was a statement from a Nixon tape of a 1972 conversation in which the Prèsident had commented that his daughter, Tricia Cox, should avoid "anything that has to do with the arts because they're Jews, they're left-wing."

Senator Jacob K. Javits termed the comment "extremely distasteful," but went on to say, "In all fairness, he has done more for the national arts foundation than any other President, but I find this reference in the transcript terribly disheartening. Obviously, he has mental associations that are highly distasteful. I can't explain it. I must say," he added, "this isn't the only thing I can't explain."

Arts officials around the country took more or less the same position—a puzzled reaction. As Louis Sudler, chairman of the Chicago Symphony Orchestra, put it, "His actions belie his words."[95]

Nancy Hanks wrote her own statement and released it throughout the agency and to the press when it called:

> Miss Hanks has no prepared statement. She has been concerned through the day with budgets, space planning, and other program commitments. She assumes that the President's and his family's support of the arts and enjoyment of them through the years speaks more to the point than the words in the transcript.[96]

Ford Supports Council's First Decade

A few days later, on August 9, 1974, Gerald R. Ford became President of the United States and Washington shifted gears. One of the first special events of the new administration was the tenth-anniversary celebration of the creation of the National Council on the Arts, beginning on September 3, 1974. The Council held open sessions, reviewed its past endeavors and principles of action as an advisory body, and looked at the changes that had taken place in the country in relation to its cultural life. Roger Stevens and other past members of the Council joined Nancy Hanks at the Council table in the Sheraton-Carlton meeting room. The mood was one of warm satisfaction for a task accomplished by the Council—that of helping to gain national public acceptance for the arts.

Michael Straight recalled earlier attitudes when he commented that "Artists are basically anti-political and the government was regarded as the Philistines who would foster all kinds of mediocrity." But, as Nancy Hanks pointed out in her remarks to the Council, a change in this attitude had taken place, due to the fierce independence which the Council members had maintained since the first group was appointed. "One sees," she commented about the ten-year period, "threaded throughout an equal commitment to diversity, a belief in the importance of individual creativity, yet a deep concern about the cultural institutions of the nation . . . a respect for the political process coupled with a determination that its activities and those of the Endowment must be nonpolitical."

A new group of Council members was announced at the meeting, including Angus L. Bowmer, Van Cliburn, Jerome Robbins, Thomas Schippers, Gunther Schuller, George C. Seybolt, Harry M. Weese, and Delores Wharton.

The Council's Bicentennial Committee announced recommendations for a variety of new endeavors to highlight the arts in the coming celebration: the publication of a newsletter from the Program Information Office to be called *The Cultural Post;* a media program of films highlighting the state and national picture in the arts; plans for grassroots community arts activities; and other projects, including "City Spirit" which jazz pianist and Council member Billy Taylor thought could help bring together all the artistic elements of a community. As always, when the Bicentennial was discussed, there was some concern expressed. Former Council member R. Philip Hanes, Jr., questioned whether the Council committee's efforts might become associated with the official government committee's record of activity, which he felt had not been outstanding. Nevertheless, the Council voted to approve the recommendations of the Bicentennial Committee "in principle."[97]

The anniversary Council meeting, like others, was accompanied by lively social events. On this occasion there was a reception at the Kennedy Center before the new musical presentation, *Mack and Mabel,* where President and Mrs. Ford joined the past and present Council members and many of the Endowment staff to herald the cultural accomplishments of the Council since 1964. "I'm a converted individual," the President explained again as he genially shook hands with everyone. "But I don't apologize. Converts are known sometimes as better advocates than those brought up in the religion."[98]

The *New York Times* picked up Ford's comments and supported his promise "to do infinitely better" for the program. "The record of growth has been steady up to now," the editorial stated, "and the National Endowment for the Arts has distributed its funds with greater imagination than its parallel agency, the National Endowment for the Humanities, which has been overly timid and traditional. Congress authorized $100 million for the arts last year, a sum now reduced to $74.7 million. Considering that his money must be divided among hundreds of dance, theater, and musical organizations and museums all over the United States, it is barely enough to keep the house lights on and the artists performing. State, city and private aid cannot let up in the essential effort to foster innovation in the performing arts."[99]

In late October, Deputy Chairman Michael Straight wrote a long article for the new "Arts and Leisure" section of the *New York Times*, taking a considered look at the state of publicly supported arts after the wrenching traumas of the Vietnam War and Watergate.[100] He pointed out that America's artists were reaching out for wider audiences, larger roles, and more participation in the whole society. "The conclusion of the agonizingly long war in Vietnam and of the trial of a President, now seem to offer the promise of an increase in creativity that interlocks with social concern." He wrote that architects were once again committed to city planning, that opera companies and symphony orchestras were performing in public parks during the summertime, that dance companies which once had rarely left New York City were now enabled to tour the United States, giving performances, master classes, and school demonstrations. He mentioned the 1500 poets who were encouraging youngsters in classrooms all over the country under the Artists-in-Schools program, plus the hundreds of filmmakers, actors, craftsmen, folk singers, and others involved in the same classroom program which both encouraged creativity in youngsters and a sense of the artist's worth in himself.

He described how the Western Opera Company, an affiliate of the San Francisco Opera, had toured Alaska and visited 16 communities with *La Traviata* and *The Barber of Seville*, including the Eskimo village of Kivalina with a population of 188 people. He mentioned the Guthrie Theatre of Minneapolis touring the northern plains states with *Tartuffe*, and the chamber musicians under the auspices of Young Audiences playing Mozart and Bartok in 12,000 classrooms. "When the Ontological-Hysteric Theater applies for funding, no government bureaucrat is heard muttering that its productions are too esoteric," he stated.

Straight continued to make his point that the claim of each participant in the Endowment's grants program was strengthened by others. "None of these institutions sees any of the others as rivals in securing its share of a fixed sum in Federal patronage." He singled out a few to make his point more graphic—direct support to "The American Shakespeare Theater in Stratford, Connecticut, and to the Cell Block Theater in New York City; to the Metropolitan Museum and to the Norwegian-American Museum in Decorah, Iowa; to the Juilliard School and to the Harlem School of the Arts; to the Metropolitan Opera and the Mississippi Opera; to the Boston Symphony and the Kalamazoo Symphony; to the New York City Ballet and to the Chuck Davis Dance Company in the Bronx; to the Philadelphia Composers Forum and the Electric Stereopticon in DeKalb, Illinois." Each of these grantees, he explained, "is considered and supported in its own social context. But quality in performance remains a central criterion to the panels of professionals who make artistic judgments for the Endowment."

Straight added that while, in the past, artists had been concerned that federal assistance might lead to stifling of creativity or political control, the danger no longer seemed threatening. Of more concern, he felt, was the very real and present danger that "private supporters—the foundations, the corporations and individuals—will conclude that the financial future of the arts is secure and will cut back their contributions." Such an occurrence, Straight thought, would undermine the central premise of the government aid to the arts and all the arts would suffer in consequence, since government support was a relatively small proportion of the total financial assistance to the field. He continued, "The Endowment currently contributes 15 to 40 percent to the budget of small theater, dance and opera companies that are of national significance. In contrast, its grants amount to only two cents in every dollar spent by the Boston Symphony; four cents in every dollar spent by the Metropolitan Opera Company; roughly a half cent spent in every dollar by the Art Institute of Chicago; eight cents in every dollar spent by the American Ballet Theatre; and one cent in every dollar spent in operating the Metropolitan Museum." Private philanthropy, he underscored, was still the main source of revenue for these national treasures.

Should private philanthropy falter and government aid have to come to the rescue, Straight felt, the arts would face difficult times in which these national treasures would become rivals. "Should this happen," he concluded, "the best hope for the arts will still center, not in a static approach that seeks to balance the books of a few major institutions, but one in which the objective is to raise the general level of esthetic awareness in the nation and, thus, to create a society within which the great artists of the future may grow."

Growing State and Community Arts Agencies

In this period of the early 1970s, both the state arts agencies and the community arts agencies were growing vigorously. With this growth came the inevitable consequence of a desire to handle more of their own affairs, of dissatisfaction with the system of federal assistance as it was then organized,* and the

*The legislation had been amended to stipulate that 20 percent of the agency's appropriation (excluding the Treasury Fund) was to be directed to state arts agency efforts, while 75 percent of the 20 percent was to go to the 50 states and five jurisdictions in "bloc" amounts with a minimum of $200,000 available to each agency.

pressing need for more funding to support the exploding arts activities all over the country.

In early July 1973, William Nemoyten, chairman of the National Assembly of Community Arts Agencies, sent a memorandum to his constituents through the Associated Councils of the Arts in which he told them that the NACAA executive committee had approved a resolution earlier in the year that was sent to the Arts Endowment, "calling for its adoption of a more substantial program of support for community arts agencies." The memorandum continued, "There is no doubt that the receipt of a quantity of applications from community arts councils should in the long term act as a spur to the Endowment in the provision of more substantial and specific funding for community councils like ours."[101]

While neither Chairman Hanks nor the directors of the state arts agencies were enthusiastic about direct funding of community agencies by the federal government, the chairman nevertheless agreed that the Nemoyten proposal for stepping up the volume of requests might be a good idea and she directed the Federal-State Program director, Clark Mitze, to draft a letter for her indicating her approval. She also encouraged the Program Information Officer to consider an information bulletin for the communities.[102]

The following year the brewing problems and misunderstandings among the federal, state, and community arts agencies became more critical. The Federal–State Program office held its fall panel meeting in Columbia, South Carolina, November 6–8, 1974. The meetings were conducted in the State Arts Commission headquarters—an old, charmingly restored house that had been purchased by the state for the commission's use through the efforts of the governor. In the evening there was a dinner at the governor's mansion and the Arts Commission presented him with a gift in appreciation for his support. Nancy Hanks was in attendance and spoke briefly after the commission chairman, Terrell Glenn, made the presentation. On the face of it, the program was friendly and hospitable.

However, there was a strong undercurrent of unrest and dissatisfaction which surfaced in the daytime meetings in resentful comments. There were complaints about "partnership" as a euphemism for federal control, about the difficulty for the states to fulfill some of the partnership requests, not for lack of desire but from sheer inability. There were complaints about breakdowns in communication, about publications such as program guidelines arriving too late to give adequate planning time; about the purposes of the "program development" grants; about the problems of Artists-in-Schools; about the need for uniform accounting procedures; about too little and too much flexibility; about funding assignments and artists' needs; about a "defective" budget procedure and the need to put certain funding supports into the individual program budget areas rather than taking them from the Federal-State budget allotments; and tensions between what constituted a "national" program, and therefore a national responsibility, and what was more properly a state responsibility. There was even a somewhat overheated motion to ask the Endowment chairman to urge Council members to attend the Federal-State panel meetings. The South Carolina Council member, Henry Cauthen, felt that an aggressive effort to do so should be made.[103]

It was obvious that the whole relationship between the federal and state program was under stress. The state agencies were no longer as dependent on federal block grants, which had done their job of stimulating state legislated money for the agencies. There seemed to be an almost adolescent jockeying for power and effort to throw off the federal yoke.

The Arts Endowment staff had not been unaware of the unrest. The Federal–State office staff brought a series of position papers[104] to the South Carolina meeting and indicated its willingness to enter into discussions about future approaches.

At that date the basic grant for the state agencies was set by law at 15 percent of the Arts Endowment program funds to be allotted in equal amounts to the 55 state arts agencies, but requirements were quite vague. In the nine-year history of the awards there had been little effort to influence the states' applications. In fiscal year 1975 there had been, however, three states whose applications were viewed with enough concern by the staff and the program panel to be returned for some specific changes. "This trend . . . of helping each state improve its administrative and programming abilities" must continue, the position paper stated.

There was a suggestion made for an earlier application date for the basic state grant, with an opportunity for meetings and discussions with several states in a region, plus the Federal–State staff, the regional coordinator, and any others concerned. There was also a proposal to discuss the several Endowment programs being run by the states (Artists-in-Schools, Dance Touring, Program Development Community Assistance) and the advisability of their being added to the basic state application.

There was a proposal to work out an accounting system through which the states would be able to process cash requests through a local certified bank. There was a frank statement that the Program Development project, which evolved in the summer and fall of 1973 to help states and regional organizations alleviate staff shortages and move into new program areas, had been put together without input from the Federal–State panel. The original proposal had stated:

> The demands on state and regional arts agencies to provide professional leadership and assistance are increasing. It is therefore the objective of the Endowment during the next several years to provide the means of strengthening state and regional arts agency program development efforts, particularly in the areas of bicentennial programming, a variety of state-initiated programs, and the coordination of Federal-State programs such as Dance Touring and Artists-in-Schools. To reach this objective the Endowment initiated a program in fiscal 1974 to assist the states in the addition of professional staff.
>
> The Endowment will respond to individual state or regional arts agency proposals

> for professional staff for programming in cases where the positions cannot be immediately funded from state or regional resources. While the scope and mix of the program development activity may vary, *its central character must be professional effort in developing or strengthening* specific programs. In general, activities such as public relations, grants-processing, and general office administration will not be funded.
>
> One individual could serve more than one program field, if qualified to do so. Nonprofessional support resources may also be granted in terms of limited secretarial help and travel directly related to the program development staff; however, the majority of the funds are to be expended for the salary of the professional programming person(s).
>
> It is anticipated that for fiscal 1975 grants will be made *up to* $20,000 including Dance Touring coordination.* Grants will most often be for lesser amounts.† It is anticipated that the grant level will remain the same in fiscal 1976.
>
> State arts agencies should particularly note that this "Program Development" category falls within what has been noted as amounts available to the Endowment for making "other grants to state and regional groups." As a result of Congressional action, *all* grants under this provision must be made on a one-for-one matching basis. *However,* if monies for program development are essential and matching funding is impossible, the National Council on the Arts has recommended that funds for program development (on a partially or completely nonmatching basis) should be sympathetically considered *in the state plan* for the basic state agency grant.
>
> It should be noted that the National Council on the Arts is in complete agreement with Congressional legislative history and with what it understands to be state arts agency long-range planning that federal monies to the states should be on at least a matching basis. The Council has recommended encouragement for increased matching funds from the states while at the same time allowing for the flexibility of funding on a nonmatching basis should the occasion merit.[105]

These position papers read like the bureaucratic statements they had to be, but under the heading "Special State Grants" there was a hint of the kind of problems the federal office was facing.

> There has been a noticeable lack of imaginative applications under the Special State Grants portion of the Federal–State Program for the past year. The majority of the applications have fallen into the category of projects that should have been funded through the Basic State Grant but were not due to a lack of planning. Other areas of requests have been for special meetings, research and similar types of projects where need was determined after total commitment of state funds had been made. In other words, the Special State Grant fund is in danger of being totally committed to being an extension of the Basic State Grant to the more aggressive states.

The papers concluded with a statement on "New Directions." "The

*The basic administrative requirements of the Dance Touring Program in this transitional stage will continue to be arranged with the individual state arts agencies and regional organizations through the Dance Program office and funded through the Federal-State Partnership Program. States are encouraged to think in terms of supplementing the basic administrative functions needed for Dance Touring with Program Development activities in dance geared to the state's or region's local needs.

†There will be a few states in which the funding level will be raised to accommodate the requirements of the Dance Touring Program during this transitional stage.

Federal-State Partnership Program has been primarily a 'reacting' operation, as has been the role of the entire Endowment," it explained.

> The association between Federal–State staff and the states has gradually changed as the States' programs have become larger and more complex while more Federal–State staff time has been devoted to satisfying the needs of the growing Endowment. In early 1970, the Federal–State staff consisted of two people and each State's allotment from the Partnership Grant was $36,363. There was approximately $100,000 for additional programs for the States. In FY 1975, each State received $200,000 and additional State programs total more than $3 million. Obviously, the old time one-to-one, eyeball-to-eyeball type of administration has become outmoded.
>
> New administrative ideas have been initiated, such as the Regional Coordinator Program, to heighten the communication and the partnership between the Endowment and the States. Recently, new assignments have been made within the Federal–State staff to provide better service. These efforts are beginning to assist the States in getting better results from all Endowment programs.
>
> However, there remains a great need for decisive action by the Endowment if the benefits of the partnership with the States are to be realized—action that requires the Federal–State Partnership to consider the directions of its present programs *and* possible new directions.[106]

The position papers touched on regional development and mentioned the three working organizations—Mid-America Arts Association, Upper Midwest Regional Arts Council, and Western States Arts Foundation—plus an additional regional project covering South Carolina, Mississippi, and Kentucky. All of them were new, eager, hard-working, sometimes a little abrasive in their enthusiasm to get the job done.

> A strong regional program is often penalized because it is doing the job too well. If one organization receives grants from several Endowment programs to tour, exhibit, teach, display, etc., there is a tendency to add up all of the awards and say, "They're getting too much money." There is a line between serving the Endowment by using their programs, and serving their region. We must not make the mistake of looking at the pieces, but must be aware of the total effect of their program. Is it working? Are they assisting the States and the communities? We must be aware that money paid to a regional organization to tour a ballet company, a symphony orchestra, or a theatre is also badly needed working money for those artistic organizations. Thus, the regional groups are actually assisting NEA in its effort to support the artistic organizations.[107]

The position paper went on to point out that the regional organizations needed better administration and coordination of the Arts Endowment grants through the Federal–State office. Unified accounting procedures for all regional programs were important; statements of purposes, goals, and procedures should be made; and the roles of the state arts agency participation in more than one regional program needed clarification as well as the roles of the regional coordinators and regional projects.

There was also a position paper on Community Development which posed another puzzling and sometimes threatening jurisdictional problem for the state arts agencies, even though it was made clear that these community activities (other than those specifically organized through the Federal-State Partnership, Expansion Arts, and Special Projects) had a low priority with most Endowment programs.[108]

Hanks Reacts to State Agency Problems

The dissatisfaction among the executive directors and chairmen of the state arts agencies was not lost on Chairman Hanks and she went to work to try to improve the situation. On January 31, 1975, she issued a memorandum to state arts agency directors, with copies to the chairmen of Endowment panels and all program directors, entitled "Growing Pains—and Medicines," in which she outlined what the problems were, in her view, and the steps she was trying to take to overcome them. Like all the Hanks memoranda, it was written in a chatty style with a minimum of bureaucratese.

> In recent years we all have faced the administrative challenge of growth. The most difficult situations have been caused by growth, not in funding levels—as many suppose—but by interest in the arts (expressed often in vastly increased applications and inquiries at the federal and state level). In facing the challenge, we all have tried to retain the special quality and character befitting the special fields we serve and to develop essential administrative machinery without becoming bureaucratic.
>
> At the Endowment, we've had some success and some problems. Appropriate questions concerning certain Endowment difficulties have been raised by individual grantees, by institutions at museum meetings, by the states in Winston-Salem, by the Federal–State Panel at its South Carolina meeting—and by me!
>
> While at the Endowment we have made progress, I am far from satisfied on many points—and flat-out disturbed about certain critical problems that have continued to plague us and our constituents (that's you!). Among the worst of the problems—for us and for you—has been the excessive time involved in processing applications, grants and cash requests. *This problem has developed basically out of our inability to obtain sufficient staff to handle the dramatic increase in the volume of applications*, from 6,000 to nearly 20,000 in two years. Procedures and deadlines were also factors, though minor in comparison to staff. And the moves, which put us in three separate buildings for a while, and still have us in two, didn't help much either!
>
> I have talked at length with several people about our problems and corrective steps being taken. At the suggestion of Terrell Glenn, chairman of the Federal–State Panel, I am writing you to explain what we're doing for two reasons: 1. to give you hope that delays in processing will be reduced; and 2. to let you know our experience as it may be helpful in your own planning.
>
> - We have a management Task Force, chaired by a management expert, with membership drawn from present and former Council members.
> - Improvements and reorganization recommendations are now being implemented, and we can begin to see the time when real results will appear.
> - The Grants Office has been augmented and we are now implementing procedural reforms which Jim Thomas described during our discussions at the ACA meeting in Winston-Salem last September.

- Speeding up our response to cash requests has been the first order of business. Revised procedures have been developed and will be put into effect immediately. You will be receiving information and instructions regarding the new procedures from Clark Mitze in the next few days.
- We have taken a series of actions to insure that all Basic State Agency grants for FY 1976 will be released early in July 1975: 1. The application deadline was moved to February 1, providing more time to resolve questions prior to Council review in May; 2. Endowment staff will meet with representatives of all SAA's in regional meetings to discuss and resolve questions, thereby eliminating much of the need for letters, telephone calls and other time-consuming efforts of clarification.
- With the most helpful cooperation of the Office of Management and Budget, we have been assured that we will be able to continue to move grants in July 1976, even though it will be the period of transition to the new federal fiscal year.
- We are working on a letter of credit arrangement which would cut down on paper and time by permitting State Arts Agencies to draw funds directly from a participating bank in your area. We plan to have letter-of-credit procedures operating in one or two states by June of this year.

In addition to improving our own procedures here at the Endowment, we are moving to help applicants and grantees avoid unnecessary mistakes that delay grant actions and cash payments. The first of a series of workshops to be presented jointly by the Endowment and State Arts Agencies took place in Boston on January 29. This session—hopefully a pilot for others—also permitted the Endowment, the Massachusetts Arts Council and area applicants to compare federal and state requirements and to discuss specific problems concerning particular applications or grants.

We also plan to share with the State Arts Agencies some very helpful recent findings of our auditors. We believe that a large percentage of audit problems can be corrected by a few relatively simple modifications of your procedures.

Underlying these and other actions to solve specific problems is a more general strengthening of management here in the Endowment. Following the work of the Management Task Force, which was considered in depth by the Council, we are reorganizing the management functions of the Endowment. There is now an Assistant Chairman for Management, Richard Contee. He comes to us from private industry with a background in administration, advertising, and fund-raising. (I am impressed both with his abilities and his impatience for results!) There is a new office of Program Development and Coordination, headed by Larry Reger. This office will give full time to such [things] as guidelines and deadlines and new program concepts. There is an office of Congressional Liaison, directed by Liv Biddle, former Deputy Chairman of the Endowment. You know how much we need Liv's help!

The memorandum mentioned new staff assistants in the Grants Office and the coming publication of *The Cultural Post*. In conclusion, Hanks wrote:

We in the Endowment are all determined to get the administrative wheels running smoothly, so you and we can turn more time and energy to the program questions that require our joint attention. We hear—and value—your thoughts on these matters, as we have valued your role in pushing toward administrative solutions. Whatever the subject, if it concerns you, and us, and the fields we all serve together, let me know.[109]

The National Assembly of State Arts Agencies (NASAA)

The restlessness on the part of the state arts agencies continued, however. In the spring of 1975 the National Council on the Arts met in Seattle, Washington, and at the meeting several members of the National Assembly of State Arts Agencies (NASAA) were privileged to make a presentation on behalf of their colleagues and regions to the Council. The NASAA chairman, S. Leonard Pas, Jr., introduced the six directors and one chairman who had been selected by the NASAA board for the task.* The jurisdictional problems of the federal and state agencies seemed to be the crux of the areas of conflict and Anthony S. Keller, executive director of the Connecticut Commission on the Arts, outlined his views on sharing roles and on the special problems of the state agencies as "brokers" of the arts. (Keller's article and various other statements to the Council were printed in a newsprint tabloid, entitled, *Cultural Inquirer.*)

> In the November 16 *New Republic*, Michael Straight attempted to define the jurisdictional differences between the National Endowment for the Arts and the state arts agencies. He said:
>
> "The Endowment has provided direct support only to professional artists and to arts institutions that are national or regional in scope. Local arts organizations and nonprofessional artists have been supported through block grants given to the *state* arts agencies. Over the past five years the increased funding that the state agencies have obtained from their legislatures has kept pace with the Endowment's own appropriations. So year by year the program has gained in depth. In Alabama for example the Endowment supports no theater companies; but 15 community theaters are supported by the Alabama Arts Council. In South Dakota 300 communities are participating in programs of the state Arts Council."
>
> I'm afraid Mr. Straight, in seeking a simple definition, has *over*simplified—for which I can hardly blame him. The definition is a very elusive one. But if *he* errs on the side of oversimplification we can't expect anyone less conversant with the subject—or less sympathetic—to do otherwise. And that suggests to us that the Council, the Endowment staff, the state arts agencies, the Congress and the public might benefit from a careful review of the roles government is assuming for the nation's cultural development at the federal and state levels.[110]

Keller described the situation in his own state of Connecticut where financial aid with "no strings" was being given to dozens of the Arts Endowment's regular, professional and institutional grantees, including the American Shakespeare Theatre, the New Haven Symphony Orchestra, and others. At the same time, he pointed out, the Endowment is also supporting neighborhood organizations that are local and nonprofessional, and which get major support from the state arts agency. Functions once considered as state and municipal respon-

*Maryland, James Backas; Massachusetts, Louise Tate; Washington State, James Haseltine; Ohio, James Edgy; Tennessee, Normal Worrell, Connecticut, Anthony Keller; and Iowa, Wayne Norman, chairman.

sibilities have been absorbed into federal funding. Keller goes on to say that he believes:

> . . . that the Endowment has often failed to recognize in this unanimity of stated goals and similarity of program direction some opportunities, the exploitation of which would significantly strengthen the arts in this country. Instead state arts agencies often feel they are seen as one more constituency group—like the symphony orchestras, the theaters, the museums, the neighborhood arts organizations. This misunderstanding is reflected clearly in our funding relationship to the Endowment. Outside of the block grant (required by Congress in order to assure some geographical variety in the allocation of federal arts dollars) and the Endowment-initiated programs needing management at the state level, state arts agencies are treated within the generality of applicants and grantees—which, we believe, is inappropriate. With a "normal" grantee, the *ultimate destination* of the grant once it has left Washington is the grantee itself. The state arts agency, on the other hand, is almost always acting as a point of organization and *redistribution* once funds have been received from the Endowment. If the Endowment staff took this very significant difference into account—and recognized that the state councils need to exert *double the administrative effort* and be given *twice the lead time* required by a "normal" grantee—the idea of making supplementary funding available competitively through the various Endowment programs (in line with their regular deadlines) would be dropped in favor of a more effective system.

He felt that the grantor/grantee relationship had been accepted too easily by both the Endowment and the state agencies.

> At their best, however, the state agencies are not simply conduits for government funds. They are a unique, new instrumentality for assessing the cultural needs of a state and seeing to it that tax dollars spent on the arts really go to work for people. They are brokers who generate and redistribute funds, coordinate resources and parlay important local models of cultural development into statewide practice.[111]

Arts agencies throughout America, Keller explained, were creating an essential delivery system for the nation's professional arts resources, encouraging participation by citizens and state governments *on their own terms*, and giving artists new work opportunities within communities.

> The survival and development of important American arts institutions and ongoing programs are, by no means, the exclusive province of the Endowment. On the contrary, state-generated and state-appropriated funds in substantial magnitude, will have to come into play if the trend toward oblivion, projected by the 1974 Ford Foundation report on 166 American performing arts organizations, is to be reversed . . . [State arts agencies] can be seen as protectors of the Endowment's interests, though this is hardly the most noble way of describing the relationship. . . .
>
> At this point, the state agencies see some operating paradoxes within the Endowment that might benefit from objective analysis. Why for example have federal programs directly affecting community development in our states tended to bypass the state structure? We have been delighted to see City Options, Edges, and Spirit reach out for local response. But would there not be greater hope of permanent effect from these efforts if development through a state agency were encouraged? And why are the state arts agencies so peripheral in the federal Expansion Arts program?

> The Endowment response to these questions would probably be 1. "Some of the state arts agencies are not ready to take on additional responsibilities of this kind."—to which the answer, for many of us, is "Give us staff support and we'll manage the programs effectively with full public accountability." Endowment response No. 2 may be "We don't want to impose programs on the states."
>
> But you *do* impose. City Spirit—in itself a glorious idea—is a classic example of a community action program conceived, immaculately, at the federal level and presented to the grassroots with no midwife in attendance to assist with the delivery. The state arts agencies were omitted from the planning and implementation but they are now at stage center when the roof begins to cave in. They have been repeatedly consulted by local representatives to attempt to deal with the Endowment's intentionally loose (and, I think, inadvertently inconsistent) program definition—and, as a result, large amounts of state staff time have been spent gaining nothing but frustration for ourselves and the confused applicants. Thus, both an exciting program innovation and a major investment of energy have been compromised, as have the potential benefits of the program. The state agencies have been unable to provide the needed information to their local clients and the results have, in many cases, been misdirected or nonparticipatory applications. In many cases, too, contrary to what appears to be City Spirit's intent, power has remained in exactly the same hands where it had rested before, except some names of quasi-community leaders have been exploited to dress up a proposal.
>
> City Spirit was a brilliant stroke, and the Council, Nancy Hanks and her staff deserve full credit for bringing it to the public. As an idea and a point of view it is extremely important and for that reason its initial trial is worthy of careful assessment. City Spirit is a program that can work and work well. There is no example that better suggests the importance of joint federal-state planning and implementation. Indeed, there are no apparent alternatives to joint planning and implementation if we are really trying to provide quality service to our mutual clientele.[112]

Other presentations to the National Council by the state agency representatives covered audience development, the individual artist (with more appointments to advisory panels), art in public places, the battle for artistic excellence, planning for the future, and "The Endowment Connection"—which exemplified the concern of many of the state arts agency leaders that not enough attention was being paid by the federal representatives to the wellspring of contemporary culture within the states and their own communities.

The ferment in the states was an inevitable outgrowth of maturing programs and leadership, a ferment that was also being felt within the Endowment staff as program directors jockeyed for funding and new power bases, and some of the friendly cooperation of the earlier years slipped away in bureaucratic maneuvering.

Tenth Anniversary of the Arts Legislation

Ten years after the bill creating the National Foundation for the Arts and the Humanities was signed by President Johnson, the Arts Endowment celebrated the anniversary on September 29 and 30, 1975, at the LBJ Library in

Austin, Texas. "The weather was magnificent, the participants thoughtful and provocative, the audience responsive, and the subject both a celebration and a challenge. The occasion was the symposium on 'The Arts: Years of Development, Time of Decision,' co-sponsored by the LBJ Library and the University of Texas."

The event not only rounded off the first decade of the Arts Endowment functioning but it also gave the opportunity to assess the progress made in the arts in that period and to consider what directions should be followed in the future. It also created a forum for spectacular national press coverage shepherded by Florence Lowe.

For some of the participants the program began with a barbecue luncheon at the Johnson ranch where Lady Bird Johnson was the gracious hostess for nearly a hundred guests, including members of the National Council on the Arts who were attending the program, a few Endowment staff members on Texas duty, and other guests, symposium participants, and friends. It was a hospitable beginning for the celebration of the decade in which one of President Johnson's initiatives had come to praiseworthy fruition.

Buses took the guests from the Hotel Driskill in downtown Austin to the ranch, over the sun-drenched Texas countryside and past the quiet Pedernales River to the fabled ranch—where the house seemed surprisingly small and homelike to be the center of such an imperial presence. Mrs. Johnson moved graciously among the guests, shaking hands with each one. She pointed out the beauty of the river flowing beyond the sloping lawn, showed visitors the house, and served the luncheon in a large annex building which must have seen many prandial celebrations of struggles and victories in the Johnson presidential years. The Texas sky was wide and blue overhead, and in the field beyond some children were flying kites. For many of the guests, it was a moment of culmination, not only for the arts but for many of the aspects of the good life which had been an abiding effort of Johnson's domestic policy.

That evening the guests and many University of Texas students and Austin residents, plus assembled symposium participants, were treated to an outdoor musical extravaganza staged on the Johnson Library plaza under the Texas stars by the University Symphonic Band, the Wind Ensemble, and combined choral groups. Later the University Symphony Orchestra performed in the LBJ Auditorium.

The next morning—Monday, September 29—the University Longhorn Band sounded the musical welcome and Library Director, Harry Middleton, opened the conference with a reminder to the audience that the symposium on the arts, like those that had preceded it on education, civil rights, urban affairs, energy and the environment, also carried the imprint of President Johnson. Middleton explained that Johnson had wanted "this library housing the record of his work to fill a purpose beyond study of the past. He wanted this institution to be an active and creative center for the consideration and discussion of ideas that are of concern to us as a people."

After preliminary welcomes by the President of the University of Texas, Lorene Rogers, and the assistant archivist, Daniel J. Reed, it was time to get to conference business. Dean Elspeth Rostow of the Division of General and Comparative Studies and chairman of the Symposium Committee, introduced the keynote speaker, Beverly Sills. Sills was a member of the National Council on the Arts at that time, and one of its most faithful and articulate supporters. Herculean efforts had been made behind the scenes to spring her out of a recording schedule so that she could come to Austin for the keynote speech, which went right to the heart of the national situation—the arts in September 1975.

> The arts are flourishing in this country. There is no crisis in the arts. There is a money crisis—a big difference. In 1965, the National Endowment for the Arts functioned with a $2.5-million budget. Ten years later we have a $75-million budget. We cannot be complacent or satisfied, because there are a great many cities in this country that don't give one nickel toward their own cultural institutions. The arts are still considered a dispensable luxury.
>
> Why are we so loathe to change our priorities? Why are wars never underfinanced, although museums are closing the doors? Why does a war never go out of business for lack of funds, when the Metropolitan Opera may have to do that in a very little while?
>
> The defense budget is $103 billion. Now I would suggest that the United States would not collapse on its backside with a budget of only $100 billion, and I would suggest $1 billion perhaps to wipe out one of the killer diseases—heart, cancer, mental retardation. And I would suggest another billion to improve our educational facilities. There's a terrible shortage of doctors, and our young men and women can't get into medical schools because there's no room for them. And then I would suggest a $1 billion appropriation for the arts.
>
> Lastly I'd like to talk about the American artist because I am one, and obviously everything I see is through the eyes of the American artist. The American artist is part of our national heritage. Unlike our other natural resources this one will continue on as long as civilization exists, and it doesn't cause any air pollution.
>
> As recently as 25 years ago, if the name was unpronounceable, the artist was automatically considered great. Today plenty of us with very pronounceable names are doing just fine, and the snobbish stupidity that if it comes from Europe of course it's better is a dead issue.
>
> We can, should and must take pride in what we have given birth to, raised and cultivated. Our artists, our museums, our singers, our dancers, are among the best in the world today, and they are our greatest strength. They can give us the world of peace and beauty we dream of, because art is the signature of a civilization.[113]

There were three panel presentations during the symposium, all with sterling participants.[114] The first dealt with "Art and Politics." The presenter was James Backas, executive director of the Maryland Arts Council, and the moderator was John Hightower, former chairman of Advocates for the Arts and onetime head of the New York State Council. William B. Cannon, dean of the Lyndon B. Johnson School of Public Affairs was the summarizer.*

For the most part this panel discussion centered on three hard issues: the amount of financial support the government should be giving to the arts; the arts community's political constituency; and what threat of control comes with government support.

Kirk Douglas and Thomas Fichandler called the current level of federal support "piddling" and inadequate for the needs of the field. Both Senators Pell and Javits, co-authors of the legislation to continue at the $75 million level for another two years, agreed.

"We ought to be devoting not less than $250 million to the arts, even now," Senator Javits observed, but he added, "let me tell you at the risk of no applause but as the voice of reality that there's no sentiment in Congress for a billion dollars for the arts." He warned, in addition, against trying to take money from the defense budget. "If you try that, you're giving yourself at least a 100 percent handicap." Federal funding will grow, he felt, only if the public is involved.

Senator Pell believed that the "arts community has done a tremendous job of increasing its arts constituency around the country," and Fichandler felt that Congress was far behind the people in recognizing arts needs.

Representative Mickey Leland, pointing out that he came from the biggest, and poorest, black district in the state of Texas, echoed the urgent messages of Kirk Douglas and Donald Weismann and expressed the hope "that the people of Texas would rise up and tell their legislators that it's high time we started spending money on things like the arts and humanities."

Moderator John Hightower felt that there was a general ignorance on the part of the arts-interested public which had been largely unaware of the political process necessary to implement appropriations for cultural support.

Senator Javits offered the remedy, with Senator Pell concurring. "There is nothing a congressman will listen to more than letters from home." They added that the other practical piece of political advice they could offer was to cite not only the spiritual benefits of the arts, but the economic ones as well, the "usefulness for all the people who will not be employed in the production of food, manufactured goods and raw materials. That will be about 85 percent of our people in another 10 years," he predicted.

*The first panel also included painter Darby Bannard; Kirk Douglas, actor, director, and producer; Thomas Fichandler, executive director of the Arena Stage in Washington, DC; Arlen Gregorio, state senator from California; Jacob Javits, U.S. senator, New York; Mickey Leland, stage representative, Texas; McNeil Lowry, former vice president of the Ford Foundation; Claiborne Pell, U.S. senator from Rhode Island; Donald Quayle, senior vice president of the Corporation for Public Broadcasting; and Donald Weismann, professor of comparative studies at the University of Texas at Austin and a recent member of the National Council.

John Hightower then introduced a question that had lurked in assessments of the Arts Endowment for a decade and had threatened the passage of the early legislation. "Can freedom of the arts be compromised by too much government support?"

The possibility troubled Senator Gregorio who felt that too much money might compromise artistic expression because "in order to make sure they are efficient and cost-effective, you start with the kind of bureaucracy that I think in the end will be a great danger unless it is carefully controlled."

Other panelists discounted the risk and Senator Javits thought that to run any real danger of political interference, budgets would need to approach the 50 percent level of support, a possibility too remote to be discussed.

Later in the conference sessions, Michael Straight commented that Senator Gregorio had "seemed to be the ghost at the feast." But the caution was shared by others, too. Moderator Hightower, for example, while acknowledging that there had been little political interference to date, nevertheless warned about the subtle pressure of bureaucratic control. Donald Quayle wondered whether the widespread "visibility" of radio and television might hamper some of their experimental development in the arts.

In his summation, Cannon concluded that "art and government" have made an accommodation of a good sort," although "subtler forms of control and censorship" could be the "clouds on the horizon which we still have to watch for," just as direct censorship had been the concern ten years previously.[115]

The second panel was built around "Art and the Participant," with Michael Straight as the presenter and Charles C. Mark, editor of *Arts Reporting Service* and a former Endowment staff member, as the moderator. The summarizer was Kenneth Prescott, chairman, Department of Art, University of Texas at Austin.*

Straight plunged into the heart of the problem at once. "What is it like," he asked, "to earn your living as an artist in America?" He challenged the artists on the panel with the statement that he felt it was the artist's obligation to find both the will and the means to communicate with the public because "the American people will only support that which they understand and value."

There was conflicting opinion among the performers, visual artists, and administrators on the panel about the importance of communication.

James Wyeth maintained that "the most important role for the artist today, or for me at least, is to paint, and for a dancer to dance, and an actor to act, and to do it to the best of his ability, and everything else is secondary."

*Other participants were: Maurice Abravanel, musical director and conductor, the Utah Symphony; Schuyler Chapin, former manager, Metropolitan Opera Company; Ann Colbert, president, Colbert Artists Management, Inc.; O'Neil Ford, architect; Richard Hunt, sculptor; Judith Jamison, dancer; Robert Merrill, opera singer; Joshua Taylor, director, National Collection of Fine Arts, Smithsonian Institution; and James Wyeth, painter.

On the other hand, dancer Judith Jamison felt that it was very important that the public understand what goes into the artist's presentation. She cited the Coordinated Residency Program of the Arts Endowment, with its performance, master classes, and lecture demonstrations as "fantastic." She added, however, that she did not believe it would work for painting.

Joshua Taylor believed that a painter did need a public as much as a performer, and offered the suggestion that "communication" can create a community of feeling and understanding. The artist should be free to do it his way, but there should be some feedback so that the public will be able to understand the artist's efforts.

Schuyler Chapin emphasized the importance of institutions in the whole scheme of communication for both the visual and the performing artists. "If the institutions are allowed to go under," he warned, "the opportunities for reaching the public will not only diminish but could possibly disappear."

The question of limited room at the top—always a frustration for the aspiring artist—was addressed by Ann Colbert and Richard Hunt, both of whom warned against excessive expectations. Chapin, however, felt this situation was improving and opportunities in the performance area, at least, had opened up in large part as a result of the support of the Arts Endowment. "The art of opera has exploded in the last 10 years," he said.

> Straight summed up the experience of the decade this way: "Ten years ago . . . dancers were earning an average of $4,000 a year, when they were working. Agnes de Mille testified the dancers ate sawdust . . . . Ten years later, the artists may not be living on cake and caviar, but they do have bread and cheese. The reason is not that they are being supported. It is that they are earning it." And communities across the country are benefiting: "Symphony orchestras are playing in shopping centers and parks." Museums are reaching out in new ways "to hundreds of thousands of new art lovers. Non-profit professional theaters, which existed only in handfuls . . . are today functioning in 50 cities. Dance companies . . . are touring in every state . . . 2,000 poets are at work in our schools; for the first time in American history, it is possible to make a living as a poet."

Faced with so much conflicting opinion among the performers, the visual artists and the administrators, the summarizer paraphrased the ' King of Siam, "they concluded in conclusion, they concluded long ago." He listed the points as he heard them. The visual artist seems to work best in isolation until his work interacts with the public. He or she may not need to actively try to help the society to understand painting or sculpture. The performing artist, on the other hand, must have public understanding of the work and craftsmanship, training and dedication which culminate in a performance. If there is no appreciation and understanding, there is no audience. During the 10 years of its existence the National Endowment for the Arts, it was felt, had helped create an environment in which the artist can perform and works of art be enjoyed and appreciated far more widely in the country.

There was discussion on the role of the institutions and the performer. "It seemed self-evident that performing artists could not perform without institutions," the summarizer commented, "and yet, we have a contrary view that indeed they have and they could." It was also pointed out that arts institutions had become stronger than they had been a decade earlier, and that this growth was due in great measure to the influence of the agency.[116]

Nancy Hanks, as presenter of the third panel, picked up Michael Straight's theme. "The most important question for the next ten years," she said, "is how to strengthen the connection between the arts and the communities, the cities and their neighborhoods, the states, the schools, the universities, the foundation." With Roger Stevens as moderator, each of these issues was discussed.*

Throughout the symposium there were occasional questions and comments from the floor. One of these comments was from Mrs. Whitney Young in the audience. She was concerned for the frequently diminishing role of the arts in the schools. "When there is a cutback in funds, the first thing that is looked at in the budget is what they call the 'frills' . . . . Is there anything the Endowment can do to mobilize public sentiment?"

Hanks predicted an advocacy function in the future but felt that such a function should be the decision of the community and the parents and "the voices have not yet been loud enough." Rosalind Russell added that if parents would be as vocal about the arts in the schools as they had been about busing, they might be listened to.

On the subject of the enlarging role of business, Roger Stevens pointed out that corporate contributions had greatly increased—to about $100 million a year. He added that he felt the advice from the art and politics panel could be applied to the interaction with the business community as well. "Write the chairmen of the boards. They are even more responsive than politicians."

There was much support for the work of the volunteers, particularly the Community Arts Council movement whose growth, according to Hanks, had been "fantastic," growing from perhaps 100 councils a decade earlier to 10 to 20 times that number. The panel urged that these community councils be representative of all elements of a community, and pointed out the economic advantages of supporting the arts. Hanks also talked about artificial barriers and even hostility between the academic and professional worlds. Gerald Bartell pushed for more imaginative professionalism in dealing with the media.

While none of the participants downgraded the importance of money in

*Other participants were Gerald A. Bartell, chairman, American Medical Buildings, Inc., and chairman, Wisconsin Arts Council; Sarah Caldwell, artistic director, The Opera Company of Boston; Jack Kroll, senior editor, *Newsweek*; Rosalind Russell, actress; Billy Taylor, musician, composer; and Thomas Willis, music critic, *Chicago Tribune*. The summarizer was Peter Garvie, dean, College of Fine Arts, University of Texas at Austin.

developing the arts, Roger Stevens warned against the assumption that "if we only had sufficient money, the problems of the arts would be solved."

Billy Taylor agreed that the kinds of community support have nothing to do with money. "It has to do with the kinds of places we can offer where people can perform," he said, "the kinds of support we can offer in terms of encouraging their efforts."[117]

Senator Hubert Humphrey, the former Vice-President, took the platform to urge support for the arts as he had done for years in the halls of Congress. He spoke eloquently of his years of effort on behalf of federal aid for the arts.

> Despite the much greater political strength the arts now carry in Congress, it will be difficult . . . to substantially increase funding for them to the levels they merit. But we can, and I believe we will, achieve those increases in time . . . . There is no way to put the genie back in the bottle . . . . People everywhere have seen and felt the impact of the arts. I hope that today the message is clear out of this symposium . . . When the next election is up, ask every single member that seeks to have a seat in Congress or in the state legislature or in City Hall, whether or not they are willing to do a little more to lift the life of the American people . . . with the arts and humanities.

He went on to encourage the use of the Comprehensive Employment and Training Act (CETA) to aid unemployed artists and artisans. "I think an imaginative city government could produce a remarkable employment program," he said and outlined a dozen projects, from performances in veterans' hospitals to the teaching of handicrafts. "No nation has a greater opportunity in this century to advance the arts and the humanities than the United States, blessed with a multiplicity of peoples, with a variety of life styles, with diverse cultures and ethnic groups." The bicentennial year, he felt, offered the chance to launch a massive national effort "to bring to the American people the great benefits, indeed the joys, of the arts. Let's join together to get it done."[118]

Mrs. Lyndon Johnson received an enthusiastic welcome as she modestly made her way to the platform to conclude the proceedings.

> The greatest satisfaction for me, as I know it would have been for Lyndon, is to see that the legislation signed ten years ago struck a note deep in the hearts of all the people, and that the goals set then have been broadened and strengthened through the Nixon and Ford Administrations. . . . It seems to me there are two kinds of people whose lives are touched by the Endowment. The talented people, many of them young, who are being given the opportunity for fulfillment and expression, come by the thousands across the land. Then there are those like me, who listen and watch and are enthralled by the magic, and we come by the millions.
>
> Well, we've heard from the experts on the condition and future of the arts. One of the messages that came through was . . . we must identify and rally the constituency . . . . I would like to add a postscript to this advice in terms of my own experience. I get letters telling me how beautiful the parks are in Washington or in some spot across the country where the flowers bloom, or where hike-and-bike trails border the riverfront. Of course I am grateful and pleased to receive those letters. But . . . what

> would count most is if those letter writers could tell that story of appreciation to the Mayors, the City Councils . . . their representatives in Congress . . . . You tell it where the decisions are made and the priorities set. I hope you will now take our story where it counts; then the happy experience of the last 10 years will grow and expand, and our lives will be richer.[119]

The symposium participants left the auditorium with a sense of challenge. Obviously, the first ten years had been successful. The critics acclaimed the agency and its activities, the public was supportive, artists and arts organizations all over the country had received federal help that translated into vigorous and expanded local assistance. Congress was benign and the budget was increasing. There were continuing questions—censorship, pressures, political compromises, but as Mrs. Johnson pointed out the agency had grown vigorously under the watchful and sensitive guidance of Roger Stevens and Nancy Hanks and had successfully avoided these shoals in the first ten years of political sailing. The Council members and the Endowment staff had been able to strike a balance. Federal support had not turned out to be the first step toward federal censorship, and funding for the arts had not been squandered.

There were worries about key institutions facing enormous deficits brought on by inflation and recession, but there were no real worries about the government co-opting or censoring the artist. This was perhaps all the more remarkable given the period in which the Arts Endowment was developing when, because of the Vietnam War, many artists (including those supported by the agency) had felt compelled to stand against the government. It was also a period when black militancy and the women's liberation movement were developing, and a great deal of the art expression of the time was controversial and sometimes offensive to many citizens. But the Arts Endowment had survived in spite of these activities—to the historic credit of the Congress and three Presidents.

Reference Notes

1. *Who's Who of American Women*, 6th ed. (Chicago: A. N. Marquis, 1970–71), p. 513, and National Endowment for the Arts (NEA), *Biographies of Staff* (Washington: NEA Office Publication, 1972), p. 1.
2. Rockefeller Panel Report, *The Performing Arts: Problems and Prospects* (New York: McGraw-Hill, 1965), pp. v, vi.
3. *Ibid.*, p. 65.
4. *Ibid.*, p. 148.
5. L. Halprin, taped interview, San Francisco, Calif., September 18, 1981.
6. K. Yasko, taped interview, Madison, Wisc., April 26, 1980.
7. N. Hanks, taped interview, Washington, D.C., January 28, 1980.
8. NEA, *Biographies*, p. 2.
9. *Who's Who in Government*, 1st ed. (Chicago: A. N. Marquis, 1972–73), p. 492.
10. M. Straight, *Twigs for the Eagle's Nest* (New York: Devon Press, 1980), p. 24.
11. M. Straight, "Government's Contribution to Creative Expression," *New Republic* (November 16, 1974).

12. M. Straight, "A New Artistic Era (If the Money Lasts)," *New York Times*, October 20, 1974.
13. *Ibid.*
14. N. Hanks, taped interview.
15. K. Yasko, taped interview.
16. See Appendix A, "Total Appropriations, Federal Funds, Through FY 1975, National Foundation on the Arts and the Humanities."
17. *America's Museums: The Belmont Report*, to the Federal Council on the Arts and the Humanities by a Special Committee of the American Association of Museums, October 1968, p. x.
18. *Ibid.*, pp. xii–xvi.
19. NEA, *1969 Annual Report* (Washington: U.S. Government Printing Office, 1969), pp. 8–9.
20. *Ibid.*, p. 9.
21. *Ibid.*
22. Andrew Glass, "She's An Artist at Getting Money for the Arts," *New York Times*, December 14, 1975.
23. Straight, "Twigs," p. 22.
24. N. Epstein, "Politics and the Arts," *Washington Post*, August 25, 1974.
25. Straight, "Twigs," p. 22.
26. M. Childs, "Personable Persuader United Hill Pursestrings for the Arts," *Washington Post*, July 1, 1970.
27. Straight, "Twigs," p. 22.
28. N. Epstein, "Politics."
29. *Ibid.*
30. NEA, *1970 Annual Report* (Washington: U.S. Government Printing Office, 1970), p. 7.
31. *Ibid.*, p. 38.
32. *Ibid.*, p. 29.
33. NEA, *New Dimensions for the Arts 1971–1972* (Washington: U.S. Government Printing Office, 1972), p. 5.
34. G. A. McLellan, *516 Ways BCA Companies Supported the Arts in '73 and '74* (New York: Business Committee for the Arts, 1974), p. 2.
35. Quotations and information on American cultural interest were taken from National Research Center for the Arts, *Americans and the Arts: Highlights from a Survey of Public Opinion* (New York: Associated Councils of the Arts, 1974), pp. 3, 8. A total of 3,005 interviews were conducted among a representative cross-section of Americans 16 years and older. This sample was scientifically drawn to ensure that all regions of the country and major demographic groups would be accurately represented and that the data would be projectable to the nation's population as a whole. The statistical confidence level from this survey was 95 percent, with a sampling error of plus or minus 2 percent.
36. NEA, Research Division, *Report #1, Employment and Unemployment of Artists: 1970–75* (Washington: NEA Office Publication, 1975), p. 9.
37. N. Hanks, "The Arts in America: A single Fabric," *Museum News*, 42 (November 1973).
38. National Endowment for the Arts (NEA), *New Dimensions*, pp. 6, 7.
39. *The Arts: A Creative Partnership*, text of the President's remarks to the Associated Councils of the Arts, Mayflower Hotel, Washington, D.C., May 26, 1971 (Washington: White House Publication, 1971).
40. NEA, *New Dimensions*, p. 67.
41. *Ibid.*
42. Information on Artrain was taken from "Art Train Weaves Its Way South," *Michigan Daily* (Ann Arbor), July 14, 1974.
43. NEA, *1973 Annual Report* (Washington: U.S. Government Printing Office, 1973), p. 17; and NEA, *1974 Annual Report* (Washington: U.S. Government Printing Office, 1974), p. 4.

44. Editorial, *Milwaukee Journal*, January 9, 1972.
45. Halprin, interview.
46. NEA, *New Dimensions*, p. 135.
47. NEA, *1974 Annual Report*, pp. 22–23.
48. "Good Talk About Good Design," *Washington Post*, March 13, 1973.
49. I. Chermayeff, *et al.*, *The Design Necessity* (Cambridge, Mass.: MIT Press, 1973), theme statement.
50. NEA, *New Dimensions*, p. 8.
51. N. Epstein, "Politics."
52. H. Zipper, Personal communication to F. Taylor, 1966.
53. NEA, *New Dimensions*, p. 29.
54. *Ibid.*
55. N. Hanks, taped interview, Washington, D.C., December 26, 1981.
56. *Ibid.*
57. *Ibid.*
58. NEA, *1973 Annual Report*, p. 15.
59. *Art Worker's News*, 6 (September 1975).
60. NEA, *New Dimensions*, p. 19.
61. "City Edges," poster published by NEA, 1972.
62. A. L. Huxtable, *New York Times*, May 27, 1973.
63. NEA, *Spaces for Living: An Overview of the Architecture-Environmental Arts Program* (Washington: U.S. Government Printing Office, 1977), p. 7.
64. "City Options," poster published by NEA, 1974.
65. NEA, *Spaces for Living*, p. 8.
66. NEA, *1974 Annual Report*, p. 4.
67. NEA, *Spaces for Living*, p. 8.
68. L. Halprin interview.
69. Quotations and information on the Bicentennial celebration were taken from NEA, *1974 Annual Report*, p. 4.
70. R. Evans and R. Novak, "From Congress, a Counterattack on Budget Control," *Hall Syndicate* (January 26, 1973).
71. Arts Section, *Newsweek* (March 26, 1973).
72. M. White, "Arguing Over the Arts," *Washington Post* March 7, 1973.
73. M. MacPherson, "Opera: More Hearings on the Arts," *Washington Post*, March 16, 1973.
74. M. MacPherson, "Subsidies and the Arts," *Washington Post*, March 7, 1973.
75. *Ibid.*
76. *Ibid.*
77. G. Gent, "3 Arts Leaders Urge Funding Set-up, Cite Crisis," *New York Times*, March 21, 1973.
78. M. Hunter, "Federal Arts Bill Faces Fund Fight," *New York Times*, April 29, 1973.
79. H. C. Schonberg, "Cash for Culture, Too," *New York Times*, March 29, 1973.
80. "32 Cents for Art," *Washington Post*, June 18, 1973, editorial.
81. "Nancy Hanks Named for New Term at Endowment," *New York Times*, September 15, 1973.
82. NEA, *1974 Annual Report*, p. 3.
83. Quotations and information on obscenity ruling were taken from S. B. Conroy, "Opening Up the Arts," *Washington Post*, September 17, 1973.
84. NEA, *1974 Annual Report*, p. 5.
85. NEA, *Museums USA: A Survey Report* (Washington: U.S. Government Printing Office, 1975); NEA, *Museums USA: Art, History, Science and Other Museums* (Washington: U.S.

Government Printing Office, 1974); NEA, *Museums USA: Highlights* (Washington: U.S. Government Printing Office, 1973).
86. NEA, *Challenge Grants* (Washington: NEA Office Publication, 1977), p. 1.
87. N. Hanks interview, December 26, 1981.
88. NEA, *1974 Annual Report*, p. 3.
89. D. Carmody, "Met Given $1 Million in U.S. Matching Funds," *New York Times*, March 3, 1974.
90. NEA, *1974 Annual Report*, p. 5.
91. Transcript of Metropolitan Opera broadcast, March 2, 1974.
92. S. Chapin letter to F. Taylor, March 22, 1982.
93. F. Taylor letter to N. Hanks, April 5, 1974.
94. "Statement of Nancy Hanks at Hearings Before the Subcommittee on Department of the Interior and Related Agencies of the Committee on Appropriations, U.S. House of Representatives" (Washington: Unpublished document, March 26, 1974), p. 1.
95. S. R. Weismann, "Arts Officials Deplore Nixon Comment," *New York Times*, August 7, 1974.
96. NEA, Office Memorandum, August 6, 1974.
97. J. Flander, "Aid for the Arts: 10 Happy Years," *Washington Star-News*, September 4, 1974.
98. J. Smyth, "Executive Arts and Applause," *Washington Post*, September 5, 1974.
99. Editorial, *New York Times*, September 8, 1974.
100. Quotations and information were taken from M. Straight, "After War and Watergate: The Sounds of Music," *New York Times*, October 20, 1974.
101. W. Nemoyten, *Memorandum* to Community Arts Agencies, distributed through the Associated Councils of the Arts, July 12, 1973.
102. N. Hanks, office memorandum to F. Taylor, July 23, 1973.
103. F. Taylor, Personal notes from the South Carolina panel meeting of the Federal–State Program office, Columbia, S.C., November 6–8, 1974.
104. Quotations and information were taken from NEA, *Federal–State Partnership Program and Funding Information Booklet* (Washington: NEA Office Publication, 1976), pp. 176–189.
105. *Ibid.*
106. *Ibid.*
107. *Ibid.*
108. *Ibid.*
109. N. Hanks, Memorandum to State Arts Agency Chairman and Directors and Federal–State Panel, January 31, 1975.
110. A Keller, "On Sharing the Roles in Cultural Goals," *Cultural Inquirer*, 1 (1) (1975).
111. *Ibid.*
112. *Ibid.*
113. B. Sills, "Remarks made at an arts symposium at the Lyndon Baines Johnson Library," Op-Ed, *New York Times*, September 30, 1975.
114. Panel Quotations and general information were taken from *Among Friends of LBJ*, newsletter of the Friends of the LBJ Library, 7 (Austin, Tex., November 1, 1975), pp. 1–16.
115. *Ibid.*
116. *Ibid.*
117. *Ibid.*
118. *Ibid.*
119. *Ibid.*

5

Opening Up the New Frontier

Once a person learns to appreciate the beauty of painting, sculpture, music, and has come to meet the great men of letters through their books, a special kind of happiness can be his.
—Roger Stevens, *Cultural Affairs* (1969)

Making the arts nationally available to men and women in every walk of life was becoming a primary emphasis of the Council and the Arts Endowment in the early seventies. Under Nancy Hanks' deft guidance, the Council had articulated its threefold purpose as the achievement of availability of the arts, cultural resources development, and advancement of the cultural heritage. The three goals provided a strong structure for handling the increasing numbers of requests that were coming into the program offices for assistance to a sweeping selection of arts activities. Without the three broad goals it would have been almost impossible to categorize and process the ferment of creativity the daily mail brought to each program director's desk.

It had been generally understood by the Council members and staff that availability was a primary function of a federal agency that had to deal with the artistic concerns of a nation. But it became more and more evident that without availability—without receptive audiences, consumer readiness, and adequate delivery systems—America's cultural resources could not grow and its cultural heritage could be neither cherished nor expanded.

Gradually the Council philosophy became committed to the urgent need to spread the country's cultural resources of the highest quality throughout every region and not let them be concentrated in the major urban centers only. Interest and assistance had to be nurtured at the grass roots level as well. It was a point of view predominant in the social liberalism of the period when provision for equal access to many kinds of opportunities for all the segments of the population was a strong legislative goal.

Roger Stevens had perceived this need very early in his chairmanship.

> We must generally decentralize the arts, making them available to more people in diverse areas, and hopefully on a year around basis. At the same time, we must increase the availability of education in the arts so that we may improve the quality of our audiences. If we achieve this widening and more discerning audience, it will follow that there will be more demand for the arts.[1]

With availability emphasized in the decision-making aspects of dispensing federal grants, the programs and projects of the Arts Endowment began to develop an impressive breadth and geographic distribution, entering the daily lives of millions of Americans with the zest of a breeze from the sea.

There were touring projects organized to take performing groups and selected exhibitions into towns and hamlets where such events had never before occurred. There were media projects to carry the message of the arts on film, radio, and television all over the nation. There were community cultural activities in storefronts and at street fairs, helped by the Expansion Arts Program. There were outreach exhibitions for museums and multi-discipline activities to knit together new alliances. There were programs to preserve America's heritage in architecture and folk arts. There were residency programs to reach into communities on a personal and extended basis. There was the Federal–State Partnership Program, mandated by the original legislation, and rooted in the concept of national availability. Finally, there was the Artists-in-Schools program which became one of the best examples of the Arts Endowment effort to bring the arts into every part of the nation on a useful daily basis.

Touring Projects

From the first years, the Arts Endowment programs were concerned with touring activities. Wider understanding, acceptance, and support of the arts, it was reasoned, would result if citizens were given the opportunity to interact with the arts within their own communities. Therefore, as the Endowment programs developed, many of them contained touring components. Perhaps the most dramatic example of the effects of sustained touring projects may be found in the area of dance.

In 1965 almost all professional performances of dance were in New York City. By 1975, as a result of national dance touring projects, administered on a cooperative basis by state arts agencies and the Endowment, many Americans in all walks of life were experiencing dance. As Nancy Hanks stated:

> Now there are most than 100 organizations reaching millions of Americans in all areas of the nation. Dance company residencies are communitywide projects, including a wide range of activities—open rehearsals, master classes, as well as full performances.[2]

As the availability of dance increased across the nation, so did its financial support. The Dance Touring Program had begun in 1968 as a $26,000 pilot program which assisted four dance companies to tour for a total of eight weeks in two states. By 1976, funding for dance touring was $3.6 million—more than one-half of the total Dance Program budget—and the amount was generating between four to five dollars locally for every Federal dollar invested (approximately $14.4 to $18 million local dollars). Of equal importance was the number of people assisted by these cooperatively generated funds. Thousands of Americans witnessed the performances of 92 dance companies that toured for a total of 432 weeks in 56 states and jurisdictions during the 1975 fiscal year. Even by the most conservative standards, the availability of dance experiences throughout the nation increased dramatically during this period, and financial support kept pace.[3]

Similar records could be cited for opera companies, symphony orchestras, and art exhibitions. In fact, the appearance of a major symphony in a high school gymnasium or a performance of a traveling opera company in a small-town community center became a somewhat commonplace occurrence by the close of 1976. In printed programs for these performances there is often reference to funding through the cooperative efforts of a local sponsoring group, the state arts agency, and the National Endowment for the Arts.

Outreach and touring projects within the Music Program were accounting for nearly 72 percent of the funding for orchestras—much of it going to youth-related programming, regional touring activities, and the expansion of public appearances in parks, prisons, factories, and other areas. Opera companies also were receiving substantial support for "satellite" operations, such as small performing ensembles of professional singers and musicians that appeared in churches, clubs, auditoriums, and parks.[4] One performing ensemble even toured on a river raft!

> The Otrabanda Company's River Raft Review takes a summer-long excursion down the Mississippi River from St. Louis to New Orleans, offering free shows to culturally isolated communities, prisons, hospitals and reformatories.[5]

Within the Expansion Arts Program, the touring segment was concerned with helping urban, suburban, and rural community arts organizations "in areas where acccess to the arts had been heretofore lacking, where there are special needs for them."[6] Under this program also, the arts were made available to audiences and participants in the inner cities, in prisons and hospitals, in small rural towns, and impoverished communities throughout the upper Midwest, Appalachia, New England, and the Southwest. One such project was described in the *1976 Annual Report:*

> The John Henry Folk Festival . . . sponsored by the John Henry Memorial Foundation with Endowment support . . . brought together folk artists and craftsmen from all over Appalachia to celebrate and share their heritage in summer gatherings.

The festival included music, arts and crafts, dance and theatre, visual arts, workshop activities, and a special program for children.[7]

Media Projects

As vehicles for the transmission of other aesthetic forms, the media of film, radio, and television are uniquely useful to widening the availability of the arts. From its beginning as a federal agency, the Endowment recognized the importance of media to the cultural life of the nation. It supported arts programs that were creatively produced and contained subject matter that was artistically worthwhile. In her 1975 testimony, Nancy Hanks enumerated the highlights of the Public Media Program.

> Involved are 32 films sponsored by state and regional arts agencies depicting the special characteristics of the arts in their locales and regions; a film for television devoted to the warmth, meaning, and beauty of American song; a major television series on American dance and another on drama. Also included are:
> — Films relating to the new discoveries in the expansion arts;
> — Films on the lives and works of living American authors;
> — The continuation of the American Film Series for television;
> — A major radio drama series being developed by groups in Wisconsin and Minnesota for national distribution.[8]

Hanks also stated that the Media Program emphasized cooperative activities with the Corporation for Public Broadcasting "aimed at increasing exposure of large audiences to excellence in the arts." In addition, the Endowment helped to encourage the development of regional film and video exhibitions and informational activities.

Through the Media Program, the Endowment had found a twentieth-century approach to expanding the availability of the arts in areas of the country formerly untouched by live arts experiences. While for some people, arts exposure through the media was an initiating experience, for others such exposure acted as a reinforcement of experiences gained from live arts encounters. In either case, the message of the arts was being presented to an ever-increasing and better-informed audience.

Expansion Arts Projects

Established in 1971, the Expansion Arts Program of the Endowment was designed to "involve thousands of people who have lived their lives remote from the traditional arts institutions, such as theatres, opera houses, symphony halls, and museums."[9] The program's major thrust was toward encouraging neighborhood groups and community cultural centers to develop the creative abilities and artistic talents of people from all economic, social, geographic, and racial or ethnic backgrounds. It was a grassroots type of program that sought to provide artistic experiences to meet the unique needs of each community—from Vermont to Hawaii, Alaska to Texas.

The inclusion of the concept of community within the Expansion Arts Program's philosophy allowed that program to fund creative endeavors that were outside the traditionally-accepted artistic mainstream. Ethnic and racially-oriented art works and crafts received public recognition and, in many cases a new respectability because of the imprimatur of government support. Moreover, many of these communities developed a sense of identity, pride, and fulfilment through artistic expressions that were unique to their needs and experiences.

Wisconsin's "Dairyland Graphics" was an example of a project solidly based in an old rural tradition which meshed with the Expansion Arts Program guideline for "the involvement of local citizens in the creative process." For decades there had been a continuing impulse in the state to use the tempting broad walls of Wisconsin's dairy barns for visual expression. Sign painters and Sunday painters for many years had delighted in filling these spaces with enormous murals and ads for pouch tobacco and beer in spontaneous and colorful folk art. In 1975, Dairyland Graphics expanded the idea in a summertime project that involved six towns, 200 people, and countless highway observers. Enormous barn-size murals emerged which depicted typical scenes and activities of the area—from cows to corn to circuses—in a "rainbow of common rhythm across the state."[10]

Accessibility and Awareness Projects

The Arts Endowment was also interested in broadening the outreach programs of museums, and in providing works of art for public places, on the theory that daily accessibility to art works would foster artistic and cultural awareness.

A survey made by the agency revealed that during the early 1970s museums were serving an increasingly broad cross-section of people. It further revealed that "more than 308 million yearly visits were made to the nation's more than 1800 museums."[11] During 1975, Endowment grants to increase the reach of museums into the communities they served ranged up to $75,000 each for a total of $1,589,888.[12] When discussing the Wider Availability of Museums category of the Museum Program, Nancy Hanks stated:

> The program had its origins in the first year of the Endowment's life, when the Council announced plans to initiate a pilot program designed to make the facilities of museums available to wider audiences and to enhance the educational contributions of museums. Today the program also encourages greater cooperation among mu-

> seums and serves to stimulate new approaches and ideas for expanded community services.[13]

The *1976 Annual Report* describes the funding categories and gives examples of projects.

> The Metropolitan Museum of Art . . . began lending to the Whatcom Museum in Bellingham, Washington; the Guggenheim Museum began lending to the Wake Forest College in Winston-Salem, North Carolina. The most successful of such programs has been continuing for years between the Brockton Arts Center and the Museun of Fine Arts in Boston.[14]

In 1966 the Endowment had launched a project called Works of Art in Public Places which brought art "works of high quality into direct dialogue with the public." The project funds were matched with local money, and cities and communities commissioned or purchased works of art for locations that they felt were suitable. In 1975, Nancy Hanks summarized the project.

> To date more than $2.25 million in Federal funds has been spent on 154 projects in 37 states. The program is becoming increasingly visible across the nation. It encourages community involvement—including significant participation—and provides an impetus for defining and giving new meaning to "public places." It serves to sharpen public awareness of the value of the arts in our everyday lives. The audience involved can include a city, a community, a state.[15]

Special Projects Activities

The Arts Endowment also concerned itself with some other innovative approaches to arts availability. In 1974, it developed the Special Projects Program "to give the Endowment sufficient flexibility in funding multidiscipline projects and those which did not fit the guidelines of other programs." The Special Projects Program, in fact, consolidated elements of a number of other programs in an effort to break through categorical restrictions and find new audiences, new sponsors, and new opportunities.[16]

Some of these Special Projects were specifically related to availability of the arts. One of these was a 1976 pilot effort to assist art centers and festivals involved in presenting professional artists or groups to the public. This category also assisted in exploring "the problems and possibilities of improved marketing, including such concerns as audience development, fund raising, and new formats and locations for public presentations." For example, in Kentucky new audiences were encouraged through support for the Regional Arts Center at Centre College. In Wilmington, Delaware, the Grand Opera House received a grant for research to identify marginal and non-attenders of performing arts events, and ultimately to find ways of reaching them. The ongoing Mississippi

River Festival of Edwardsville, Illinois, received a grant for the development and implementation of an audience development program.[17]

Within the City Spirit category, projects were subsidized that encouraged and stimulated citizen interests in the creation of community forums for discussing the arts and for planning cultural opportunities. City Spirit was also designed to explore new linkages among the arts, government, the media, education, business, and volunteer service organizations in serving the cultural needs of people within their communities. Nancy Hanks stated:

> Individual community approaches have varied from a year-long series of meetings and catalyst events aimed at developing a master plan for a variety of arts activities (Pasadena, California), to program planning by the community to "recycle" a movie theatre and nearby storefronts as a community arts center (Ashland, Kentucky), to development of an Arts Experimental Station modeled on an Agricultural Experimental Station (Tifton, Georgia). Particular attention in this case is being given to the successful format developed over the years in agriculture, whereby a rural area is given a new sense of purpose and unity through community action.[18]

Several other sections under the Special Projects Program were related to arts availability projects. The Interrelated Programs and Special Services category served to accommodate both multi-arts and service projects that did not come under other Endowment divisions. For example, in 1975, the AFL-CIO Studies Center in Silver Springs, Maryland, received support for a program of visual and performing arts activities. The Corporation of Yaddo in Saratoga Springs, New York, received a grant to subsidize short-term residencies by writers, composers, and visual artists. The Theatre Development Fund (TDF) in New York City received support for its National Development Services program through which it provided assistance to communities interested in installing the highly successful ticket voucher system that TDF had developed.[19]

Preservation of Heritage Projects

The Endowment also concerned itself with those artistic and historic factors already existing within the environment. The Architecture+Environment Program worked closely with a variety of public and private groups, including HUD, the Department of the Interior, and the National Trust for Historic Preservation. Its efforts were aimed at the development of an awareness of the artistic value inherent in many old structures, the mobilization of action to preserve the existence of such buildings, and the improvement of the environment of the places in which Americans live, through "architecture, landscape architecture, urban design, and industrial design."[20]

A 1975 fact sheet compiled by the Endowment for possible use in a tenth anniversary press packet described three projects that had potential impact on arts availability. One of the projects set up a 1974 conference in Indianapolis to discuss ways communities could preserve and adapt abandoned or underutilized railroad stations. Another conference in 1975 was sponsored in New York to consider the role of historic districts and community conservation. A third project supported a study "of the use, mis-use and possible improvement of illuminated freeway signage, and of alternative uses for the neglected space under elevated highways."[21] In addition, the fact sheet noted, communities desiring to create cultural centers or preserve historic buildings of artistic worth could receive funding assistance for planning, feasibility studies, and actual design of facilities for the arts.

Federal–State Partnership Program

One of the principal ways by which the Endowment made the arts nationally available was through the Federal-State Partnership Program—a most significant feature of the 1965 enabling legislation. The purposes of the Partnership program were described in the Endowment's 1976 annual report:

> To assist in providing arts programming at the local level, every state and special jurisdiction in the United States has a state arts agency, operating as a part of the state government and receiving state appropriations. Each serves its state or jurisdiction as the National Endowment for the Arts serves the nation: generating and distributing funds, coordinating resources, and providing assistance to artists and cultural organizations. Grants for the state arts agencies support festivals, workshops residencies, community arts agencies, touring exhibits, crafts fairs, cultural institutions, fellowships to individual artists—the host of projects which develop and strengthen our cultural resources and make them more widely available to the public.[22]

In addition to the bloc monies dispensed under the program's Basic State Agency category, there were other state arts agency grants to sustain the wide arts availability concept under other program categories: Program Development, Regional Programs, Community Development, Services to the Field, and General Programs. These categories were designed to assist in the training of state and regional arts administrators, to develop community arts agencies, to support the work of national cultural organizations, and to support specific pilot projects or other proposals that did not fall under other funding programs.

Residency Programs as a Means of Achieving Arts Availability

Throughout its development, the National Endowment for the Arts viewed the idea of resident artists—artists living and working in a community for an extended period—as an effective means of providing access to and understanding of the arts. The opportunity to see the artist at work, to learn about the art from him, and to interact with an artist on personal and artistic levels was considered to be an effective means for expanding audiences. Moreover, the presence of the artist in the community over an extended period allowed sufficient time for the local population to become acquainted with the artist and for the growth of appreciation and participation in the arts.

A 1973 Louis Harris poll, commissioned by the Associated Councils of the Arts and conducted by the National Research Center for the Arts, had generally supported the residency concept used by the Endowment. The survey revealed that 50 percent of the public, many of whom lived in small towns or rural areas, felt that there were not enough opportunities for cultural events. In addition, 42 percent of those surveyed felt that less formal creative events such as art and photography shows, street festivals, local music and drama groups, or craft groups were inadequate in their communities.

- 41 percent of the public—59.6 million Americans—felt that it was important to have more opportunities for creative events in their communities.
- 94 percent of the public—or 136.8 million Americans (adults)—felt it was important for children and young people to have more opportunities for creative events.[23]

By establishing artist residencies in a variety of community settings the Arts Endowment and state and local agencies were able to increase access to the arts for a larger segment of the nation's citizens.

The artist-in-residence concept was not an original creation of the Arts Endowment but grew out of an idea that had developed years earlier. One might say, however, that the federal agency, recognizing the potential of the residency concept for arts availability and audience expansion, packaged it for national distribution.

Historical Development of Artist-in-Residence Concept

The first artist-in-residence program in the United States had been established on the University of Wisconsin–Madison campus in 1936. Through the efforts of University President Glenn Frank and Dean Chris L. Christensen, the College of Agriculture appointed the noted midwestern American painter, John Steuart Curry, to the position of Artist-in-Residence. In comments made later, Christensen recalled the establishment of the position:

> I personally initiated the idea of this new educational venture . . . . I felt that the talent of farmers and rural people in the area of the arts should be recognized and I presented my suggested program to the Board of Regents on July 23, 1936 . . . . Education, if it is to serve to the fullest, must include many things besides learning methods of increasing our financial income. We are all realizing that income is but a means to an end, and that end is the good life.

> So it is that our educational process needs to deal with subjects that contribute to the growth of our cultural side of life, such as literature, arts, music and history as well as with practical training for the vocations.

Curry worked in this position until his death in 1946. In addition to his influence on those who observed him at work, the artist's "ten years' service with the agriculture school of this great state university saw the widening of his influence into every county and town in a genuinely artistic grass roots movement."[24]

Over the years, similar positions involving various art forms were established throughout the country. At first, universities and colleges were the leaders in this movement, but during the Fifties the idea spread to community and public school situations.

In 1949, Nina Collier of Baltimore began arranging concerts of chamber music in the city's public schools. This program, later called Young Audiences, grew in credibility and financial backing because of the support of Mrs. Rosalie Leventritt, the "grand dame" of music patrons who also founded the Leventritt International Competition for violinists and pianists. Michael Hiestand, in an article about Young Audiences, said of Mrs. Leventritt:

> Her vision was to bring chamber music ("good music," she said) to children in the fourth through sixth grades. Only professional musicians who could represent the organization in an appropriate manner, and who could communicate verbally as well as through their music, would be selected.[25]

Evidently, Mrs. Leventritt viewed the artist's ability to communicate as essential to the success of the program. Administrators of later Endowment-sponsored projects endorsed her conclusions.

Over the years Young Audiences expanded to include ballet, opera, theatre, poetry, modern dance, and mime in the short-term residency offerings.

In 1959, another residency program in music was initiated when the Ford Foundation appropriated $200,000 "to enable a limited number of young composers to spend a year in public school systems around the country, writing music to be performed by the orchestras, bands, choruses, and other musical ensembles of those systems."[26] Entitled the Young Composers Project (YCP), this program—under the chairmanship of the noted American composer Norman Dello Joio—placed 31 composers over a three-year period in secondary schools throughout the country. These composers, none over the age of 35,

> were placed at a critical time in their development, in public school systems where they could write for specific performing groups whose abilities they would directly know, and where students could share in the creation of new musical works and be provided opportunities to gain insight into the creative process. It was hoped that in return such a program would provide incentive for composers, enrichment of the musical life of the communities, and an expansion of the repertory of secondary school music.[27]

The Young Composers Project engendered many features found in later Endowment residency activities. Composers in YCP residencies created works; students observed and, to a degree, participated in the process of creation; communities interacted with the composer in personal and artistic situations; and arts educators, as conductors, were involved in the preparation and presentation of the new pieces.

Concurrent with the YCP, another residence program was developing with a somewhat different design. The Affiliate Artists Program (AAP) was more limited in its residency requirements but wider in its artistic scope. AAP, which is still in operation, "provides a young performer (singer, actor, dancer, musician, or mime) to reside in a community for four two-week periods during the year." Usually sponsored by a major organization or industry, the program's resident artists make 80 to 100 appearances in a variety of settings. Unlike the YCP, this program from its beginning focused on community residencies although school programs were often part of the artists' duties. Also notable is the provision that residencies were broken up into blocks of time and divided over the period of a year. In their "off time," artists could work on their own creations while receiving total program support. When in residence, however, they were required to devote their full attention to community arts endeavors—teaching and presentations.[28]

Three categories of residence programs were characteristic during the 1950s and 1960s. The first category included projects in the performing arts which were designed primarily to provide students and adults with opportunities to attend cultural events. In conjunction with this artistic exposure, audiences were given opportunities to meet with the artists, discuss the art form, and attend master classes, lectures, and demonstrations.

In the second category, the artist's work was again twofold. While the artist might teach, lecture, and/or demonstrate, he or she would also share the working phase of the production with students and the community. The major emphasis of these programs was on the observation by area residents and students of the artists in the act of creation and on formal exhibitions of the artist's work at the close of the residency.

The third category was one that involved students and adults in the actual creative process. In these programs artists were placed in teaching situations as guest instructors and taught classes in their areas of specialization.[29] Because of the evident successes, later Endowment residency projects would draw ideas from these project designs.

Endowment-Sponsored Community Residencies

Other kinds of residence projects in communities and other social surroundings were explored.

> The Endowment not only aids in placing professional artists in schools, but also in settings outside the traditional classroom—in alternative educational settings—especially among the underprivileged.[30]

During the 1970s artist-in-residence projects receiving Endowment support were established in numerous colleges and universities, community cultural centers, hospitals, retirement homes, and prisons. In fact, by 1976, almost every program of the National Endowment had some sort of residency component. The *1976 Annual Report* includes examples.[31]

1. The Resident Professional Dance Companies category was designed to encourage dance companies to take up residence in, and provide continuing services to, communities around the country. In addition, the Dance Touring category awarded grants for brief residencies of professional companies (periods of at least 2-1/2 days) "to provide activities including performances, open rehearsals, master classes, lecture–demonstrations, seminars, and children's programs."

2. The Arts Exposure Area of the Expansion Arts Program provided matching grants to community-based organizations that brought performances, exhibitions, and festivals to people who were normally denied access to cultural events because of economic, geographic, or physical restraints. For example, the Endowment and the Federal Bureau of Prisons co-sponsored a pilot Artist-in-Residence Prison Arts Project designed to test the rehabilitative potential of the arts in prison environments.

3. Beginning as a pilot project in fiscal 1976, the Readings and Residencies for Writers category of the Literature Program was designed to bring fiction writers and poets into a wider contact with the public. The purpose of the program was to help writers, especially those just achieving recognition, to establish new audiences and new sources of income; and to provide communities, particularly in areas beyond the large urban centers, with exposure to contemporary poets and writers. For example:

> Joe Paddock, a poet, spent nine months in the town of Olivia, Minnesota (pop. 3,000). He conducted writing workshops, inside and outside the schools, wrote a weekly column for the town newspaper, and assembled an oral history of Olivia, entitled "The Things We Know Best." The people of the town, with help from the Trojan Seed Co. located there, formed a public corporation to have the volume published. Paddock's stay in Olivia proved the value of the writer working within a community, getting to know and be known by the people there, and transmitting to them some new awareness of themselves and a renewed pride in their own ways.

4. The Music Program had funded many residency-types of projects throughout the years. Under the Independent Schools of Music, the Jazz/Folk/Ethnic, the Opera, and the Orchestra categories, numerous residency projects in community centers, public schools, and colleges and universities were accomplished.

5. The Public Media Program's category of Media Studies furthered the creation and study of film and video as art forms through short-term residencies, seminars, workshops, and conferences.

> This year a prominent filmmaker/anthropologist spent a full semester at Temple University, teaching classes in the Anthropology and Communications departments, giving lectures to the public, and involving students in the editing of his latest film.

Other Media Program funding categories sponsored filmmakers in residence at public and cable television stations in projects dealing with broadcast preparation and local programming.

6. The Community Residencies category in the Special Projects Program offered pilot projects that encouraged whole communities to sponsor artists in residence. One grant went to the Arizona Commission on the Arts and Humanities "to suppport a program of performing artist residencies in five Arizona communities." The emphasis lay in preparing the communities to become sponsors in their own rights by "awakening them to the ways in which artists' services can be made available to the whole community, and teaching them how to initiate and administer residency projects on their own in the future." Other program categories distributed subsidies to support short-term residencies by writers, composers, and visual artists.

7. The Artists, Critics, Photographers, and Craftsmen in Residence category of the Visual Arts Program gave matching grants to museums, universities, community centers, and art schools to invite nationally-known artists, critics, photographers, and craftsmen for short terms. These guest artists were encouraged to meet with people at institutions, present exhibitions of their works, and exchange ideas and information.

8. The Learning Through the Arts (LTA) category of the Education Program was a "limited laboratory program" in fiscal 1976. The intent was to support a few demonstration projects that could "serve as models for the use of artists in educational settings." The focus was on the role of the artist and on ways in which the arts could be integrated in the educational experiences of schools and communities.

> The work of artists in LTA projects indicates new possibilities for motivation of learning, understanding of other cultures, the development of personal resources and stimulation of the process of thought and expression. LTA funds artists' work with community, cultural and arts organizations. The program focuses on the needs of a variety of audiences including adults, students, the handicapped, prisoners, and diverse cultural groups.

While most of the residence categories described thus far were developed primarily to meet the needs of community adults, the Artists-in-Schools category of the Education Program was intended for another community group—the children in the schools.

ARTISTS-IN-SCHOOLS (AIS)

The Artists-in-Schools (AIS) program is a specific model of the complexity of issues that the Council members and Endowment staff faced to a greater or lesser degree with all assistance areas. This funding segment of the Education Program was the Endowment's response to the belief that arts experiences of high quality occurring early in the education of children would be influential on their future arts participation. Results from the 1974 Harris survey appeared to support the soundness of this reasoning. It pointed out that "an important influence on appreciation of the arts and attendance at cultural events later in life . . . was early childhood exposure and education in the arts."[32]

The policy of the National Council from the very beginning was to provide general arts experiences for children in various areas of the country. AIS, however, was designed to furnish such experiences specifically in the schools. Often these schools were remote from large cultural institutions—in places where access to the mainstream of arts activities was not convenient. Lydia Joel, the evaluator for IMPACT (an AIS dance project), wrote:

> The dancers . . . in stage make-up and costume . . . are in a fourth grade classroom in an inner-city Philadelphia school discussing the company's public performance of the night before. "It was a blast!" is the critical estimate of one ten-year-old.

The report continues:

> Cold rain pounds on the roof of a school gymnasium in Troy, Alabama. Inside, children watch with rapture as an artist brushed onto canvas his reactions to improvisations of their chamber music trio—professionals who've been in residence at their school for three months. The youngsters smile at the musical jokes and enjoy the response in color and stroke.
>
> In nearby Goshen, students meet casually at the feet of the school mascot, a glistening nine-foot-high eagle who perches in their school yard. It was made by their artist-sculptor in residence with the help of two pupils, and was constructed entirely of automobile bumpers bought at the auto graveyard for twenty cents a pound.
>
> In Columbus, Ohio, kindergarten children have fun clapping out the rhythms of their names, their city, and the months of the year.
>
> In Eugene, Oregon, third graders use light, texture, sound, and movement to make a film and a music tape as part of their science class study of the sea, tides, and erosion.[33]

The roots of the Endowment's commitment to early education in the arts are traceable to the second meeting of the National Council on the Arts in June 1965. At that meeting two Council observers—the Commissioner of the United States Office of Education (USOE), Francis Keppel, and the USOE Arts Coordinator, Kathryn Bloom—had both stated their interest in possible cooperative programs. The Council, after animated discussion, developed resolutions that set a tentative course toward the establishment of future residency projects:

> The National Council on the Arts recognizes that a continuing and significant flowering of the arts in America today will depend largely on education; that our schools, at all levels, primary, secondary, and college must accept the challenge to create a new and propitious environment for the arts. To this end, the National Council on the Arts indicates its concern:
> —That the arts and the aesthetic experience should represent a major part of student education at all levels.
> —That encouragement be given to such pilot programs as are designed to explore curriculum changes which will more adequately fit the needs of the gifted student, rather than forcing the student to fit himself into rigid curricula designed primarily for the academically interested . . . .
> —That resident artists and/or artist-teachers be utilized more fully in enrichment services to the community leading to raised levels of taste and understanding.
> —That existing public school facilities be made available whenever possible, for increased use by those interested in the arts.[34]

In 1966, the Endowment established the first residence project in schools in cooperation with the USOE, entitled Poets-in-the-Schools. The success of the professional poets in classrooms encouraged the National Council to recommend a broader-based Artists-in-Schools category within the Endowment's Education Program.[35]

The Office of Education, in 1969, transferred $100,000 to the Arts Endowment to finance a visual arts component. In 1970, when USOE transferred an additional $900,000, the program began a growth process that would eventually include various art forms and project sites in widely dispersed areas of the nation. As Nancy Hanks stated in 1975:

> In addition to poets, the program now involves artists in a variety of fields—in dance, in crafts, in painting and sculpture, in music and theatre, in film, in the folk arts, in design. State and city governments, local school boards, local foundations have become increasingly interested in this program, philosophically and monetarily. Bringing our Nation's artists into contact with young people has opened up new avenues of awareness, has excited the development of talent, has given many students a new appreciation of life and of themselves, a new sense of identity and purpose.[36]

Whether the Chairman's assessment of the program was overly enthusiastic is difficult to determine. Although it is possible to report the number of students, artists, and schools who participated in projects, the actual effects on participants are still open to conjecture. However, proliferation of projects during the seventies is indication that both participants and agency personnel were convinced of its effectiveness.

The development of the AIS concept meets the three basic Endowment goals of arts availability, cultural resources development, and advancement of the cultural legacy. Through this program, wide segments of the population were given artistic experiences early in their lives when these experiences are believed to be most influential; cultural institutions such as schools and art centers were supported with expanded public service in the area of the arts; and, finally, gifted young local artists were placed in situations where they would receive financial assistance and professional visibility. Conceivably, they could affect future generations of arts consumers with a new dimension of understanding of the creative process.

The growth of the program also reflected the times. The affluent economic and social conditions were favorable to the development of arts programs in communities and schools; the financial and artistic welfare of artists were abiding concerns of arts activists; and the educational philosophy of the period which advocated both cognitive and aesthetic child development—the education of the total child—caused educators to view the cooperative aspects of AIS with favor. While the conjunction of these factors seems to be responsible for the flourishing of AIS, it should be noted that program motivations on the part of the arts establishment and the education establishment were somewhat different.

Motivation for AIS: The Arts Endowment

Although the Council members and the Arts Endowment staff were interested in problems of arts availability and improvement of arts education in American schools, the main objective for artists-in-schools projects appeared to be concern for the creative, financial, and social welfare of artists. At a 1974 meeting of the National Council on the Arts, a statement was adopted that seems to confirm the artist-centered motivation.

> The Council reaffirms its belief that the success of Artists-in-Schools is based in large measure on the participation of exceptionally talented professional artists in situations where the creative process is encouraged. In-depth contact with students, adequate studio space, equipment, and supplies are essential to the success of each project. In addition, the remuneration paid to the artists and the schedule should provide the artist with the opportunity to work independently, thereby contributing substantially to the financial and creative life of participating artists.[37]

A report of the 1975 Artists-in-Schools National Conference held at Notre Dame University revealed similar attitudes from within the Endowment. Leonard Randolph, director of the Literature Program, stated:

> As AIS grows larger and stronger let us remember the *reason* for the program: the individual artist. When we began the program a decade ago we weren't thinking of AIS coordinators, state educational departments, and all that. And it is still true today that the important thing is the effect of the program on individual artists. What's distinctive about AIS is what the artist uniquely has to offer that no one else can contribute—something that can change lives, institutions, and change the artists themselves.[38]

Also motivating the Council members and the staff was an attitude that arts education in the schools of America during that period was, at best, marginal. They were convinced that the administrative and curricular structure of schools was not conducive to effective arts instruction and that arts educators were not teaching their subject matter effectively. The arts, they felt, could be taught best by accomplished practitioners. Because arts educators, during their preparation, were often required "to spend about half of their academic life studying education as a subject, and therefore deprived of opportunities to become more skilled in the practice of their art," they were often inadequately prepared in the subject matter they taught.[39] Unfortunately, this rather restrictive point of view was shared by some artist participants in the AIS projects and, at times, caused personal and professional friction between guest artists and arts educators in school situations where tolerance and cooperation were needed.

Motivation for AIS: The Education Establishment

Educators were motivated to initiate artists-in-school projects for somewhat different reasons than the federal arts agency. Unlike the Endowment staff, whose main responsibility was for the artist, educators were concerned with the development of children. They regarded arts education as a means of opening up new understanding. While they believed that traditional education programs had been effective in developing cognitive skills, these educators were seeking instructional approaches that would heighten the aesthetic senses of children and, as a result, lead them to value the arts as an important part of their lives.

Over the years, the teaching profession had also come to the realization that the walls of the school should be extended so that community resources could enrich the educational process. Numerous arts educators and school administrators who believed in this concept saw professional artists as community resources—enhancing factors in the arts education process. Therefore, in the 1960s and 1970s, numerous school systems, with state and federal assistance, cosponsored artist residency projects that were designed to provide students with arts experiences not possible within traditional programs of instruction.

Some educators also wished to change structure by moving the arts to the core of the curriculum. Advocates of this aesthetic approach to education also believed that ideas learned from experiences with the arts could be transferred to other situations in everyday life—to the education of the whole person.[40] Because the achievement of arts experiences of high quality was essential to this kind of instruction, educators gravitated to residency projects that enhanced the artistic experiences of children through direct encounters with professional artists.

While some educators and administrators recognized that changes in the curricular structures of schools might be helpful, they also felt that the preparation of arts educators could always be improved. Many of these advocates, however, believed that the study of education was necessary if arts teachers were to interest children effectively from varied backgrounds with differing interests and abilities. As a result of this belief, these educators were attracted to the cooperative aspects of AIS which, they thought, would draw on the unique abilities of both arts educators and guest artists.

One additional motivation for establishing AIS projects was the availability of federal and state funds, an opportunity that attracted many school administrators. During the early 1970s, the success of a school's administration was often measured by its ability to secure government funds. While the receipt of such grants extended the schools financial resources, the acceptance of a school for a highly visible educational project lent prestige to the school's image with the taxpayers. Because AIS projects were both highly visible and financially feasible, they became part of the total school "grant-getting" picture.

While the motivations of the Endowment and educators were somewhat different, their ultimate goal of enrichment of arts experiences was similar enough to fuse their respective intentions so that residency projects became possible in schools throughout the country.

AIS in Operation

At the center of the Artists-in-Schools program philosophy was Goethe's contention that "a man does not learn to understand anything unless he loves it." The Arts Council members had repeatedly stated that the experience of art is a basic need of the human spirit and that these experiences should be made available to all children as an essential part of their education.

> The idea is to expand the child's total personality, develop emotional attitudes and receptivity to the process of learning, and instill an awareness of creativity as a living and personal process that will remain with the child long after formal education is completed.[41]

Or, as a third-grader wrote:

> and I awoke and it was true
> I saw everything I saw
> sky of roses house of daisies a tree
> of orange a book of apples and
> I loved it all and I lived with it for
> the rest of my life.[42]

One boy's frustrated response to brotherly irritation was equally powerful:

> If I was the world
> I would shake
> James
> off.[43]

Surely, an arts education program that could elicit such sensitive poetic expression from children was worthy of consideration by any school system. Such creative responses, Endowment publications claimed, often resulted from AIS projects.

Another child, after visiting an artist at work in a community center, remarked, "Oh yes, it was wonderful, I didn't know any artists were still alive!"

Naïve as the statement sounds, it could have been made by millions of Americans in the Sixties and Seventies who lacked firsthand opportunities to meet and observe artists. The child's comment also revealed the excitement that can be gained from face-to-face encounters with artists at work on their art. In 1975, Nancy Hanks said of this program:

> It is one of the major success stories of the Endowment's ten-year history. And it is one example of an area of activity to which could profitably be devoted the entire presently authorized sums—were it not for the overriding necessity to keep working toward a well-balanced total program.[44]

As the AIS projects developed, designers tried with varying degrees of effectiveness "to make change possible within the school structure, to incorporate the arts into the standard curricula, to expand the natural creativity that is inherent in children, and to raise the esthetic sensibility of the nation."[45] While organizational factors varied according to local and state designs, all AIS projects contained the common component of interaction between students and professional artists.

The 1970 evaluation of the first visual arts AIS projects accomplished by the Central Midwestern Regional Educational Laboratory (CEMREL) described the artists' roles in three concept models.[46] First, the Teacher/Artist concept had its major emphasis on a direct or formal teaching arrangement.

> The artist would intervene directly in the school program. He would assume responsibility for teaching, at regularly scheduled times, either a selected group of students or adults or a regular class for the entire school years.

In the second concept, designated as Artist/Teacher, the artist's instructional role was more informal and was complemented by structured activities in which students could see the artist working in his school-based studio.

Concept emphasis in the third role model, the Artist/Catalyst, was placed on providing students with opportunities to witness the artist at work.

> The artist would act as a catalyst for the arts in both the school and community. These encounters would be initiated by participants and the artist had no assigned teaching responsibility. In this approach the artist would have an open studio so visitors could talk to him and observe him at work. He would schedule special exhibitions . . . provide opportunities for students to work with him on individual projects, and would conduct informal teaching situations, seminars, and workshops.

As AIS later expanded to include projects in art forms other than visual arts, these role concepts were adapted to the new requirements as well as the individual needs of schools and communities.

Artists as Teachers

In order to carry out successfully their roles as instructors, artists had to possess some special competencies. They needed a creative talent of high quality in their own disciplines and the ability to bring into the classroom their excitement with creativity and their conviction of the importance of learning by doing.

Participating artists had to have a feeling of social engagement as well, a commitment to life beyond the boundaries of their own art discipline. They had to be able to communicate effectively and explain both the artistic purpose and the process in simple terms. They had to be flexible, willing to use varied settings, ranging from classroom to community center, with the ease they felt in their own studios.[47]

Even with the most painstaking screening process for artists in the program there were inevitable problems—many of them arising from conflicts with resident educators. Some of the AIS artists reported on these stresses at the National Conference on Artists-in-Schools held at Notre Dame in 1975. One of the concerns was that arts educators seemed to consider the work of the program threatening and there was a fear for its "survival in the face of growing envy and competition from professional arts education organizations, state departments of education, and other groups anxious to take control of funds."[48]

Such statements revealed a disillusionment with arts educators and the education establishment, but were not specific reasons for day-to-day conflicts. Some of the daily frictions may have resulted because the artists themselves ignored the resident arts educators and posed a threat to their teaching positions. Other problems may have surfaced because the artists were not sufficiently sensitive to the professional status of teachers and administrators, or were cavalier in their regard for standard school operations.

A 1973 publication by the Connecticut Commission on the Arts, entitled *Artists in the Classroom*, summed up the problem in this way:

> Artists who believe they know THE ANSWER to the problems of education, or that teachers and administrators are the enemy, will fail. Similarly, if they see students as latent free-spirits in touch with their senses, ready to be sprung, artists will also fail. But if the artist works with teachers and administrators, suggesting new possibilities instead of imposing assumed truths, change can take place that will be sustained after the artist leaves.[49]

A number of artists at the Notre Dame conference appeared to understand the cooperative aspects of AIS and offered conciliatory advice:

> The challenge to us is to establish and maintain relations of mutual respect with

> the professional arts educators. They are *not* the enemy, unless the Endowment makes them so. The artist should wait and watch, work with the teachers, learn a little by observing, not just stomp in and do his art thing. The artist should take time to feel his way into the situation.[50]

But problems with AIS should not be attributed exclusively to artists. Some educators and administrators were also remiss in their regard for the cooperative aspects of residency projects. They ignored the fact that the artists brought a different perspective to the process of arts education and that, as a result, their ideas about how to teach and what to teach might vary from traditional approaches and appear nonconforming. These very points of contention, however, were the factors that made artists potentially valuable resources. The fresh ideas of artists presented educators with opportunities to investigate new approaches to arts education while allowing them chances to provide input drawn from their own expertise.

Any innovative program is subject to problems arising from human failings. However, it appears that such problems occurring in AIS projects, while disturbing, were not inhibiting to the program's general effectiveness or popularity with artists and educators.

A 1976 evaluation of AIS by the Western States Arts Foundation revealed that, "despite some procedural problems, 96 percent of the visual artists and 98 percent of the poets responded that they would agree to participate again in Artists-in-Schools." Equally interesting were the responses of school administrators and teachers. Eighty-one percent of the teachers and 90 percent of the administrators expressed willingness to participate in future projects. Evidently, a large number of the participants were pleased with the project design and results.[51]

AIS Growth

The annual reports from the Endowment and other sources contain impressive statistics concerning the growth of Artists-in-Schools during the years 1969–1976. In the fiscal year 1969, when the programming expanded into the visual arts, six artists were placed in secondary schools in various parts of the country. The Endowment, encouraged by the initial success of these projects, expanded this program in 1970 to elementary and secondary schools in 31 states. The next year (1971), visual artists, poets, filmmakers, dancers, musical and theatre artists, and experimental design artists were brought into 61 school districts in 41 states. By 1972, the Endowment was spending $1,417,897 for projects in all 50 states and the five special jurisdictions. In addition to the Endowment expenditures for 1972, the U.S. Office of Education provided $1,000,206 from Title III funds of the Elementary and Secondary Act and the Bureau of Indian Affairs transferred $20,000 to the Endowment to enable a $40,000 grant to the Institute of American Indian Art in Santa Fe (NM) for drama, documentary film, poetry, and visual arts projects.[52] By 1976, the Endowment's support for AIS had grown to about $4 million and during the 1975–76 school year "more than 2,000 artists worked in 7,500 schools with nearly one million students in all 50 states and the five special jurisdictions."[53]*

In addition to its AIS projects, the Endowment also made separate grants to various independent cultural organizations providing similar services. Such groups as Young Audiences, Affiliate Artists, and the Alliance for Arts in Education were recipients of federal assistance.

AIS Administration and Program Components

The Endowment's Education Program guidelines for 1976 outlined the Artists-in-Schools administrative procedure. They state that projects were administered through grants to the state arts agency and other cooperating organizations such as the St. Paul Council on the Arts and Sciences and the San Francisco Poetry Center, which selected the participating schools, chose the artists, and raised matching funds required by Endowment grants.[54] The *1976 Annual Report* also divided funding for AIS projects into eight program components, each of which corresponded with a different art form: Architecture/Environmental Art, Dance, Film/Video, Folk Arts, Poetry, Visual Arts and Crafts, and two pilot components for Music and Theatre.[55]

AIS and Communities

The results of residency projects in the schools were often felt by adults in the community. While some AIS components such as Visual Arts and Crafts were specifically designed to include community arts development, others produced ripple effects in libraries, hospitals, centers for senior citizens, and community arts centers. These institutions frequently invited AIS artists to present exhibitions, performances, or instruction in the arts.

Parents of children experiencing AIS projects were also influenced to seek

*In 1974, Eliott Eisner, professor of art and education at Stanford University and an outspoken critic of AIS, questioned the value of a program that serviced so few of the nation's school children. He reported that between two and three percent of the school children were involved in long-term AIS projects each year. In 1983, Joseph Prince, the Endowment's director of educational programs, generally affirmed Eisner's estimate but stated that AIS projects were never intended to cover all school children. Such coverage, he contended, would be impossible with the amount of funds available for AIS. He concluded however, that if one considers the cumulative number of children serviced by the program since its establishment and the geographic distribution of project sites, AIS coverage becomes quite impressive. (J. Prince, telephone interview, February 24, 1983.)

interaction with artists. To illustrate this idea, a poet in an Arkansas AIS project told the following story:

> I was in a restaurant fairly late one night when a gigantic man walked up to the table. He said, "My daughter tells me you're a poet." And I thought that this was the trouble I expected; but I said, "Yes, I'm a poet." And he said, "So am I," and he pushed me over and pulled out a sheaf of poems and I sat there in the restaurant reading his poems.[56]

Marlynn Likens, former director of AIS for the Oklahoma Arts Council, described how the effects of the projects sometimes sparked increased community interest. She stated:

> The name of our program evolved from artists-in-the-schools to artist-in-residence. The total concept of the artist, school, and local community arts council (if there was one established) working as a complementary unit became more important to all concerned. Parents were taking classes in the evening alongside their children, and in many instances the children were teaching the parents. Art festivals were being planned, local arts councils were being developed, and on and on and on the circle of involved people kept growing and expanding.[57]

It has often been said that schools are a direct reflection of the community. AIS projects have shown that communities may be influenced by what goes on in the schools. When children found that their interaction with artists was pleasant, informative, and aesthetically valuable, they often communicated their feelings to their parents. Parents, in turn, informed others until whole segments of the community began to develop more open attitudes toward artists and the arts. As a result of this community motivation, many artists working in the schools were encouraged to teach, perform, or exhibit in community settings so that the adult population could have access to their personal and artistic influence. This was the kind of grassroots interaction that the Endowment and state arts agencies deemed most effective for achieving increased arts availability and expanded audiences for the arts.

AIS: A Success or Failure?

Many stories can be told of Artists-in-Schools project successes: heartwarming stories about disadvantaged children expressing themselves eloquently through their art works; about citizens attending arts presentations and questioning artists about their creative process; and about project participants cooperatively creating an art work to be enjoyed by all members of the community. Stories can also be told of project failures: of program goals that were educationally unrealistic or unattainable; of artists who could not relate to their students; of teachers and administrators who refused to cooperate with resident artists; and of school boards that did not see fit to continue AIS funding after government funds were discontinued. In fact, the verdict on AIS is still not in. It remains for future evaluators to ascertain its true effectiveness, if such a judgment is possible. It does seem evident, however, that the concept of Artist-in-Schools was the product of its times—a lively response to the needs of the society, the education establishment, and the professional artists. AIS was an honest federal effort to increase arts availability for millions of Americans and to provide financial and artistic assistance for numerous artists.

Reference Notes

1. R. L. Stevens, speech to the American Theatre Association Annual Convention, Miami, Fla., August 25, 1965.
2. *Statement of Nancy Hanks, Chairman, National Endowment for the Arts, Before the Joint Hearings of the Special Subcommittee on Arts and Humanities of the Committee on Labor and Public Welfare of the United States Senate and the Select Subcommittee on Education of the Committee on Education and Labor of the United States House of Representatives on* S. *1800,* S. *1809, and* H.R. *9657,* H.R. *7490,* November 12, 1975, p. 45.
3. National Endowment for the Arts (NEA), *1976 Annual Report* (Washington: U.S. Government Printing Office, 1976), p. 21.
4. NEA, *Outreach of the National Endowment for the Arts* (Washington, D.C.: Nea Office Publication, May 1975), unpaged.
5. NEA, Interoffice memorandum from Florence Lowe to Richard Contee containing a fact sheet on individual programs for a 10th Anniversary press packet, May 1975, unpaged.
6. *Statement of* N. *Hanks,* p. 46.
7. NEA, *1976 Annual Report,* p. 38.
8. *Statement of* N. *Hanks,* pp. 46–47.
9. NEA, *New Dimensions for the Arts 1971–1972* (Washington: U.S. Government Printing Office, 1973), p. 29.
10. *Dairyland Graphics,* brochure distributed by the Wisconsin Arts Board, Madison, Wisc., 1975.
11. National Research Center of the Arts, Inc. (affiliate of Louis Harris and Associates, Inc.), *Museums USA: Highlights* (Washington: National Endowment for the Arts, 1973), pp. 3–20.
12. NEA, *1976 Annual Report,* pp. 70–71.
13. *Statement of* N. *Hanks,* p. 50.
14. NEA, *1976 Annual Report,* pp. 67–68.
15. *Statement of* N. *Hanks,* p. 51.
16. NEA, *1976 Annual Report,* p. 109.
17. *Ibid.*
18. *Statement of* N. *Hanks,* pp. 52–53.
19. NEA, *1976 Annual Report,* p. 109.
20. *Ibid.,* p. 9.
21. NEA, Memorandum–fact sheet.
22. NEA, *1976 Annual Report,* p. 51.
23. National Research Center of the Arts, Inc. (affiliate of Louis Harris and Associates, Inc.), *Americans and the Arts: Highlights from a Survey of Public Opinion* (New York: Associated Councils of the Arts, 1974), p. 21.
24. F. Taylor, "Wisconsin Pioneers—The Artist in Residence," *Wisconsin Academy Review* (June 1973), pp. 22–26.

25. M. Hiestand, "Reaching Out to the Young," *American Arts Magazine* (May 1982), pp. 24–25.
26. Contemporary Music Project, *Comprehensive Musicianship: An Anthology of Evolving Thought* (Washington: Music Educators National Conference, 1971), p. 3.
27. *Ibid.*
28. D. Bartholomew and C. Tannen, *Arteries: Articles on Community Arts Development* (Chicago: Illinois Arts Council, 1979), p. 15.
29. S. Madeja, *et al.*, *The Artist in the Schools: A Report on the Artist-in-Residency Project* (St. Louis: Central Midwestern Regional Educational Laboratory, 1970), pp. 13–14.
30. *Statement of N. Hanks*, p. 49.
31. Quotations and information on program residence components were taken from NEA, *1976 Annual Report*, pp. 21–127.
32. National Research Center, *Americans*, p. 27.
33. L. Joel, "The Impact of IMPACT: Artists as Catalysts for Change in Education," *Dance Scope* (Spring/Summer 1972), p. 7.
34. National Council on the Arts (NCA), "First Annual Report of the National Council on the Arts 1964–1965" (Washington: Unpublished report to the President of the United States, 1965), p. 27.
35. John D. Rockefeller III Fund, *Coming to Our Senses: The Significance of the Arts for American Education* (New York: McGraw-Hill, 1977), p. 222.
36. *Statement of N. Hanks*, pp. 48–49.
37. Center for Continuing Education, University of Notre Dame, *Extending the Dream: A Report of the 1975 Artists-in-Schools National Conference* (Washington: National Endowment for the Arts, 1975), p. ii.
38. *Ibid.*, pp. 10–11.
39. NCA, "First Annual Report 1964–1965," p. 26.
40. S. Shapiro, *et al.*, *Artists in the Classroom* (Hartford, Conn.: Connecticut Commission on the Arts, 1973), pp. 12–13.
41. NEA, *New Dimensions*, p. 23.
42. *Ibid.*
43. NEA, *Artists and Schools: An Overview of the Education Program* (Washington: U.S. Government Printing Office, 1977), p. 8.
44. *Statement of N. Hanks*, p. 49.
45. NEA, *Artists in Schools* (Washington: U.S. Government Printing Office, 1973), p. 25.
46. S. Madeja, *et al.*, pp. 25–26.
47. S. Shapiro, p. 88.
48. Center for Continuing Education, Notre Dame, p. 11.
49. S. Shapiro, p. 89.
50. Center for Continuing Education, Notre Dame, p. 12.
51. John D. Rockefeller III Fund, p. 159.
52. NEA, *New Dimensions*, p. 23.
53. John D. Rockefeller 3rd Fund, p. 222.
54. NEA, *Education Program: Artists-in-Schools Guidelines* (Washington: U.S. Government Printing Office, 1976), p. 5.
55. NEA, *1976 Annual Report*, p. 31.
56. John D. Rockefeller III Fund, p. 156.
57. M. Likens, "Expanding Your Horizons," *Design* (May–June 1981), p. 24.

6

At the End of Ten Years

What we were calling a culture boom in 1959
has become in 1976 a deep-rooted cultural
growth that has yet to come to full flower.
—John Canaday, *The New York Times*,
August 8, 1976

In 1965 Congress had found and declared that "the encouragement and support of national progress in the humanities and the arts, while primarily a matter of private and local initiative, is also a matter of concern to the Federal Government."[1] This was landmark legislation. Not since the American Revolution had there been so clear a public statement by any Congress of the need for government to foster the quality of life. Indeed, the legislation went further than the simple "pursuit of happiness" into the essential human need for aesthetic nourishment of the spirit.

The first decade of operation of the National Endowment for the Arts was a time for expansion far beyond the dreams of the early proponents of the legislation. There was, nevertheless, throughout a consistency of purpose among the cultural leaders and private citizens who sat on the National Council on the Arts and the advisory panels who guided the program development. Since membership on the Council and panels rotated periodically, new ideas and points of view were constantly brought to the decisions, as well as fresh approaches to the needs and yearnings of the American people. The shifting system kept the grant-making process from becoming stagnant but succeeding members never lost sight of the goals of the original Council and its dedication to quality.

With the rounding out of the decade in 1975, members of the Council undertook to draft a report of their own. They pointed out that they, and their 48 private-citizen predecessors on the Council had been honored to be selected for presidential appointments. They emphasized that they were grateful for the national tradition of private leadership which allowed them to take a central advisory position in guiding the policies and programs of a federal agency. The

Council report outlined many concerns and observations but focused particularly on the central role of the arts in the society of the seventies. This role, it stated, reflected an unprecedented demand for "fuller development and wider sharing of cultural activities, and for improvements in the environmental qualities of our cities, our homes, offices, shops, schools and countryside"—all of which demanded aesthetic judgment, talent, and resources.

The report laid out many dreams for the next decade, but its primary effort was to find ways to stabilize the economic support of institutions and to broaden the base of help largely supplied by private and local sources.[2]

The press of the period was supportive. An interesting analysis of the progress of the agency came from Thomas Willis in the *Chicago Tribune:*

> As far as I am concerned, W. H. Auden was exactly right when he defined the difference between a craftsman and an artist as: "A craftsman knows in advance what the finished result will be, while the artist knows only what it will be when he has finished it."
>
> Judging by this definition, the National Endowment for the Arts is the nation's most artistic bureau. From the beginning, it has sought its own directions and proceeded to implement them with remarkable energy and breadth of vision.

The agency, he added, that Roger Stevens built in the early years had acquired a dexterity and flexibility altogether unique in the federal establishment.[3]

Neither Roger Stevens nor Nancy Hanks would have called themselves artists but they were each, in their own ways, quintessential arts administrators. They had taste, understanding, and sympathy for artists. They had organizational skills, creative vision, a willingness to gamble on the elusive promise of talent or hint of genius. They listened to their advisors on the Council and the professional panels. They monitored the public attitudes.

In the first decade of the National Endowment for the Arts they turned the concept of government support for the arts into an art form, in and of itself—the model federal program based on local and private needs and energies, assisted with governmental strength—a flexible formula for creativity at all national levels.

When the Arts Endowment had first been established in the mid-sixties there were pockets of strength and creativity here and there around the nation, but no concerted voice. The support splintered into fiefdoms—Sol Hurok still ruled the concert management field in New York with stunning showmanship; Carol Fox and the Chicago Lyric Opera were internationally known; the Tyrone Guthrie Theatre in Minneapolis had opened just a few years before; Dorothy Alexander was pioneering regional ballet in Atlanta; in Hollywood, June Wayne had put together the Tamarind Lithography Workshop for hand-pulled prints; and about 100 college concert series dominated the booking of professional artists in as many cities and towns through the nation, accounting for about "70 percent of the booking business," according to the *New York Times*.[4]

But these oases of creativity were not enough for a parched nation, for most of whose citizens the joy and fulfilment of arts had been a distant mirage for two centuries. It was important to expand opportunities with new support for artists and the arts institutions that maintained them; it was necessary to decentralize from these pockets of strength and creativity into widened territories.

The touring programs of the Arts Endowment helped; assistance to service organizations brought new skills to the arts administrators who were emerging into a respected new profession; the cutting edge of the lively arts was being felt in the state legislatures and in community councils where funds were being carved out for regional and local arts programs that might have been ridiculed a few years before. Public service employment opportunities in the arts were explored through CETA jobs and there was a gradual shift from art celebrated in a kind of elitist vacuum to art recognized as a part of the general social fabric and economy.

Business fell into line. In a talk in Oklahoma City in 1974, Frank Stanton, then chairman of the Business Committee for the Arts, pointed out the need for the arts in setting standards of excellence and taste. He defended their usefulness as tools for recruitment of management talent and their importance in presenting a corporation's products or services with style, imagination, and individuality.

Conversely, Stanton added, business was essential to the arts. "For years, the arts have been low on the philanthropic totem pole. They survived only because the demands on the institutions devoted to the arts were minimal." But, he pointed out, growing regional arts participation and expanding interest in creative activities of all kinds had begun to put great stress on these minimally funded and marginally managed institutions. In the Sixties and the Seventies public interest had intensified in the arts and both personal participation and audiences had grown. The need for local business support was more and more critical and the advantages to business were, he said, substantial.[5]

Throughout the years of her chairmanship Nancy Hanks stressed that patronage of the arts was a legitimate, needed, and important function of the federal government. She repeatedly maintained the obligation to use federal funds to open new sources of private money, and insisted that the arts be kept in private hands where, she felt, they belonged. She made these points at every public appearance—before Congress, in talks to state arts agency directors, to America's mayors. "In America we have this unique pluralism in arts support—federal–state–municipal–private sources." She pounded home the point that federal help could only be effective with strong local commitment and partnership.

As the first decade neared its close, there were hundreds of such partnerships functioning all over the nation, opening doors for artists, widening audience opportunities, improving community values, including real estate, and providing welcome tax breaks for business. One well-publicized example was a joint Arts Endowment–Exxon Corporation program for young American conductors. This was a long-range effort to develop directors for American symphony orchestras. It placed six outstanding young conductors (men *and* women) with six of the leading orchestras in "special positions designed to give them appropriate musical and administrative experience to qualify as future music directors." The program was administered by Affiliate Artists and in the first year reached the National Symphony of Washington (D.C.), the Atlanta Symphony, the Milwaukee Symphony, the Pittsburgh Symphony, the St. Paul Chamber Orchestra, and the San Diego Symphony.[6]

A program such as this was an antidote to another growing tendency in the early Seventies, namely, looking at the arts as a business, with the annual 'bottom line' as a determining factor for orchestras, ballet companies and museums. Some years before at a Senate subcommittee hearing, Agnes de Mille had said:

> It is supposed by the layman that what is good in theater makes money, and that the obverse is equally true. That is a point of view reaffirmed by all the commercial media, since it is their chief yardstick for success. And, usually, it is valid. But what is misleading in the argument is the element of time. Commercial enterprises pay off quickly. Symphonic music, opera, ballet, and great repertory are designed to last and expected to pay off long hence—with immortality.[7]

The long view, the long gamble on future immortality was essential to the successful functioning of the National Endowment for the Arts and, by and large, the agency had been able to achieve this perspective. As a result of Roger Stevens' straightforward efforts and Nancy Hanks' persuasive powers with Congress, the Arts Endowment had become a standard for what a federal agency can and should be: both catalyst and support for the needs of a nation.

Obviously, not everyone was convinced by either rhetoric or solid results. The painter Larry Rivers had been widely quoted as saying that the activities of the Arts Endowment were like the efforts of a gorilla to thread a needle.[8] Another painter, John Wilde, felt that federal funding might be more harmful than helpful and lead to the triumph of mediocrity, although he was less doubting about "official support of the museums, theaters, orchestras, libraries, etc., which bring to the public work that has already been created and proven its merit."[9]

By and large, however, the presence of the Arts Endowment was an encouragement to artists and arts organizations. The grant dollars, although minimal in terms of the national budget, were a major catalyst for growth and change. Museums and symphonies that had drifted along, financially marginal for years, depending for existence on the nineteenth-century concept of private largesse from a handful of donors, were suddenly brought into the twentieth-century world with the need for grant applications and fund-raising techniques. Responsibility for providing financial support moved from the individual patron to the corporations, foundations, and various levels of government as new developments and technology in the arts changed older patterns.

There was evident pleasure and satisfaction with the emerging visibility of the arts as a national asset. Community activities, such as summer arts festivals, became commonplace in towns across the country. Local theatre groups expanded with local business support and old movie houses were refurbished into new civic centers. Inner-city arts activities brought new purpose to half-abandoned areas. Touring grants made national bookings possible for professional dance, opera, and theatre companies.

Neither Roger Stevens nor Nancy Hanks ever wavered from their conviction that the arts should remain in private hands and that federal funding was a catalyst only for private funding to help institutional needs. For the individual artist its purpose was to buy time for future creativity. Nor did either chairman flinch from supporting projects of high risk in a turbulent period in the century. Grants were consistently made for urban theatre and storefront art and to well-recommended artists who often produced protest poetry and other controversial literature.

At the November 1975 Joint Hearings, Nancy Hanks took stock of the decade served by the Arts Endowment and tabulated the expansion and activities of cultural institutions.

- Resident professional theatres had grown from 15 to 50.
- Resident professional dance companies had increased from 10 to 60.
- There were about 25 regional film centers where none had existed a decade earlier.
- Orchestra and opera seasons had expanded.
- Museums had increased in number; the quality of their offerings and community services had improved.
- Art centers in communities and on college campuses had proliferated.
- There were many struggling literary magazines bringing young writers to the attention of the public.[10]

The Arts Endowment had also encouraged a tremendous outreach of programs during the decade, and at the same Joint Hearings the Chairman stated that she estimated that just under 50 percent of the agency's funding was going for such purposes to increase access and availability.

> The Federal investment provides an essential and unique catalyst for progress. The strength of that catalyst has been tested by the Endowment in a time of economic hardship and uncertainty. It has proved over and over again its effectiveness.[11]

It was evident that for the first time in two centuries George Washington's statement that the arts are "essential to the prosperity of the State and to the ornamentation and happiness in human life" was being tested. Throughout the nation audiences were growing. Both private and community resources were expanding financial support in an attempt to keep up with the demand. The federal commitment had moved, over the decade, from a total of $2,534,308 in fiscal year 1966 to $74,750,000 in fiscal year 1975—mathematical symbols for a national enthusiasm. Public approval seemed clearly behind the "right" of John Adams' grandchildren and great-great grandchildren "to study painting, poetry, music, and architecture."

The decade had been a long but finally joyous journey to a frontier that for 200 years had seemed an unobtainable dream.

Reference Notes

1. Public Law 89–209, 89th Cong., National Foundation on the Arts and Humanities Act of 1965, Sec. 2(1).
2. Report by the National Council on the Arts, draft of interoffice memorandum, September 27, 1975.
3. Thomas Willis, "A Decade of Arts Subsidy Faces a Time of Decision," *Chicago Tribune*, September 28, 1975.
4. E. Bolwell, "Campuses Drawing Cream of the Arts at Premium Prices," *New York Times*, January 15, 1968.
5. "Give a Buck to ART," remarks by Dr. Frank Stanton, Chairman, Business Committee for the Arts, to the Oklahoma City Rotary Club and the Allied Arts Foundation, Oklahoma City, January 29, 1974.
6. "Exxon, Endowment Announce Program for Young Conductors," NEA News Release, November 25, 1974.
7. *Hearings Before the Special Subcommitte on Arts and Humanities of the Committee on Labor and Public Welfare, United States Senate*, 90th Congress, 1st sess. on S. 2061, August 15 and 16, 1967 (Washington: U.S. Government Printing Office, 1967), p. 447.
8. David Dempsey, "Uncle Sam, the Angel," *New York Times Magazine*, March 24, 1974, pp. 19ff.
9. John Wilde, "An Open Letter to Howard Schuman, Administrative Assistant to Sen. William Proxmire," *Capital Times* (Madison, Wisc.), April 20, 1979.
10. *Statement of Nancy Hanks at the Joint Congressional Hearings*, November 12, 1975, pp. 8, 9.
11. *Ibid.*, p. 76.

EPILOGUE

There is no way to put the genie back into the bottle.
—Hubert H. Humphrey, Speech, University of Texas at Austin, 1976

As the years following the Bicentennial unfolded, the personal contributions of Roger Stevens and Nancy Hanks as chairmen of the Arts Endowment in its formative years came more clearly into focus.

Stevens was the architect who took the raw material of federal legislation and created an agency devoted to progress for the arts, quality of execution, and welfare of the individual arts. Hanks was the facilitator who listened to the calls for help from the field, attended to Congress and its political goals, and subtly moved the Arts Endowment into a position of extraordinary political strength—to a point where neither the administrations of President Carter nor President Reagan were able to stem the pressure from the arts constituency to maintain federal assistance. The skills of these two chairmen in using federal funds as a catalyst to raise local monies and stabilize organizations with local financial support gave the Arts Endowment its strong partnership with public and private sectors and its political clout. This strength was implicit in the original one-for-one matching grant concept. It was implicit in the Treasury Fund method that raised three local dollars for one federal dollar, and carried to ultimate force by the Challenge Grant, which urged matching *new* nonfederal dollars to federal dollars to strengthen the financial and administrative capacity of the nation's cultural institutions.

Hanks was often criticized for maintaining too tight control of the power base in the federal agency and not relinquishing decision-making to the states, which were clamoring for a larger role. The criticism, which came for the most part from state representatives, may have been just; however, her methods won increasing funding from Congress, which in turn supported more activity on the state level and enabled her critics to perpetuate their fault-finding.

Budget escalation after the Bicentennial underscores the success of the agency tactics. Following the "transition quarter" of July 1, 1976 to September 30, 1976, when the federal government changed the date of its fiscal year, allocations grew steadily. In 1976 the appropriation for the arts was $82 million, plus shared staff administrative funds; in 1977 it was $94 million plus the administrative funds: in 1978 it was $123,850 million (and for the first time the statement "such sums as may be necessary" appears for administrative funds). In 1979 the appropriation (in millions) was $149,585; in 1980 it reached $154,610; in 1981 it peaked at $158,795; in 1982 it dropped back to $143,040 and remained at the $140-million mark the following year.

On August 29, 1977, Nancy Hanks announced her resignation from the chairmanship, to take effect on October 2.[1] During the interim period of about a month the deputy, Michael Straight, continued as head of the agency until the White House should announce the new appointment. It was a turbulent time. Livingston L. Biddle—a deputy under Roger Stevens who was currently the staff director of the Senate subcommittee on Education, Arts, and Humanities—was selected by President Carter as incoming chairman, pending Senate approval of the appointment.

The appointment of the man who had been close to Senator Pell for many years triggered "a sweeping series of charges" from Straight. He was quoted in the *New York Times* as believing "that the arts endowment and its twin, the National Endowment for the Humanities, have become politicized by vested interest, pressure groups, Congress and the Carter Administration. . . . The cancer of political interference has begun to undermine the credibility of the endowments," he claimed.[2]

Biddle went to the nomination hearing of the Committee on Human resources of the United States Senate, November 2, 1977, and stressed the concept of partnership between government and the private community as basic to the law that created the Arts Endowment, quoting the Declaration of Purpose at the beginning of the Act, which stated that support for the nation's cultural progress was to remain "primarily a matter of private and local initiative." He spoke of the strictures against federal interference, of the guidance to the agency by a Council of private citizens, and of the review process by private citizen panelists. He recognized that there had been criticism of the Arts Endowment as too "elitist" and took on the challenge directly.

> We find words like "elitism" and "populism" being used to suggest a polarization of the arts. Some suggest that elitism applies to the quality of our major arts institutions, our orchestras, our opera companies, our dance and theatre organizations, our museums. And some suggest that "populism" applies to an opposite and perhaps equally separate domain—the State and local organizations which represent the arts at

> the grassroots. And some even suggest that battle lines should be drawn and alternatives chosen.
>
> I am convinced a very different approach is needed, a different means of defining our cultural goals. It seems to me that "elitism" can indeed mean quality, can indeed mean "the best"—that is a proper dictionary meaning for the word. And "populism" I would suggest can mean "access." Access to the arts all across the land.
>
> Why not bridge these two words—why not join them in harmony, rather than in discord?—and simply say that together they can mean "access to the best."[3]

In the same speech, Biddle spoke of the "distinguished wife of our Vice-President, Mrs. Joan Mondale, who does so much to advance the cause of the arts." Indeed, after she was tapped by President Carter to be the honorary chairman of the Federal Council on the Arts and Humanities, "Joan of Art," as she was inevitably nicknamed, proved herself a tireless supporter of cultural activities. Her appointment, *Variety* conjectured, was a move that was "expected to boost the Administration's posture concerning cultural activities."[4] Whether or not this appointment was an example of the "cancer of political interference" that Straight had predicted, the Arts Endowment found its budget sharply increasing. There were no complaints from the arts constituency in the nation.

Biddle named three deputy chairmen to assist him: David Searles for policy and planning, James Edgy for cooperation with state and local governments, and Mary Ann Tighe for programs. The new team encountered a fresh problem in January of 1978 when the President, in his State of the Union address, proposed to create a separate cabinet-rank Department of Education, and the new department was to have jurisdiction over both Endowments. Such legislation had already been proposed in the Senate where Senator Pell supported it; his counterpart art supporter in the House, Representative John Brademas, opposed it. At this time, widespread national reaction arose against subordinating the two Endowments to Education and the agencies ultimately remained independent.[5]

By the close of Nancy Hanks' final term there had been considerable resistance to some of the procedures of the Arts Endowment in relation to the national arts field. In an interview some years later, Ana Steele, one of the agency's longest-term staff members,* likened the resistance to the swings of a pendulum. At the close of Roger Stevens' tenure, she recalled, the federal–state relationship was strained; then, when Hanks took over the helm, there was widespread rejoicing. The state leadership felt that her background with the Associated Councils of the Arts would give her a more sympathetic attitude toward state problems and needs.

"By the end of her eight-year term the relations had gone downhill," Steele recalled. "When Biddle came in there was much the same applause and excite-

*In 1983 Ana Steele was associate deputy chairman for program and director of program coordination.

ment." By the end of his term the relationship had once again deteriorated, but picked up when Frank Hodsoll was appointed in 1981. "Perhaps it has to do with the federal–state struggle, which is timeless and endless," she concluded.[6]

In response to these pressures from the national arts constituency, the Biddle team set about to make revisions in the advisory panels in order to bring in new flexibility and greater representation from minorities and women and, inevitably, changing points of view. Previous budget levels for eligibility standards for applicants were also discarded in response to complaints from the field that they were restrictive.

The effort on the part of the Biddle administration to foster more widespread aid to the arts was highlighted in December of 1978 by a 14-member task force on Community Program Policy, which was set up to review programmatic relationships between the agency and arts organizations and to recommend policy for community-based programs. Soon after, the agency expanded the regional representative program from ten to twelve areas and began the search for two new representatives.[7]

Steele recalled that while she felt there were no dramatic program changes under Biddle and his program deputy, Mary Ann Tighe, there were definite emphases, such as concern for the individual artist and more assistance to "availability," with a good deal of funding going toward touring and media program activities that provided broader access. The dance touring program, always one of the most productive but sometimes controversial Endowment undertakings, received a new set of guidelines aimed at relieving concerns of the dance field and providing qualitative review.[8]

When Biddle took over the office of chairman, he initiated a policy by which program directors who had been in office for five years or more were automatically rotated off, and new program directors were hired to replace them. The so-called "five-year policy" was probably designed largely as a means to reorganize the team to his own needs, a perfectly defensible action on the part of a new chairman. Because it was called a policy, it created trouble among the staff and in the field that had continuing repercussions greater than such a legitimate personnel action should have called for.

Inevitably, new program directors, new Council members on the legislated rotation, and new panelists in response to the new agency panel policy, brought program changes. Many of these changes had been long sought but virtually given up as unobtainable. For example, in music, where a new program director, composer Ezra Laderman, had been appointed, several initiatives were established for chamber music, for choral music, for the performance of new music, and for support to recital sponsors—long an endangered species in a highly competitive field.[9]

But the major program shift in Biddle's tenure was moving of the opera section out of the Music Program into a department of its own. "The opera panel," Steele said, "had voted to get themselves out of music on the grounds that they were [not just music but] a distinct multidisciplinary hybrid art form. They wanted their own program, co-equal with dance, music, literature, and the visual arts." The music program deputy brought the suggestion to a Council meeting, saying that a resolution would be presented at the May meeting. Steele was put in charge of "staffing out" the proposal "because I was the neutral corner," she said. "Believe me, people had strong feelings. . . . Everybody had a point of view and was convinced that theirs was absolutely right. All of them thought I was on the other guy's side. I was bribed and yelled at, taken out to dinner and threatened. It was just outrageous. I knew I must be doing exactly the right job, because I figured that if they all think I'm on the other side, then I must be doing something right! Anyway, we did bring the [resolution] to the Council, and it was one of the most breathtaking Council discussions ever. For three or four hours you could have heard a pin drop. At one point they were so split that they turned to Livvy and asked him to tell them what he thought. I guess that they were thinking that if, in fact, we have a tie vote, what will he do? He called a coffee break!

"When they got back, the thing just played itself out, with a split vote in favor of separating opera, marrying it to musical theatre, and making it its own thing."[10] In July of 1978 the National Council for the Arts approved the new program for Opera/Music Theater. Sometime later James D. Ireland Jr. was named program director.[11]

In October 1978 challenge grants were announced, with 133 cultural institutions receiving $30 million for fiscal year 1979. Congress had increased the challenge segment of the budget from an $18 million appropriation to $30 million. It was thus possible for new participants in the project and additional states to be included in the three-to-one matching plan which was expected to generate at least $100 million for participating institutions.[12]

Other major program initiatives continued from the previous decade. The Federal Design Assembly, meeting for its 4th Washington session, held a conference in September 1978 and were urged on by President Carter in a press statement. "Good design," the President was quoted as saying, "can help us meet our commitment to improve the efficiency of government."[13]

George Stevens, Jr., turned over the office of director of the American Film Institute, as that organization passed its 12th year, and became co-chairman of the board. He acknowledged the chronic deficit of about $400,000. "Despite its many successful programs," he wrote in the *New York Times*, "the Film Institute is insufficiently supported by the National Endowment which founded it, and by the film and television industry which, had they been more forward-looking *would* have founded it." It was the "Catch-22" problem that had plagued the Institute from its inception.[14]

By 1980 the nation and the federal government were facing increasing difficulties with recession and inflation. Belt-tightening was the rule for most federal agencies, but the final appropriation for the Arts Endowment that fiscal year climbed to $154,610,000.

With the coming of another new administration, and the conclusion of Livingston Biddle's tenure as chairman, the agency was suddenly confronted with a different and, for a time, very threatening set of problems. The Reagan administration came into office promising budget cuts. One of the prime targets was the National Endowment for the Arts, an extremely small agency that was remarkably visible and important to a large and supportive public. The new budget director announced that the agency's funding would be slashed to $88 million, and the general impression went out that within another year or so such a "frill" in the federal budget—as a program to support the cultural life of the nation—would be cut out entirely.

According to the Office of Management and Budget submission that went to Congress, the rationale was that the Arts Endowment had become the first resort for artists and arts organizations, and that it was driving out private money. Since the rationale was exactly the reverse of everything the National Council and Endowment had battled to achieve for 16 years, the implication that support of the arts was low on the list of administration budget priorities sent out shock waves. There was an immense adverse reaction from the arts constituency and the press throughout the nation. President Reagan then created a Presidential Task Force to look into the condition of both the arts and the humanities and appointed Charlton Heston, the film actor and former member of the National Council on the Arts, and Hanna Gray, president of the University of Chicago, as co-chairmen.

Heston was quoted in an interview in *American Arts*. "The White House was originally a little surprised at the level, the *volume* of response in the arts community and at how clearly audible it was. After all, vastly more important sections of the economy feel the same anxiety at having their piece of the pie diminished, but have not been heard as clearly. And I said to them, 'You have to recognize that people in the arts are highly visible, usually fairly effective communicators. You're going to hear from them.' I suppose this task force is one of the results."[15]

The staff of the Arts Endowment prepared a voluminous briefing book. Once again the mission was outlined. "The National Endowment for the Arts is intended to encourage and assist . . . the *development* . . . *preservation* . . . *wider availability* . . . and *broader support* . . . of excellence in the arts in America." The report emphasized the agency's role as catalyst, in partnership. "While our role is responsive, it is not passive. Many initiatives are required to be responsive to the needs of artists, cultural institutions, and the public."[16]

The ultimate result of all the hue and cry about the Presidential Task Force, which concluded its meetings in September 1981, was that "In the end," as Charles Christopher Mark wrote in *Arts Reporting Service*, "they educated themselves to believe that the present NEA and NEH methods and programs were about as good as the human mind can conceive under the pressure of time and politics."[17]

But, as Ana Steele recalled, "It was living through it that was tough. It was very tough on Chairman Biddle. People were saying 'why doesn't that man get out because he's a lame duck?' The chairman was torn trying to figure out whether he should in fact leave, though he was not at all sure that would help, and felt that it might, in fact, make things worse—in the short- and long-term life of the agency." The agency staff had to sit still and wait it out. There was nothing to be done and, while the arts field representatives were demanding to know why the National Council on the Arts was not taking a firm stand, the Council members were being told by their lawyer that they had to be careful because, in a sense, they were considered federal employees when they met as a body.[18]

Francis S. M. Hodsoll was announced as Biddle's successor in September 1981 by the White House and confirmed by the Senate in November. His background was that of a career civil servant with minimal involvement in the arts. He was a Yale graduate with a Stanford degree in law, had been a Foreign Service officer, a Commerce Department official, a member of the Reagan–Bush presidential campaign team, and deputy to White House Chief of Staff, James A. Baker.

Senator Pell reported that he knew him, liked him, and hoped that he would run the Endowment as efficiently as Biddle had done. Nancy Hanks told an inquirer that she felt the arts background was not necessary if he listened to what the professional panelists and professional staff had to say. There was generally willingness among arts administrators who met with him to accept him for his abilities, administrative strengths, and connections on the Hill.

Like the chairmen who preceded him, Hodsoll began to make his mark on the agency. Even though the Endowment budget was somewhat reduced from the 1981 peak of nearly $159 million, it was not slashed. Hodsoll pressed hard for the need for partnership between private industry and the federal government. In a time of fiscal austerity he maintained that the Endowment had to maintain its commitment to individual artists and smaller organizations that would be most harmed by cutbacks. He believed they were at the "cutting edge" of the arts, "pushing the edges of the current esthetic criteria."[19] He tightened the agency administration, hired an excellent new group of program directors to fill a number of slots that had opened up. He took a much more active part in the final decision on grants than previous chairmen, and even rejected a handful of applications which the advisory panels and the Council had recommended. The challenge-grant machinery was enlarged and strengthened. Opportunities opened for local arts groups that had never participated before. By the time the agency moved into new headquarters in the Nancy Hanks Center of the refurbished Old Post Office at 1100 Pennsylvania Avenue, NW, it was moving smoothly as an integrated part of the vast federal machinery. To some observers, however, the Endowment appeared to be more concerned with financing art than with art itself. Anne G. Murphy, executive director of the American Arts Alliance—a consortium of some 350 theater, dance, and opera companies—commented that "the emphasis has moved from art to dollars."[20] Unchecked, such a development could insidiously undermine the importance of the agency.

Other signs of growth and change were apparent. The National Assembly of State Arts Agencies appeared to be defining its mission and functioning with less complaint about Endowment policies. Six of the dozen regional representatives who had been working throughout the country as spokesmen for the Endowment and advisors to applicants, were relieved of their assignments.[21] President Reagan appointed Daniel J. Terra, a retired industrialist, to the nation's first ambassador-at-large post for cultural affairs through the State Department. Reagan also set up a President's Committee for the Arts and Humanities whose mission, it was said, was to stimulate more support for the arts and humanities from the private sector (in response to the loss of federal dollars in budgets of both Endowments). The committee was also to honor patrons in the private sector. Andrew Heiskell, former chairman of Time, Inc., was appointed to head the committee, and Joseph Krakora, former dance program director at the Arts Endowment, was named executive director.

When Nancy Hanks left the chairmanship in 1977 she was asked by the *New York Times* what accomplishment made her proudest of her term in office. "Encouraging private leadership, private initiative and private money," she replied, "a fundamental, traditional idea which is in contrast to every other government in the world. And my, how it's worked," she added, "because people have pride in their institutions and their communities."[22]

A few years later Frank Hodsoll reiterated this philosophy in his chairman's statement in the *Annual Report*. "Over the past decade and a half, in part as a result of increased contributions from all sources, the arts have flourished and grown. Neither the government nor the private sector alone can give the arts the support they need to maintain their present momentum. But clearly a partnership can accomplish more than either can do alone; for each has strengths that complement the other."[23]

Today, it seems evident to the arts constituency and the general public alike that the tentative, small agency first chaired by Roger Stevens in the 1960s has become the acknowledged focus of leadership in the arts in the 1980s. Although vastly different in concept from the subsidizing councils and cultural bureaus of other Western nations, it has, by utilizing the strength of private funding and the American impulse to form associations and volunteer aid, achieved much the same result as these long-established European entities. No other cultural supporting source in America has maintained so consistently a universal view, encompassing all art forms, from the traditional music, theater, dance, visual arts, literature areas to the growing media activities and the emerging interdisciplinary "performance arts." The agency rewards excellence and creative imagination. It is the strongest catalyst for garnering private dollars and has remained flexible and responsive. A grant from the Endowment is always an artistic cachet for the recipient—whether individual or organization. In spite of great misgivings when it was first legislated, and in the face of considerable criticism and paranoia on the part of many artists and administrators, it has remained relatively free of political pressure. The battle between "elitism" and "populism" continues to see-saw. Conservatives and liberals are found in both camps. There is no ready answer; there probably never will be. The strength of the arts in any society has always been in their power to implement dreams, give new life to ancient realities, bring fresh insights into our society. Such attributes are not political.

As the Arts Endowment has moved through its second decade as part of the federal pantheon, it has become increasingly apparent that the original legislation with its checks and balances, its multiplicity of administrative controls combined with first amendment openness for ideas, has created a responsive tool for the nation's cultural welfare, as flexible and open to changing ideas and approaches as the arts themselves. The process as designed was not complex. There was the chairman, appointed by the President with Senate approval, whose four-year term overlapped into successor administrations; there was the National Council on the Arts of 26 members appointed by the President for six-year terms, thus assuring diversity of opinion; there were panels of professional practitioners of the arts, numbering about 500 people from all disciplines, appointed by the chairman with advice of staff and Council; there was the Arts Endowment staff of some 300 civil service employees, with program directors generally in the "excepted" category and therefore frequently changing. In addition, links with state arts agencies were forged by both financial and cultural mutual concern. It was a system well-designed to respond to different needs and attitudes, but to resist purely political pressure.

Throughout the second decade, priorities set by the first Council were maintained on a continuum, expanding and modifying as changing and growing cultural activities of the nation shifted directions. Concerns of the individual artist—always the root and source—were emphasized over and over. Avant-garde and "performance arts" activities were nurtured. The Arts Endowment continued its mission in spite of the threat of potentially inhibiting budget cuts in the federal program resulting from a national economy wobbling under the twin pressures of inflation and recession.

Audience growth was fostered: "availability of the arts" in all its ramifications of aid to touring, educational outreach programs, and help for regional institutions and state development continued to function. With a resilient, vigorous partnership system of federal, state, public, private, and community organizations, with challenges for new money, and imaginative new uses for funds long available in traditional ways for the arts, new and different alliances were being welded.

As Vice-President Hubert Humphrey declared, the genie was indeed out of the bottle. America had worked through its years of considering the arts only as a practical necessity. It had come to recognize them as an economic necessity as well. Finally, the legislation of the National Endowment for the Arts had identified national support as a cultural necessity for a civilized nation. With the approval of millions of people, the continuing concern of the federal government with the cultural affairs of a vast and creative country had become an intrinsic part of American life.

Reference Notes

1. National Endowment for the Arts (NEA), *1977 Annual Report* (Washington: U.S. Government Printing Office, 1976), p. 5.
2. Grace Glueck, "Endowment's Head Decries Politics," *New York Times*, October 12, 1977.
3. L. L. Biddle, Statement at Nomination Hearing Before the Committee of Human Resources of the United States Senate, November 2, 1977.
4. "Tap Joan Mondale for Fed Arts Post," *Variety*, March 1, 1978.
5. "Carter Favors U.S. Education Dept.; Fear Swallowing of Endowments," *Variety*, January 25, 1978.
6. A. Steele, Taped interview, Washington, D.C., March 15, 1983.
7. NEA, Press release, February 1, 1979.
8. NEA, Memorandum, April 26, 1978.
9. NEA, Press release, May 15, 1980.
10. A. Steele, Interview, March 15, 1983.
11. NEA, Press release, July 24, 1978.
12. NEA, Press release, October 10, 1978.
13. NEA, Press release, September 1978.
14. George Stevens, Jr., "The Founding Director Grades the Film Institute at Age 12-1/2," *New York Times*, January 6, 1980.
15. "Living and Thriving Forever," interview with Charlton Heston, *American Arts*, July 1981.
16. NEA, "Briefing Book on the National Endowment for the Arts for the Presidential Task Force on the Arts and Humanities," June 1981.
17. *Arts Reporting Service*, 275 (September 21, 1981).
18. A. Steele, interview, March 15, 1983.
19. Robert Pear, "Reagan's Arts Chairman Brings Subtle Changes to the Endowment," *New York Times*, April 10, 1983.
20. *Ibid.*
21. *Arts Reporting Service*, 295 (June 28, 1982).
22. "Nancy Hanks Honored for Arts Role," *New York Times*, November 11, 1977.
23. NEA, Chairman's Statement, *Annual Report*, 1981.

Appendix A: National Foundation on the Arts and the Humanities

Total Appropriations, Federal Funds, through FY 1975

	Arts	Humanities	Administrative
Fiscal 1966			
Program Funds	$ 2,500,000	$ 2,500,000	$ 727,000
Funds to match private donations	34,308	—	
(Subtotals)	($ 2,534,308)	($ 2,500,000)	
Fiscal 1967			1,019,500
Program Funds	$ 4,000,000	$ 2,000,000	
State Agencies (bloc)	2,000,000	—	
Funds to match private donations	1,965,692	106,278	
(Subtotals)	($ 7,965,692)	($ 2,106,278)	
Fiscal 1968			1,200,000
Program Funds	$ 4,500,000	$ 3,500,000	
State Agencies (bloc)	2,000,000	—	
Funds to match private donations	674,291	325,257	
(Subtotals)	($ 7,174,291)	($ 3,825,257)	
Fiscal 1969			1,400,000
Program Funds	$ 3,700,000	$ 3,700,000	
State Agencies (bloc)	1,700,000	—	
Funds to match private donations	2,356,875	1,262,473	
(Subtotals)	($ 7,756,875)	($ 4,962,473)	

(continued)

Appendix A (Continued)

	Arts	Humanities	Administrative
Fiscal 1970			1,610,000
Program Funds	$ 4,250,000	$ 6,050,000	
State Agencies (bloc)	2,000,000	—	
Funds to match private donations	2,000,000	2,000,000	
(Subtotals)	($ 8,250,000)	($ 8,050,000)	
Fiscal 1971			2,660,000
Program Funds	$ 8,465,000	$ 11,060,000	
State Agencies (bloc)	4,125,000	—	
Funds to match private donations	2,500,000	2,500,000	
(Subtotals)	($ 15,090,000)	($ 13,560,000)	
Fiscal 1972			3,460,000
Program Funds	$ 20,750,000	$ 24,500,000	
State Agencies (bloc)	5,500,000	—	
Funds to match private donations	3,500,000	3,500,000	
(Subtotals)	($ 29,750,000)	($ 28,000,000)	

	Arts Authorization	Arts Appropriation	Administrative Funds
Fiscal 1973			
Program Funds	$ 28,625,000	$ 27,825,000	$ 5,314,000*
State Arts Agencies (block)	6,875,000	6,875,000	
(Subtotal—Program Funds)	(35,500,000)	(34,700,000)	
Treasury Funds**	4,500,000	3,500,000	
Total Funds for Programming	$ 40,000,000	$ 38,200,000	
Fiscal 1974			
Program Funds	$ 54,000,000	$ 46,025,000	$ 6,500,000*
State Arts Agencies (block)	11,000,000	8,250,000	
(Subtotal—Program Funds)	(65,000,000)	(54,275,000)	
Treasury Funds**	7,500,000	6,500,000	
Total Funds for Programming	$ 72,500,000	$ 60,775,000	
Fiscal 1975			
Program Funds***	$ 90,000,000	$ 67,250,000	$ 10,783,000*
Treasury Funds**	10,000,000	7,500,000	
Total Funds for Programming	$100,000,000	$ 74,750,000	

Appendix A (Continued)

	Arts Authorization	Arts Appropriation	Administrative Funds
Fiscal 1976			
Program Funds***	$113,500,000	$ 74,500,000	$ 10,910,000*
Treasury Funds**	12,500,000	7,500,000	
Total Funds for Programming	$126,000,000	$ 82,000,000	
Transition Quarter July 1, 1976–September 30, 1976			
Program Funds***	—	$ 33,437,000	$ 2,727,000*
Treasury Funds**	—	500,000	
Total Funds for Programming	—	$ 33,937,000	
Fiscal 1977			
Program Funds***	$ 93,500,000	$ 77,500,000	$ 11,743,000*
Treasury Funds**	10,000,000	7,500,000	
Challenge Grants**	12,000,000	9,000,000	
Photo/Film Projects	4,000,000	—	
Total Funds for Programming	$119,500,000	$ 94,000,000	
Fiscal 1978			
Program Funds***	$105,000,000	$ 89,100,000	
Treasury Funds**	12,500,000	7,500,000	
Challenge Grants**	18,000,000	18,000,000	
Photo/Film Project	2,000,000	—	
Administrative Funds	such sums as necessary	9,250,000	
Total Funds	$137,500,000	$123,850,000	
Fiscal 1979			
Program Funds***	—	$102,160,000	
Treasury Funds**	—	7,500,000	
Challenge Grants**	—	30,000,000	
Administrative Funds	—	9,925,000	
Total Funds	such sums as necessary	$149,585,000	
Fiscal 1980			
Program Funds***	—	$ 97,000,000	
Treasury Funds**	—	$ 18,500,000	
Challenge Grants**	—	$ 26,900,000	
Administrative Funds	—	$ 12,210,000	
Total Funds	such sums as necessary	$154,610,000	

(continued)

Appendix A (*Continued*)

	Arts Authorization	Arts Appropriation	Administrative Funds
Fiscal 1981			
Program Funds***	$115,500,000	$113,960,000	
Treasury Funds**	18,500,000	19,250,000	
Challenge Grants**	27,000,000	13,450,000	
Administrative	14,000,000	12,135,000	
Total Funds	$175,000,000	$158,795,000	
Fiscal 1982			
Program Funds***		$103,330,000	
Treasury Funds**		$ 14,400,000	
Challenge Grants**		$ 14,400,000	
Administrative Funds		$ 10,910,000	
Total Funds	$119,300,000	$143,040,000	

*These funds were jointly provided to the National Endowment for the Arts and the National Endowment for the Humanities until the two agencies were administratively separated in 1978.
**Federal funds appropriated by Congress to match nonfederal donations to the Endowment.
***Not less than 20 percent of Program Funds are required to go to state art agencies and regional arts groups.

Appendix B: National Council on the Arts

Nancy Hanks*
Chairman

Michael Straight
Deputy Chairman

Members whose terms expired in 1976

Maurice Abravanel
Conductor, Music Director

Kenneth Dayton
Corporate Executive

Charles Eames
Designer and Film Producer

James Earl Jones
Actor

Charles K. McWhorter
Attorney

Beverly Sills
Opera Singer, Music Director

E. Leland Webber
Museum Director

Robert Wise
Producer–Director

Members whose terms expire in 1978

Richard F. Brown
Museum Director

Henry J. Cauthen
Educational Television

Clint Eastwood
Actor, Director, Producer

Judith Jamison
Dancer

James D. Robertson
Investment Banker

Rosalind Russell*
Actress

Billy Taylor
Jazz Musician

Eudora Welty
Author

Anne Potter Wilson
Arts Patron

James Wyeth
Painter

Members whose terms expire in 1980

Angus L. Bowmer
Educator, Theatrical Director

Gunther Schuller
Composer, Educator, Conductor

Listings current to 1977.

*Deceased, as of 1977.

Van Cliburn
Concert Pianist

Jerome Robbins
Choreographer

Thomas Schippers
Conductor, Music Director

George C. Seybolt
Corporate Executive, Museum Official

Harry M. Weese
Architect

Dolores Wharton
Arts Patron, Author

MEMBERS WHOSE TERMS EXPIRE IN 1982

Martina Arroyo
Concert and Opera Singer

Willard L. Boyd
University President

Hal C. Davis
Musician, Union Official

J. C. Dickinson, Jr.
Museum Director

William H. Eells
Businessman

Harold Prince
Director-Producer

Franklin J. Schaffner
Film Director

Geraldine Stutz
Corporate Executive, Fashion Leader

FORMER MEMBERS

Marian Anderson 1966–72
Elizabeth Ashley 1965–66
Robert Berks 1969–70
Leonard Bernstein 1965–68
Anthony Bliss 1965–68
David Brinkley 1965
Albert Rush-Brown 1965–70
Jean Dalrymple 1968–74
Agnes de Mille 1965–66
Rene d'Harnoncourt 1965–68*
Richard C. Diebenkorn 1966–69
Duke Ellington 1968–74*
Ralph Ellison 1965–66
Paul Engle 1965–70
O'Neil Ford 1968–74
Virginia B. Gerity 1970–72*
Lawrence Halprin 1966–72
R. Philip Hanes, Jr. 1965–70
Huntington Hartford 1969–72
Reverend Gilbert Hartke, O.P. 1965–66
Helen Hayes 1966–69; 1971–72
Charlton Heston 1966–72
Richard Hunt 1968–74
Ruth Carter Johnson 1969–70
Herman David Kenin 1965–68*
Eleanor Lambert 1965–66
Warner Lawson 1965–68*
Harper Lee 1966–72
Jimilu Mason 1966–72
Robert Merrill 1968–74
Gregory Peck 1965–66; 1968–74
William L. Pereira 1965–68
Sidney Poitier 1966–70
Richard Rodgers 1965–68
Rudolf Serkin 1968–74
David Smith 1965*
Oliver Smith 1965–70
John Steinbeck 1966–68*
Isaac Stern 1965–70
George Stevens, Sr. 1965–70*
James Johnson Sweeney 1965–68
Edward Villella 1968–74
Donald Weismann 1966–72
Nancy White 1966–72
Otto Wittmann 1965–66
Minoru Yamasaki 1965–69
Stanley Young 1965–66*
Roger L. Stevens, Former Chairman 1965–69

*Deceased, as of 1977.

Staff of the National Endowment for the Arts—1975

Office of the Chairman

Chairman
Nancy Hanks

Selena Hoyle
Marjorielaine Menke

Staff Assistant
Fred Lazarus

Robin Clawson
Jeff Hackler
Anne Hartzell
Robin Murphy

Deputy Chairman
Michael Straight

Beth Alexiou
Cynthia Moreno-LaCalle

Executive Assistant to the Chairman
John Clark

Julie McClennan

Congressional Liaison
Livingston Biddle
Anne Murphy

James Brookens
Gay Garth
Anne Johnson

Assistant to the Chairman/Press
Florence Lowe

Virginia Ballenger
Patricia Fisher
Phillip Kopper
Ben Ruhe

General Counsel for the Arts
Robert Wade

Valerie Adams
Susan Liberman
Marigrace Soinski

Program Development and Coordination

Director
Lawrence L. Reger

Louise Remmey
Pat Sanders
Eleanor Snyder

Bicentennial Coordinator
William Weld

Jane Blitch
Lee Fleming

PROGRAM AREAS

Architecture + Environmental Arts

Program Director
Bill N. Lacy

Assistant Director
Robert McNulty

Assistant Director
Roy Knight

Helen Brooks
Joan Campbell
Chris Chamberlain
Birch Coffey
Paul Hildebrand
Nancy (Robbie) Langham
Nancy Moore
Alece Morgan
Betty Principe
Pam Stalling
Susan Wagner
Merrill Ware

Federal Design

Design Awareness and Education
Lani Lattin

Jane Clark
Gail Harper
Nancy Lucia
Nancy Moore
Joan Shantz
Mary Williams

Federal Graphics
Jerry Perlmutter

Cynthia Stana
Barbara Streett

EDUCATION
Program Director
John Kerr

James Allison
Michael Blumenthal
Clark Kellogg
Jane Paulson
Stephanie Singer
Lee Woodbury

EXPANSION ARTS
Program Director
Vantile Whitfield

Assistant Director
Gordon Braithwaite

Greta Graham
Lizzie Green
Allen Hile
Margo Koines
Henrietta Sanford
Jennifer Walz

LITERATURE
Program Director
Leonard Randolph

Lois Moriarty
Patricia Stuffle
Knox Turner

MUSEUMS
Program Director
John Spencer

Assistant Director
David Ryan

Susan Barton
Linda Bell
William Bodine
Scotty Godfrey
Donna King
Lena Luck
Patricia Pickles
John Ruddy
Elizabeth Weil
Robert Wilson

SPECIAL PROJECTS
Program Director
Stephen Sell

Assistant Director
Stephanie Sills

Marion Dockery
Debbie Dokken
David Hawkanson
Lisa Kuhn
Rosemary Taromino

Folk Arts Director
Alan Jabbour

VISUAL ARTS
Program Director
Brian O'Doherty

Assistant Director
Richard Koshalek

David Bancroft
Jean Efrom
Mary Fahey
Vicki Fern
Maria Goodwin
Rodney Goldstein
Julia Moore Jackson
Dana Rust
John Seeley

Crafts Coordinator
Elena Canavier

Patrick Fisher

OFFICE OF FEDERAL–STATE PARTNERSHIP
Program Director
Clark Mitze

Assistant Director
Donald Dillon

Assistant Director
Phillip Hyde

Pat Abreu
Marilyn Biggs
Carolyn Green
Jean Handsberry
Constance Lally
Joanne Pearlstein
Cyndy Read
Robin Tryloff

OFFICE OF PERFORMING ARTS AND PUBLIC MEDIA
Director
Polly Buck

Katherine Noonan

DANCE
Program Directors
Joseph Krakora
Don S. Anderson

Robert Altman
Deece Graham
Janet Oetinger
Elaine Parker
Joan Randolph
Kriss Schaffer

MUSIC
Program Director
Walter Anderson

Assistant Director
Ralph Rizzolo

Nancy Clarke
Gregg Fisher
Tonya Gay
Robert Gordon
Marjory Hanson
Susan Hoagland
Kathy Keffer
Ted Libbey
Rose Morgan
Andrew Wentzel

PUBLIC MEDIA
Program Director
Chloe Aaron

Paige Amidon
Ron Green
Perrin Hurst
Laura Jevnikar
Bob Kanter
Kathy Kline
Gary Kreisberg
Nancy Raine
Gertrude Saleh
Melissa Widekehr

THEATRE
Program Director
Ruth Mayleas

Eliza Migdal
Sandy Schreiber
David Visser

OFFICE OF THE ASSISTANT CHAIRMAN/ MANAGEMENT
Assistant Chairman/Management
Richard Contee

Georgia Chumas
Robin Huggins
Sue Wilbern

Special Assistant for Policy Systems and Analysis
Thomas Freeman

Special Assistant
Edward Wolfe

ADMINISTRATION
Administrative Officer
Robert Sims

Barbara Callander
Melva Hill
Earnestine Horne

Staff Development Officer
Kathleen Bannon

Program Aides
Therese Allen
Patricia Angelucci
Philip Bergstresser
Delma Beverly
Sally Bird
Patricia Chrzanowski
Dwain Dillard
Rebecca Fulmer
Annette Gales
Diana Gallop
Eugene Goss
Deborah Horner
Ellen Kidder
Sandra LaBelle
Lynne Leopold
Morris Lewis
Katherine McGregor
Parthenia Monagan
Stacey Paleologos
Linda Peterson
Elizabeth Strauss
Susan Wortman

Interior Design Specialist
Herbert Kubli

Correspondence Supervisor
Rene Hill

Monica Brady
Annette Davis
Margaret DeLartique
Lois Hamlin
Mary Martin
Effie Morton
Barbara Perdue
Vera Powell
Almeta Pratt
Diane Williams
David Walter

BUDGET
Director
Jon Yellin

Toni Adelinis
Tom Castonguay
Laura Chassy
Joyce Chisley
James Ireland
Norman Kraft
Joan Walker

EVALUATION
Director
Chuck Kirk

Carolyn Lee
Kathy Plowitz

Audit Liaison
Mike Elderkin

GRANTS
Grants Officer
James Thomas

Assistant Grants Officer
Carolyn M. (Sue) Johnson

Grants Project Officer
Wilbur H. Potter

Suzanne-Michele Austin
Richard G. Belcher
Michele E. Morris
Roxann Snyder
Mary Terhorst

Applications
Ellen Burbank
Rex D'Costa
Kathleen M. Gauss
Lawrence S. Jenkins
William Junk
Michael Schneider
Kathi J. Sheppard
Stephen A. Stone

Grants
Donna M. McLaughlin

Robert O. Costin
Pauline A. Fortune
Carolyn J. Green
Kathryn E. Guy
Geoffrey Henderson
Linda A. Moore
Ralph Michael Pezzullo
John Ruddy
Melva Skokes
Ann Sturdevant
Susan L. Tyykila
Cantwell Walsh

Reports & Review
Aida R. Schoenfeld
Carol Brosnan
Hortorance Fletcher
Edward J. Foye

PLANNING
Director
Ana Steele

Anne Clark
Ed Cox
Madelyn Mailman
Pam Doong Walsh

PROGRAM INFORMATION
Director
Fannie Taylor

Ludy Biddle
Ilona Croft
Ann Guthrie
Robert Hartmann
David Hausmann
Janice Johnson
Jeanne Krohn
Robert Mackie
Tim Radford

Library
Chris Morrison
Mary Pratt

RESEARCH
Director
Harold Horowitz

Rena Hall

SECRETARY TO THE NATIONAL COUNCIL ON THE ARTS
Luna Diamond

Elizabeth Norwood
Sue Shanks

INDEX